John Jardine, Father Sangermano

The Burmese Empire a Hundred Years ago

John Jardine, Father Sangermano

The Burmese Empire a Hundred Years ago

ISBN/EAN: 9783337173050

Printed in Europe, USA, Canada, Australia, Japan

Cover: Foto ©ninafisch / pixelio.de

More available books at **www.hansebooks.com**

THE
BURMESE EMPIRE
A HUNDRED YEARS AGO

AS DESCRIBED BY

FATHER SANGERMANO

With an Introduction and Notes by

JOHN JARDINE

JUDGE OF HER MAJESTY'S HIGH COURT OF JUDICATURE

AT BOMBAY

LATE JUDICIAL COMMISSIONER OF BRITISH BURMA, AND PRESIDENT
OF THE EDUCATIONAL SYNDICATE OF BRITISH BURMA :
AND SOMETIME DEAN OF THE FACULTY OF ARTS
IN THE UNIVERSITY OF BOMBAY

Westminster

ARCHIBALD CONSTABLE AND COMPANY

14 PARLIAMENT STREET, S.W.

MDCCCXCIII

CONTENTS

RELIGION OF THE BURMESE

MORAL AND PHYSICAL CONSTITUTION OF THE BURMESE EMPIRE

BURMESE CODE

INTRODUCTION

DURING all the past Burma has been a land of attraction to
men of adventure, a region of delight to those, like the old
travellers, whose eyes sought after what is picturesque and
strange. This far-off part of India was, indeed, even in the
later centuries, hardly known to the European merchants
who had seen the cities under the dominion of the Great
Mogul, and the castles and church towers which at Ormus,
Goa, and other points along the coasts, marked the rising
power of the Portuguese. To the people of India Burma
had been known as the Golden Land from remote time, and it
may very likely be that this old region was the Golden Cher-
sonese of Ptolemy. Here, on the shores where the rivers
Salween and Sitang join the sea, a number of powerful colonies
from India, planted 2000 years ago, were engaged in constant struggles with the native tribes. The ruins of Golana-
gar, the town of the Gaudas or people from Gour in Bengal,
are still to be seen. Here, in the time of the Emperor
Asoka (the third century B.C.), came the Buddhist missionaries
Sona and Uttara, from the Council of Patna, to preach that
faith which ultimately spread among the primitive peoples
surrounding the colony. Albeit the Hindu communities fell
in the end under the people of the land, they contrived
for a time to establish powerful kingdoms, and left a strong
impress of their own religions, science, and literature on the
minds of these Talaings of Pegu. In that country also, as
in India and Cambodia, the conflict between Buddhism and
Brahmanism lasted long. Although in the course of centuries

the former became the prevalent religion of Burma, gaining converts on all sides, the ancient powers of the Brahmans can be traced in the history as well as in the ruins of old cities, in the popular traditions and on the carven stones, such as those which Dr. Forchhammer saw at Thatôn, one of which reveals an early endeavour to compromise disputes, where the Dravidian immigrants from the south of India portray Vishnu in his ninth incarnation as Buddha, the Enlightened One. We have in these early facts of history apparent proof of the high antiquity of the influence of India over the various nations dwelling in Burma; whether or no the legends and traditions which describe an ancient incursion of Indians from Kapilavastu, under a royal leader of the Kshatriya caste, by the landward route through Manipur, and the founding of the dynasty at Tagaung (possibly the Tugma metropolis of Ptolemy), are to be treated as mere fable, or, as Sir A. Phayre, following Lassen, inclines to believe, as enshrining some foundation of fact, and accounting for the early use of Sanskrit in names of places and terms of art and law.

There is now more general agreement of scholars as to the races of men whom these Indians, colonists, and missionaries encountered in Burma. Into the upper region of the Irawadi the dominant race, now called the Burmese, had descended from Central Asia, which tract their physical resemblances and affinities of language with the people of Tibet show to have been the home of their forefathers. The clans became more or less welded into tribes, as among their 'younger brothers' the Chins of to-day; and in course of time we find dynasties of kings reigning at Tagaung, Panya, Pagan, and Prome, and others ruling the remoter countries of Arakan and Toungoo. The Tibeto-Burman tribes had, however, to contend with the Tai or Shan people, which in its different branches is perhaps the most widely spread of any race in the Indo-Chinese peninsula, including as it does the Ahoms of Assam, the Laos of Zimmé, and the Siamese. Face and language point to racial

connection with China, and the history and tradition of these
tribes tell of an earlier home ages ago in Yunnan, of a Shan
kingdom in the north of Burma, with its capital at Mong Maw
Long on the Sheveli river, and another Shan kingdom of Tali,
which fell under the conquering hand of Kublai Khan in A.D.
1253. Nearer the sea, along the coasts and in the fertile
plains bordering the great rivers and creeks, were found
another race, the old dwellers of Pegu and the country
round Moulmain, who call themselves Môns. These obtained
the mastery of the delta, driving out the Taungthu tribe
who originally tilled its soil, and establishing themselves so
firmly there as to check for some centuries the ultimate
conquest by the Burmans, who in contempt styled the Môns
' Talaings,' or people ' trodden under foot,' and proscribed
their language, after Alompra in 1757 had taken Pegu, and
the Môns had made common cause with the British in 1824.
The Talaing language, which, it is said, is likely to die out, as
the nation tends to merge in the Burmese, belongs to the
Môn-Annam group of those languages which use tone or
variety of pitch of voice, where we employ inflection to
modify meaning. Captain Forbes has shown that the language of the Talaings and the Cambodians was originally
one, and that before the intrusion of the Siamese the Môn-
Annam monarchy dominated the deltas of the rivers Irawadi,
Salween, Menam, and Mekong. There is a theory held
by Sir A. Phayre and others that the Talaings and their
language came from Telingana, in the south of India. But
the researches of later scholars have shown that the Môn and
Cambodian tongues are connected with those of China. It
is true, however, that the Talaings were in closer touch than
the Burman or Shan races with the higher civilisation of India
—firstly with the Indian colonies where Brahman views prevailed, and next with Buddhist missionaries, who began their
teaching there, and soon became involved in conflict with the
Brahmans. During the first five or six centuries of our era,

when Buddhism had spread over India, there was constant intercourse between the Coromandel coast and the opposite shores of the Bay of Bengal ; and when the persecutions began to rage in India against Buddhism the victims sailed for refuge to the ports on the Burman side.

Conquered at last, and ill-treated by the Burmese kings, the trodden-down Talaings can apply to themselves what Seneca wrote of the Jews in the Roman Empire: '*Victoribus victi leges dederunt.*' It was to the Talaings of Thatôn that about 450 A.D. the greatest Buddhist divine, Buddhaghosa, the author of the *Visuddhi Magga*, or Path of Holiness, brought a complete set of the Buddhist Scriptures in the Pali language from Ceylon. It was from Thatôn that the ecclesiastic went who converted King Anoarahta of Pagan to the orthodox Buddhist faith ; it was to Thatôn that the royal convert sent an embassy to procure the Scriptures, the Tripitaka ; and on meeting with a refusal, and invading the Talaing country, and razing this mother-city of Burman Buddhism to the ground with all its pagodas and ancient buildings (A.D. 1057), it was thence he carried off to his own capital the thirty-two elephant-loads of the Scriptures and the 1000 monks, and gave that impetus to pure Buddhism in the Upper Valley of the Irawadi, which some writers treat as the first real planting of the faith in that region. It was a Talaing monk of Dala, opposite Rangoon, Sàriputta (*obiit* 1246 A.D.), honoured by the King of Pagan with the title of Dhammavilâsa, who compiled the first of the Manu Dharma-shasters known to the Burmese literature, the Dhammavilâsa promulgated in Pagan. It was the Talaing or half-Shan king of Martaban, Wagaru (*obiit* 1306 A.D.), who caused the edition of this famous Code of Manu which bears Wagaru's name to be compiled—the same which the Talaing jurist Buddha-ghosa translated two centuries later, and which the King of Toungoo adopted in 1580. It may therefore be said that the Burman races are indebted to India for their religion, their literature and their law, received chiefly through the Talaings dwelling on the coasts and estuaries, and in close communication with the Hindu colonies which Anoarahta overthrew at last. By these same channels of religion, literature, and law, came also the astronomy, astrology, computation of time, the arts of medicine and divination, and the alphabets known at the present day, all which bear the Indian sign and superscription.

Until intercourse with the nations of Europe began in later times, these influences of India were the most powerful that affected the contending Burmans and Talaings, from whom also the foreign civilisation spread to the Shans and other tribes connected with the Chinese—a development which still goes on so prominently as to be discussed in the Census Report of 1891. The greatest influence of all was and is the Buddhist religion, with which came into the northern valley, according to Sir A. Phayre's opinion, the simple handicrafts, spinning and weaving, and the cultivation of the cotton-plant. Before, however, dealing with the vast effects of this mighty agency, it were well to estimate the conditions, material and moral, of the peoples before its advent. We wish to know what kind of institutions the Burmans possessed before the great changes of Anoarahta's reign. To this inquiry the learned Dr. Forchhammer gives an answer which is in general agreement with the opinions of our historians, and of those officials who have studied the rules and customs of the wilder tribes now under the Queen's sceptre. The Chins of to-day reflect the Burman as he was of old. We find them divided into many clans, according to occupation; the unity of the family is preserved by the worship of a family ghost. To this manes are made over offerings of rice, beer, pork, and buffalo-flesh in safe-keeping, to be enjoyed by the giver in the world to come. The Chin also propitiates other spirits (not manes) of evil propensities, who dwell in houses, forests, rivers, and trees. These are the real indigenous Nats or demons of the tribes, carefully to be distinguished from the ogres, fairies, and dryads, the rakshasas, devas, and brahmas introduced through Buddhism and the Tantra school of India. Among these Nats is Maung Zein, who in an image-house in old Pagan, is made to kneel before Gaudama Buddha. The Burmans affirm that this Zein was one of their chief Nats before they became Buddhists ; and, as Forchhammer observes, it is an admirable act of religious policy on the part of the Burmans that, after adopting Buddhism, and probably moved by a lingering fear of his power, they began to stultify it by changing him into a devoted pupil and adorer of Gaudama. By a converse process the seven evil spirits appear in a Buddhist law-book as seven kinds of witches and wizards. Like beliefs are found among the wilder Karens and Shans ; and among the Kachin tribes whose rites are described by Mr. George in the Census Report of 1891. These frontier people, he says, worship Nats or spirits, of whom the numbers are endless, for any one may become a Nat after his death. This general worship of the powers of nature was widely common all over Central Asia until the Buddhist religion spread there, as is testified by that learned Orientalist, Rehatsek, in his *Essay on Christianity among the Mongols.*

'The powers of nature had from the most ancient times been personified among Asiatic nations, and, according to them, not only the earth and its bowels, but also the sky, is full of spirits, who exert either a beneficent or maleficent influence on mankind ; accordingly, it is no wonder that this belief was current not only among the Mongols, but also the Zoroastrians and Hindus. Every country, mountain, river, brook, tree or any other object of nature was by the Mongols believed to have a spirit for its tenant ; not only violent natural phenomena, such as thunder, earthquakes, hurricanes, and inundations, but also bad crops, epidemics, all kinds of other diseases and evils, such as sudden attacks of epilepsy, lunacy, etc., were ascribed to the wrath of these gods, who are divided into many classes, greatly differing in power and effect.'—*Journal of the R.A. Society*, Bombay branch, vol. xiii. pp. 152, 181.

This Shamanism appears not to differ much from Taoism, the belief of the great majority of the Chinese, on which Confucianism and Buddhism have been grafted. Rehatsek adds that although the spread of Buddhism and Islam has greatly curtailed this extensive faith in demons, it has by no means entirely disappeared from among the Mongols and Tibetans, with whom it still prevails in the midst of Buddhist tenets and ceremonies, nor have its traces entirely vanished from the wandering Mussalman tribes. According to Mr. Leland, similar beliefs survive among some of the ignorant classes in Italy, pagans in two senses of the word—those who delightedly believe in fays and talismans and spirits, and call this creed of theirs the *vecchia religione*, in spite of the Catholic Church and all the Christian centuries. Bishop Bigandet tells us that although Buddhism has a hold over the imagination and sentiments of the better educated, the Burmans all publicly and privately indulge in the worship of the Nats. Almost every city has its own patron spirit; and each household is under the guardian care of the family Nat. If calamity overtakes a Burman, he considers it to be the work of unfriendly Nats; and when he wishes to begin any important undertaking, he propitiates these direct representatives of the old animistic worship, the present cult of the Karens, Chins, and other wilder tribes. Still, we read in the Census Report of 1891 that Nat-worship is a decaying and despised religion, and that both Buddhism and Christianity have increased at its expense. Without giving up their aboriginal rites, the tendency of the unconverted races is to pass into Buddhism. The Chins, for instance, are not Buddhists, yet when living among Burmans they join in the Buddhist festivals, in the building of monasteries, and in the support of monks; they also prefer to secure by a visit to the great Shway Dagon Pagoda at Rangoon the blessings of the Tavatimsa heaven. The census returns show a Buddhist population of 6,888,075 persons; the proportion being 9056 out of every 10,000, that of the Nat-worshippers being only 221. The Nat-worship is contrary to the principles of Buddhism; and although in Central Asia the Buddhist priests have organised the various kinds of spirits according to Hindu views, and act as exorcisers, magicians, and astrologers, in Burma the occult sciences are relegated to the Brahmans, Burma being the only Buddhist country in which the religious order is prohibited from such studies and arts. Gaudama of old classed them with palmistry, fortune-telling, oracles, and charms, as lying practices, and censured those who gain their living by such means, whom, it may be remarked, the law of England treats as rogues and vagabonds. It will, perhaps, be objected by the reader that in Christendom, even so late as the time of Burns, of Walter Scott, and the Ettrick Shepherd, the ancient beliefs in malicious or capricious ghosts and demons, and in the spells and charms of witches, lingered in the land, —survivals of opinions which had once ruled the masculine intellects of such eminent Christians as Chief-Justice Hale, Sir Thomas Browne, and John Wesley. Yet it is beyond the reach of doubt that the dogmas, sacraments, and morals of the Christian religion had a constant, penetrating, and weighty force; and it is to be noticed that writers on Burma impute many effects on character, customs, and law to Buddhism. Mr. Eales in his Census Report does indeed conclude that 'the Buddhism of Burma at the present day is but a thin veneer of philosophy laid over the main structure of Shaman- istic belief.' On the other hand, Major Temple says with greater caution: 'The Buddhism of Burma, as understood by the laity, may be well compared to the Christianity of the Russian moujik. In both of these countries the imported civilised religion has not yet succeeded in completely ousting the uncivilised Shamanism that preceded it.' The fact appears

to be that the influences of the good and bad Nats are confined to the passing *events* of life, to good luck and calamity ;
the conduct of life, the moral sentiments, and the theology of
the people are dominated, not by the old superstitions, but by
the religion of Gaudama. It seems generally admitted that
Buddhism in Burma has been a civilising institution ; and, as
Forchhammer tells us, the Burmans have in past centuries
been zealous Buddhists ; their ways of life, their social and
private institutions, are thoroughly Buddhistic, and they would
resent the idea of having still the tatters of their former
savage condition clinging to them. But I have been unable to
find any full estimate of the changes wrought by Buddhism
or a summing-up of its elevating results. This desideratum
is analogous to the absence of anything like a full account
in the histories of India of the effect of Buddhism on laws
and social life : scholars have been more fascinated by the
theology and the ecclesiastical polity. Bigandet remarks that
Gaudama paid little attention to the dogmatical portion of
religion, but laid the greatest stress on morals ; and there is
abundant proof that the great ethical commands of the
Buddhist system, as well as the formulas and creeds, have
become familiar to the Burmans and Talaings, and more or
less to the wilder tribes. The incessant teaching of the five
binding precepts, not to kill, nor steal, nor tell a lie, nor
drink intoxicating liquor, nor commit adultery, must have had
wide effect. The children of Burma are taught in the monasteries to read religious books, and the habit is kept up on holy
days, and when they bewail the death of friends. 'They,
without being aware of it, imbibe religious notions and become
acquainted with some parts of the religious creed, particularly
with what relates to Gaudama's preceding and last existence.'
I quote my venerable friend Bishop Bigandet ; and as to the
persuasion towards virtue contained in the Life of Gaudama,
whoever desires to know more should read his translation of
the Burmese Legend, which, as Dr. Rhys Davids states,

adheres very closely to the orthodox books of the Southern Church, introduced into Burma from Ceylon in the fifth century of our era.[1] The learned Prelate's notes and essays are on all hands treated as authority about Burmese Buddhism, combining, as they do, long experience of men and things with sagacious and judicial reflections. He describes the sermon preached by Gaudama to a Nat, the specimen given by Sangermano, as a fair sample of similar performances; and this sermon is a compendium of almost all the moral virtues. Buddhism he calls 'a moral and practical system, making man acquainted with the duties he has to perform in order to shun vice and practise virtue.' Again, 'It will not be deemed rash to assert that most of the moral truths prescribed by the Gospel are to be met with in the Buddhist Scriptures.' The wonder therefore disappears that the Legend of Buddha should have been adapted into a Christian form by St. John of Damascus, and the saintly hero canonised by the Pope of Rome as St. Josaphat, to whom, according to Colonel Yule, a church at Palermo is dedicated. Monier-Williams believes the Buddhists to have been the first to introduce total abstinence from strong drinks into India. Rehatsek, after ascribing the civilisation of the Mongols to their conversion from Shamanism to Buddhism, writes : 'It is almost incomprehensible how the savage Mongols, who were accustomed to massacre whole populations in order to secure their rear from enemies, zealously submitted to a religion inculcating gentleness and kindness to all created beings, and how a nation that loved to raze cities to the ground, and to convert cultivated plains into deserts to obtain pastures, should have eagerly built temples, established convents, introduced useful institutions, and practised religious duties.' The

---

[1] To those who believe, with Tennyson, that the poets see 'through life and death, through good and ill,' I would commend Sir Edwin Arnold's *Light of Asia*. No prose descriptions of the varied landscapes of Burma, with which I am acquainted, approach Mrs. Hemans's verses in ' The Better Land.' All the scenes she imagines are beheld in Burma.

tendency of the religion must have been the same among other savage tribes. Buddhism also supplies the mind with ideas of vastness and solemnity, not without elevating effect. The Burman woman, with her rosary in hand, may be heard any day repeating the formula about Vanity or Vanities—the words 'Change, Pain, Illusion.' The other sentence of the three gems, wherein the weary soul takes refuge, is equally familiar: 'Buddha, the Law, and the Communion of Saints.' We are told by Bigandet that the fervour and love with which Buddhists speak of the Law must be witnessed to be realised: in conversation regarding their faith they are sometimes moved to tears. This law, discovered by Buddha, governs the whole universe physical and moral, in heaven above and the earth beneath, through the operation of cause and effect. The dewdrop is formed, and the heart is tranquillised, and the practice of virtue is rewarded by means of causes that are alike in the manner of their operation. One must suppose that several generations passed away to their long home before the worshippers of ghosts and demons and tribal gods, people addicted to blood-feuds, and as ignorant of letters as the wilder Karens and Chins and Kachins of to-day, accepted a gigantic philosophical theory like this of Dharma.

Turning aside from the *tendencies* to what is known of the practical *results* of Buddhism in Burma, we find two of great importance—a general diffusion of education through the teaching of the monks, and the elevation of the character and position of women. The genius of the religion disregards caste, allows no difference between man and man except what is proved by superiority in virtue, and insists on imparting knowledge to all. The Census Report of 1891, which is the latest official document I have come across, speaks of the exertions of the monks in matters of education in those terms of praise with which we have long been familiar; they seem willing, even in the newly conquered province, to combine the new with the old, to attempt a reconciliation between science and religion. The elevation of woman is rather more perplexing, as the theology treats marriage from the ascetic point of view: a wise man is to avoid it as if it were a burning pit of live coals, and to wander lonely on the path of life, like a rhinoceros. These counsels of perfection were met in India by the same sort of arguments that Chaucer puts into the mouth of the Wife of Bath in his *Canterbury Tales.* According to Monier-Williams, they checked the spread of Gaudama's religion. The people murmured and said, 'He is come to bring childlessness among us, and widowhood and destruction of family life.' All the same, Buddhism admits of nuns and lay sisters; and its love of equality comes to their aid. On so interesting a subject I am constrained to quote at length from the writings of the learned and impartial Bigandet. 'Who could think,' he asks, 'of looking upon the woman as a somewhat inferior being, when we see her ranking, according to the degrees of her spiritual attainments, among the perfect and foremost followers of Buddha?' Again, 'In Burma and Siam the doctrines of Buddhism have produced a striking, and to the lover of true civilisation a most interesting, result, viz., established the almost complete equality of the condition of women with that of men. In those countries women are not miserably confined in the interior of their houses, without the remotest chance of ever appearing in public. They are seen circulating freely in the streets; they preside at the comptoirs, and hold an almost exclusive possession of the bazaars. Their social position is more elevated in every respect than that of the persons of their sex in the regions where Buddhism is not the predominating creed. They may be said to be men's companions and not their slaves. They are active, industrious, and by their labours and exertions contribute their full share towards the maintenance of the family. The marital rights, however, are fully acknowledged by a respectful behaviour towards their lords.'

The reader acquainted with the tendencies and some of the

results of Buddhism will perhaps be perplexed when he hears of the cruelties perpetrated in wars, or in the reigns of terror by some of the absolute monarchs. These atrocities, as well as the corruption and insecurity which despotic government caused, are depicted by Sangermano, and bewailed by our Envoys in their narratives. The King of Burma was the secular head of the religion, and it may doubtless be argued that he ought to have felt the restraining hand of Holy Church. It would, however, be unjust to blame religion for the secular crimes of uncontrolled kings: it is simpler to impute them in Burma to Oriental despotism. Over these tyrants the religion cast its terrors when it proclaimed the unchangeable effect of evil action; and in the law-books, which were often compiled by men of the sacred yellow robe at the behest of kings, we find long quotations from the Scriptures explaining the difference between dharma, or rule according to law, and the sinful decrees of passion and brute force. These Codes, originally based on the famous Codes of Manuic India, thus became saturated with Buddhist ethics; and one of the most visible results is the elevation of women in matters of status, marriage, and inheritance. The testimony of these law-books to this great social change is ignored by most writers, although in the general absence of original Burmese literature, except a few lyrics, these Dhammathats are, as Dr. Forchhammer pointed out, the only literary works which disclose to the student the practical effect of a religious system upon the social and political growth of the Talaings and Burmans. It must, however, be confessed that Buddhism did not abolish slavery in Burma or Siam; and our Envoys notice with pity a revolting incident of insolvency, whereby the wife or daughter might be sold at the suit of a creditor, and thus condemned to the public brothel. Turning from these non-feasances of the Buddhist Church, we must put in the other scale the religious toleration noted by Sangermano which allowed the Italian Catholics, and, later on, the American

Baptists, to confer benefits on the people, before we had gained
any territory in Burma. Sometimes one sect of Buddhists has
prevailed on the king to persecute the rival sect : but, as a rule,
theological hatred shrank from taking human life, round which
the religion sheds a sanctity. The Bishops and Abbots often
interposed between the monarch or governor and the people,
for purposes of humanity or justice ; and at the present day
religious fanaticism is almost unknown among the Buddhists,
and rival sects live with each other on friendly terms. To
avoid prolixity, I must now conclude my remarks on the racial
origins and Indian institutions affecting Burma, and turn to
the next great cause which more and more sways life and
thought there—the intercourse with Europe ending in the
conquest by England, and the regulative effects of our law and
administration, which may fitly be compared to those of the
Romans. It has been no part of my aim to discuss Buddhism
in general, and I leave untouched the questions whether the
Gaudama of the Legend was a real person or a solar myth,
whether Buddhaghosa the divine is a mere name and allegory,
and other matters of dispute in religion and philology.

In his *Narrative of the Mission to Ava* in 1855, Colonel Yule
supplies a singularly full and accurate account of the intercourse
of the Burmese countries with Western nations, to which, and
also the last chapter in Phayre's *History of Burma*, I refer the
reader, abridging here what otherwise I might have to say.
The first European traveller of modern times seems to be
Nicolò de Conti, a noble Venetian of Damascus, who travelled
by Persia, India, and Ceylon to Sumatra, whence, after sixteen
days' sailing, he reached Tenasserim, which district he says
abounds in elephants and a species of thrush. He then crossed
to the Ganges, and next went up the river Racha (Arakan)
to the city of that name. Then he journeyed over ' mountains
void of all habitations for the space of seventeen days, and
then through open plains for fifteen days more' to the river
Irawadi and the city of Ava, where, he remarks, the king rides

on a white elephant, and the women, as well as men, puncture
their flesh with pins of iron, and rub into these punctures pig-
ments which cannot be obliterated, and so they remain painted
for ever. The Burman women have now given up this habit of
tattooing, which the Chin women retain. The traveller was
not strictly correct in saying that all worship idols: it is interesting to read about the devotion to the three gems. 'When
they rise in the morning from their beds they turn towards the
east, and with their hands together say, "God in his Trinity
and his Law defend us."' About 1496 we find Hieronimo de
Santo Stephano of Genoa in the city of Pegu. War was going
on with Ava; and he had to wait above a year to get payment
from the king for his merchandise. In the sixteenth century
the Portuguese appear; and we find them often serving as
mercenaries in the wars between the kings of the Delta. One
of these military adventurers was the celebrated Ferdinand
Mendez Pinto, who mingles romance with his history. Cæsar
Frederike, a more trustworthy traveller, left Venice in 1563,
and spent eighteen years in the East. He refers to the capture
of Yuthia by Bureng Naung (A.D. 1569), and the return of the
conqueror to Pegu with the spoils of Siam, Frederike being an
eye-witness of 'his tryumphs and victorie, which coming home
and returning from the warres was a goodly sight to behold,
to see the elephants come home in a square, laden with gold,
silver, jewels, and with noble men and women that were taken
prisoners.' He describes the two cities of Pegu, the old and
the new: the houses built of cane and thatched with leaves,
the magazine or *godon* of brick, used as a common store by
the merchants, the crocodiles in the ditch, the four white elephants, the gilded shrines with the four statues of gold, silver,
brass, and copper alloy. He got an exaggerated notion of an
army, mustering 4000 elephants and 80,000 harquebusses; the
difficulty usually felt in a campaign, the problem of feeding
so great a multitude seemed to him nothing great, as these
troops would eat anything, 'very filthie or otherwise, all

serveth for their mouthes, yea, I have seen them eat scorpions
and serpents,' like the King of Cambay in *Hudibras*,

> 'whose daily food
> Was asp and basilisk and toad.'

In 1583 Gasparo Balbi, a Venetian jeweller, visited Pegu
with a stock of emeralds. He gives a lively account of all
that he saw: of Negrais with its swarms of flies, Cosmin the
haunt of tigers, Dala with the ten large rooms full of royal
elephants, 'the faire citie of Dagon' [Rangoon] with the long
approach to the glorious pagoda, rising high in air like the
Campanile at Venice. Then he sailed by Syriam, where the
ruined walls showed traces of the war of 1567, and at length
reached Pegu, where in solemn audience he gave the king an
emerald.

Ralph Fitch, a London merchant, who after staying at Aleppo,
Ormus, Cambay, Goa, and some places on the Ganges, reached
Negrais in 1586, confirms many statements of Frederike's and
Balbi's. 'Three days after, we came to Cosmin, which is a very
pretty town, and standeth very pleasantly, very well furnished
with all things. The people be very tall and well-disposed:
the women white, round-faced, with little eyes; the houses are
high built, set upon great high posts, and they go up to them
for feare of the tigres, which be very many.' He went on to
Pegu, and, like Frederike, who says the king 'far excels the
power of the Grand Turk in treasure and strength,' he was
impressed with all he saw of a pomp and magnificence which far

> 'Outshone the wealth of Ormus and of Ind.'

In the letters of these old travellers, Pegu stands forth as a
right royal abode

> 'Where the gorgeous East with richest hand
> Showers on her kings barbaric gold and pearl.'

Rubies were in such quantity, 'that they know not what to do
with them, but sell them at most vile and base prices.' 'The
merchandises that go out of Pegu are gold, silver, rubies,

sapphires, spinelles, great store of benjamin, long pepper, lead, lacca, rice, wine, some sugar.' The trade was conducted through brokers, and the practice of selling a debtor's wife and children as slaves is mentioned. There seems to have been a thriving import trade. Sometimes opium came from Cambay; and once a year a ship arrived from Bengal, and another from Madras, with bombast cloth. Martaban traded with Malacca. Wool, scarlets, velvets, opium, and chickinos came from Mecca, and the King of Acheen's ships brought pepper. But the Pegu king was menaced by the naval power of Arakan. Fitch went a journey of twenty-one days from Pegu to 'a very faire and great towne,' where merchants from China came 'with great store of muske, golde, silver, and many other things.' 'I went,' he writes, 'from Pegu to Iamahey, which is in the country of the Langeiannes, whom we call Iangomes.' This remote city is Zimmé, or, as our Foreign Office, which has established a consulate there, now spells it. Chieng-mai. Thither the East India Company's factor in Siam sent in 1618 one Thomas Samuel to open up a trade. The place had been captured from Pegu by the King of Siam; but after the fall of Pegu, the Burman king took possession of Zimmé, and carried off Samuel among other prisoners to Pegu, where he died. During the seventeenth century the Madras authorities of the East India Company started factories at Syriam, Prome, and Ava; and for a great part of that period the Dutch had establishments at the same places. In the great collection of Dutch archives made by de Jonge, we find a letter of 1608 from the King of Arakan, self-styled Salimscha. Kaiser of Pegu, and traces of contact with the famous Portuguese adventurer Philip de Brito, who afterwards ruled at Syriam.

The 'interlopers,' as the East India Company's servants called the private traders from England, soon appeared on the scene; and in 1687 the Company sent Captain Weldon in a ship from Madras to drive out the English settlers at Mergui, then under Siam, by force. In a disturbance that followed some Siamese were killed ; and seventeen Englishmen who were in the town were massacred in revenge. After this, British subjects were for a long time excluded from Siam. In 1695 Mr. Fleetwood and Captain Lesley went as envoys from Madras to Ava, and in 1709 Mr. Allanson was sent there by Governor Pitt. For the succeeding period, including the reign of Alompra and his conquest of Pegu, the parts played by the English and French in that war, the capture of Syriam from the French in 1756, and the massacre of the English at Negrais in 1759, the best authority is Major Michael Symes' *Embassy to Ava in* 1795. In the following year Captain Hiram Cox, our Resident at Rangoon, visited the King Bodoahpra, or, as Sangermano calls him, Badonsachen. The entertaining and thoughtful narrative of Symes throws much light on the period, and in many respects supplements Sangermano's account of the Burman Empire. The next events of importance are the war of 1824, which led to the annexation of Arakan and Tenasserim by the British, and the sending of Mr. John Crawfurd on an embassy to Ava in 1826, of which he wrote a journal, which is very good reading. The narrative of Sir A. Phayre's mission in 1855, soon after the second war which gave us the province of Pegu, the city of Rangoon, and all the Delta, was written by Yule, and is in every way of conspicuous merit. This work stands in point of time between Sangermano and the official *Gazetteer of Lower Burma*, compiled by Colonel Spearman. Since this *Gazetteer* was published, Upper Burma has been conquered, and the Burman monarchy has come to an end. Great events like these strike those that make them : they have created a new and wider interest in the country, and added to the value of Sangermano's work as a description of a state of things now receding far into the past.

Sangermano's residence in Ava and Rangoon from 1783 to 1806, while the Burman monarchy was in full power and

undismembered, enabled him to understand the Burman and
Talaing nations. He was one of the earliest of that type of
Christian missionaries who, in order to influence the people,
set themselves to study their languages, literatures, and institutions; and who were thus enabled to place at the
service of the English officials much information, of the
utmost use, first to the administrators, and afterwards to
scholars. I may add to what is said of Sangermano's life in
the Prefaces to the two earlier editions the notice of him
written by Major Symes, to illustrate the above remark.
Symes says: 'Among the foreigners who came to pay their
respects to the English gentlemen was an Italian missionary,
named Vincentius Sangermano, who had been deputed to this
country, about twenty years before, by the Society de Propaganda: he seemed a very respectable and intelligent man,
spoke and wrote the Birman language fluently, and was held
in high estimation by the natives for his exemplary life
and inoffensive manners. His congregation consisted of the
descendants of former Portugeze colonists, who, though numer-.
ous, are in general very poor; they, however, had erected a
neat chapel, and purchased for their pastor a piece of ground
a mile from the town, on which a neat, comfortable dwelling
was built and a garden enclosed. He is indebted for his
subsistence to voluntary contributions of his flock; in return
for their charity he educates their children, instructs them
in the tenets of the Romish faith, and performs mass
twice a day at the chapel. From this reverend father I
received much useful information.' It seems to be the fact
that Symes and Sangermano went into matters of learning in
their talks, as appears from another passage where Symes
notices the resemblance of a Persian edition of the Arakan
Code to the Burman version of the Manu Shaster of India.
'I was so fortunate,' says Symes, 'as to procure a translation
of the most remarkable passages, which were rendered into
Latin by Padre Vincentius Sangermano.' It only remains to

add that the reputation of the Italian priest has stood the test of time. He is treated as an authority by Bigandet and every writer on Burma: he is cited also by Dr. Kern and most of the historians of Buddhism. The above considerations appear ample to justify the offer to the public of a new edition of his work.

The notes I have appended to Dr. W. Tandy's translation of the Italian text will, I trust, not interfere with the charm of Sangermano's story. Many of them are proofs of the accuracy of his observations: others throw side-lights on his views of things, especially where I cite the three historians of our embassies—Symes, Crawfurd, and Yule, whose interesting folios are not easily accessible to the general reader, and are less available for reference because, like Bishop Bigandet's book on Buddhism, they are wanting in indexes. These inconveniences attend some works of research produced in the last decade, Forchhammer's *Notes on Archæology* and my series of *Notes on Buddhist Law*. The Blue-book containing the Census Report of 1891 is full of novel information on the subjects of ethnology and languages, with which Sangermano dealt according to his lights. Since his day, also, the natural history of Burma has received full and scientific treatment. In editing this work I have, where the limits of space allowed, aimed at supplying the results of most recent inquiry ; and elsewhere have stated the source where the student of any branch of learning may find it treated. This aim is rendered more difficult, seeing that on many points where research is recent, the authorities propound varying theories and come to different conclusions. In matters of history I have here and there supplemented the author by reference chiefly to Sir A. Phayre's *History of Burma* ; and while avoiding the vast questions about Buddhism upon which great scholars like Kern, Oldenberg, Monier-Williams, Rhys Davids, and Senart raise discussion, I have tried to answer those which arise out of the ordinary life of the people of Burma, by quotations from local authorities, *e.g.* Bigandet, Forchhammer, Forbes, and Scott. The Italian phonetic spelling of Burmese and other names has been retained, as this affords evidence of the pronunciation in Sangermano's time. To assist the student, I have in many instances inserted in brackets the spelling of kings' names and technical terms used in Phayre's History and Hardy's books on Buddhism, and have given the names of most places of importance as commonly spelt. An index to the work has been supplied. The reader will also observe that here and there I have endeavoured to show what changes have come over the people, so that he may contrast and compare times present with times past.

Sangermano dwelt in Burma during the period of the French Revolution, the Reign of Terror, the European wars that followed, and the Irish Rebellion of 1798. In India many things were allowed under British rule, such as criminal punishment by lopping off the feet, the sale of slaves, and the burning of widows, which in course of time were abolished by such reforming Governors-General as Lord Cornwallis and Lord William Bentinck. The criminal code of England was extremely sanguinary, as is noticed by such different men as Yule and Heine; and the whole condition of society in the United Kingdom, as well as in most parts of Europe then, was far behind what it is now. The crusade against colonial slavery had hardly begun. Facts like these must be borne in mind to balance what Sangermano says of the character of the people. It is only fair to the Burmans and Talaings to record that many competent judges think that the amiable Italian hardly does justice to their better and more agreeable qualities. Happily, two great changes have taken place, let alone the general increase of enlightenment. Slavery with all its cruel opportunities is abolished, and there is no such thing as the sale of a wife or child for debt. Despotism has given way to just rule : the sale of public offices, the favouritism, the corruption, the licentious treatment of women which went on under the wilful king whose character Sangermano paints in such dark colours, exist no more. These abuses were far less prominent, indeed, in Upper Burma under the rule of the milder prince to whose court Phayre and Yule journeyed in 1855. Security of property and person is now established with the law over the whole land; and if we compare what the Director of State Education says in the Census Report of 1891, of the order of monks, with the estimate 'of the religious by Bishop Bigandet in 1880, we may fairly hope that the removal of the burden of despotism has infused a freshness of beneficent energy into these common school-masters of the people. Two causes, said the learned Bishop, made the Talapoins incomparably idle: the first a physical one, the relaxing heat of the climate; the second a moral one, the tyranny of the despotic government which, by making property insecure, destroyed the incentive to work, with all the useful moral discipline that labour affords. 'He who is suspected of being rich is exposed to numerous vexations on the part of the vile satellites of tyranny, who soon find out some apparent pretext for confiscating a part or the whole of his property, or depriving him of life, should he dare to offer resistance.' This sentence skims the philosophy of history. A vivid picture of the state of things about Rangoon in 1813 is found in the journal of Mrs. Judson, the wife of the American missionary. 'The country,' she writes, ' presents a rich and beautiful appearance, everywhere covered with vegetation, and, if cultivated, would be one of the finest in the world. But the poor natives have little inducement to labour, or to accumulate property, as it would probably be taken from them by their oppressive rulers.' The change from despotic violence to the rule of law must in time elevate the character of the subjects, and the English in Burma cannot reasonably expect the upward progress to be completed in one generation or even two.

In concluding this introduction I must express my thanks

to my friend Mr. Taw Sein-Ko, a native of Burma, and at present Lecturer in the University of Cambridge, for the learned aid I have received from him, and my hopes that he will resume on the spot his researches into the recondite lore of the Indo-Chinese countries when the Educational Board of Burma has, as it now proposes to do, changed itself into a University for all the countries and tribes of that part of the Queen's empire.

JOHN JARDINE.

LIST OF THE PRINCIPAL WORKS REFERRED TO

BIGANDET, The Right Rev. P. *The Life or Legend of Gaudama, the Buddha of the Burmese.* 2 vols. Third edition. London, 1880.

British Burma Gazetteer. 2 vols. Rangoon, 1880.

Burma Census Report, 1891. Rangoon.

CRAWFURD, JOHN. *Journal of an Embassy to Ava in 1827.* London, 1829.

DAVIDS, Dr. T. W. RHYS. *Buddhism.*

Early Voyages and Travels. See Hakluyt's *Voyages, India in the Fifteenth Century*, and Purchas' *Pilgrims.*

ELPHINSTONE, Hon. MOUNTSTUART. *The History of India.*

FORBES, Captain. *British Burma and its People.*

FORCHHAMMER, E. *Jardine Prize Essay on Burmese Law.* Rangoon, 1885.

—— *Notes on the Early History and Geography of British Burma.* Rangoon, 1883 and 1884.

—— *Notes on the Languages and Dialects spoken in British Burma.* Rangoon, 1884.

FRANCKLIN, Major WILLIAM. *Tracts on Ava.* Compiled from Papers of Captain Hiram Cox. London, 1811.

GRAY, Professor JAMES. *Ancient Proverbs and Maxims, from Burmese Sources.* London, 1886.

GRIFFINI, Father D. M., *Della Vita di Monsignor Gio. Maria Percoto.* Udine, 1781.

HAKLUYT's *Voyages.* Vol. ii. London, 1810.—The Voyage of Master Cesar Frederick into the east India, and beyonde the Indies, Anno 1563.—The long, dangerous, and memorable voyage of M. Ralph Fitch, marchant of London.

HARDY, R. SPENCE. *The Legends and Theories of the Buddhists.*

India in the Fifteenth Century. By R. H. MAJOR. Hakluyt Society, 1857.—Travels of Nicolò de Conti and Hieronimo de Santo Stephano.

JARDINE, JOHN. *Customary Law of the Chin Tribe.* By Maung Tet Pyo. Rangoon, 1884.

—— *Notes on Buddhist Law, with Translations.* Nos. 1 to 8. Rangoon, 1882, 1883.

JUDSON, ANN H., *An Account of the American Baptist Mission to the Burman Empire.* London, 1827.

KERN, Dr. H. *Geschiedenis van het Buddhisme in Indie.* Haarlem, 1882.

MASON, Dr. F. *Burma, its People and Productions.* 2 vols. Theobald's edition. Hertford, 1882.

MAUNG TET PYO. *Customary Law of the Chin Tribe.* Rangoon, 1884.

PALLEGOIX, Monsignor. *Description du Royaume Thai ou Siam.* Paris, 1854.

PHAYRE, Sir ARTHUR P. *History of Burma.* London, 1883.

PURCHAS' *Pilgrims.* Edition of 1625, Book 10.—Voyages of Gasparo Balbi, Cæsar Frederike and Ralph Fitch.

REHATSEK, E. ' Christianity among the Mongols.' *Journal of the Bombay Branch of the Royal Asiatic Society.* Vol. xiii. 1877.

ROST, Dr. R. Article on ' Pali.' *Encylopædia Britannica.*

SHWAY YOE (J. Scott). *The Burman, his Life and Notions.*

SPEARMAN, Colonel H. See *British Burma Gazetteer.*

SYKES, Lieut.-Colonel W. H. *Notes on the Religious, Moral, and Political State of India before the Mahomedan Invasion.* London, 1841.

SYMES, MICHAEL ; Major in His Majesty's 76th Regiment. *An Account of an Embassy to Ava in* 1795. London, 1800.

THEOBALD, W. See Dr. F. Mason's *Burma, its People and Productions.*

YULE, Captain HENRY. *A Narrative of the Mission to the Court of Ava in* 1855. London, 1858.

PREFACE TO THE SECOND EDITION

In nearly every history of Burma, or account of the Burmese people, the reader finds allusions to Sangermano and often extracts from his book. But he is puzzled to make out who Sangermano was and when and where he lived, and is sometimes left in danger of supposing wrongly that Sangermano's remarks apply to the present times. If, attracted by the interesting matter that every author finds in him, the reader goes to the libraries to get Sangermano's book, he learns that there is no copy. If he goes to a private person reputed to have a copy, he returns disappointed, the copy having perhaps been lent long ago to some one else who never returned it. For several years this was my experience.

A few months ago I discovered that Colonel Spearman, of the British Burma Commission, had a copy, and he obliged me by the loan of it. This is the volume from which the present edition is reprinted by order of the Chief Commissioner, after obtaining the consent to this republication of the Right Rev. P. Bigandet, Bishop of Ramatha and Vicar Apostolic. It was deemed right to refer to him as being the present head of the Roman Catholic mission in Burma.

Cardinal Wiseman's preface to the edition of 1833 informs us that Father Sangermano arrived in Burma in 1783, and returned to Italy in 1808. Becoming President of the order of Barnabites at Arpinum, his native city, he employed himself in preparing his work for publication, but was prevented by his death in 1819. Bishop Bigandet informs me that this happened at Leghorn as he was about to sail for Burma, and that during his stay in Italy he was graciously treated by Joachim Murat.

c

king of Naples. The Roman Sub-Committee of the Oriental Translation Fund undertook to publish and translate the manuscript. The orthography was kept except in a few well-known names : hence the proper names are to be read as in Italian. In this reprint no alterations have been made.

The Oriental Translation Fund was instituted in 1828 under the patronage of King William IV. In the binding of Colonel Spearman's copy I find a prospectus showing that Sir Gore Ouseley, the Vice-President of the Royal Asiatic Society, was its Chairman, and John Shakespear and Dr. Rosen its Secretaries. ' This copy was printed for the Right Honourable the Earl of Clare, Governor of Bombay, a subscriber.' The motto of the Fund was ' Ex oriente lux.' Fifty years have passed and no second edition has been issued.

During this half century much has been added to our knowledge of the subjects described by Sangermano. The Burmese legend of Buddha has been translated and edited by Bishop Bigandet. The history of Burma has lately been written by Sir Arthur Phayre ; and before this edition issues from the press the learning of Dr. Forchhammer will have thrown light on the Burmese Dhammathat or Code of Law in his edition of King Wagaru's code and his essay on Buddhist law. But all this increase of knowledge does not detract from the real value of Sangermano's work or lessen its charm. Even when he describes the abstract notions of the Buddhist religion, or the dry rules of law, we feel his contact with the people : we learn how the religion influenced their life, and how the despotic and capricious administration of the law produced results which the Dhammathat would never suggest. Sangermano's thoroughness is notable. He gets his account of Buddhism from a treatise drawn up by the king's uncle in 1763 : he translated much of the Buddhist canon with the help of a former pôngyi learned in Pali. He went direct to the Burmese annals for his history ; and his version of the Burmese Code, called the Golden Rule, shows that he used some such Dhammathat as the Manu Sara Shwe Myin, and took much trouble to understand it. Between 1768 and 1780 several new versions of Dhammathats had been compiled by learned Burmans such as Kyaw Deng ; and it is probable that a scholar eager to get at their real meaning would have found some of these lawyers or other learned men competent to teach him. Sangermano proceeded to make an abstract of one of these codes ; he seems not to have aimed at precise translation ; but after comparing his abstract with the Wagaru and the part of the Wonnana Dhammathat found in our Notes on Buddhist Law, I would be well inclined to treat this abstract as valuable in suggesting meanings of doubtful passages. There is now little oral tradition to explain the Dhammathats, at least in British Burma : but in Sangermano's time there must have been plenty : he was familiar with the king's officials, he had Pali scholars at his elbow, and he noticed the way the Burmese judges applied the law. In these several respects he had advantages which European scholars miss nowadays. Sangermano appends a few notes showing instances where the law was administered contrary to the code, and his earlier chapters on manners must be read in connection with it. I greatly doubt whether Dr. Richardson, who in 1847 translated the Manu Kyay Dhammathat (dated A.D. 1760), had seen this abstract. It is the only popular account of Burmese law that has ever been written ; it appears to be a useful manual of that law as understood in Rangoon a hundred years ago ; it fairly reflects the spirit of the Dhammathats, and in these respects seemed to me likely to be of such use to the officers freshly appointed to the British Burma Commission that I advised that it should be reprinted. On the other hand, I must remark that until it has been thoroughly compared, section by section, with the Dhammathats, it cannot be treated as equal to those originals or as a safe guide to settlement of doubtful questions. It is curious that nearly all later writers on the Burmese avoid mention or statement of the law ; so that information on the simplest questions hardly exists except in judicial decisions.

At the end of the book are two notes, compiled by the Roman sub-committee, to show the progress of Roman Catholic missions in Burma. I add a third, compiled from an Italian book lent me by Bishop Bigandet, Griffini's *Vita di Monsignor Percoto,* published at Udine in 1781.

The reader will time after time remark how some generalization of Sangermano's seems as true now as in his day. Burmese medicine, *e.g.*, has not advanced; 'they have themselves no regular surgeons.' But the trade in rice, the great wealth of Burma and principal export of the port of Rangoon at present, is not mentioned at all in the account of trade.

JOHN JARDINE.

RANGOON, *5th April* 1884.

THE following work was drawn up by F. Sangermano, partly during his residence as a missionary in Ava, and partly after his return to Europe. He was sent out as a missioner in 1782, and in the July of the following year arrived at Rangoon, whence he proceeded directly to the city of Ava. But shortly after he was remanded to Rangoon, which was the scene of his future missionary labours. The cause of Christianity was greatly forwarded in this place by his exertions. He completed the church of St. John, which had been begun before him, as well as the college of the missionaries; both of which were built of brick. He superintended the college as long as he remained there; and under his direction it was very prosperous. It contained fifty students, who were instructed in several branches of learning and science; so that besides some ecclesiastics, it has produced skilful engineers, physicians, and even pilots. There is at present a young Burmese practising as a surgeon in Rome who received his education in this institution.

F. Sangermano was greatly esteemed by the natives of Rangoon: in particular, the Viceroy and his consort honoured him with many marks of distinction. The latter would often come to his church to be present at the Catholic ceremonies, especially those of Holy-week: and sometimes she would pay a visit to the Superior in his College, and hold long conferences with him on religion; so that it was thought that she would become a Christian. On these occasions she always came with her guards and her whole court. Her guards remained in the square opposite the college, but the rest of her suite entered with her.

F. Sangermano was also well known to the foreigners who frequented Rangoon, particularly to the English. From one of the latter he had a commission to make a chart of the port of Rangoon, which he executed with so much ability as to receive a pension for life from our Government. He also experienced great attention from the English authorities when at Calcutta on his return home.

The individual who had given him the above-mentioned commission procured for him a letter of recommendation from the Governor-General, by which all English captains were required to afford him every facility for his return. He arrived in Italy in 1808; and after having got through the business which had recalled him home, endeavoured to return to his missionary labours. But the state of the times prevented him; and he was finally established as president of the college of his order at Arpinum, his native city. Here he employed himself in preparing the following work for publication; but his death in 1819 prevented the execution of his designs. His manuscript remained in the hands of the Barnabite Fathers, and would probably have never been presented to the public had not the Roman sub-committee of the Oriental Translation Fund undertaken its translation and publication. Although the primary regulations of this Society seem to sanction the publication of none but Oriental works, the Roman sub-committee felt themselves warranted in proposing this history to the parent committee, on the ground that it is chiefly made up of translations from important Burmese writings, whereof probably copies do not exist in Europe.

The following note found among F. Sangermano's papers, after the work was partly translated, indicates the original documents he has principally followed.

' 1. The Burmese cosmography has been extracted almost entirely from a book expressly composed for the elder brother of the reigning monarch, by a Zaradò or master of the Emperor, wherein he succinctly describes the system of the world, as taught by Godama, according to the expositions and opinions of the most celebrated Burmese Doctors.

' 2. All that is related of the ancient Burmese monarchs, and of the foundation and subsequent history of this kingdom, has been faithfully copied from the Maharazaven, that is, the great history of the kings.

' 3. In what I have said of the superstitions, astrology, religion, constitutions of the Talapoins, and the sermons of

Godama, I have not followed the tales and reports of the common people, but have carefully consulted the classical writings of the Burmese, known by the name of Kiam. The chapters on the rules of the Talapoins and the sermons of Godama contain an abstract of all that is worthy of notice in the three Kiam, called Vini, Padimot, and Sottan. I have translated nearly the whole of these books with the assistance of an Ex-Talapoin of the name of Ubà, who was one of the most learned of that order in the vicinity of Nabek, where for several years our seminary was situated. He has also taught the Palì language to two of my scholars, one of whom is at the present time labouring in the work of the mission at Rangoon.'

Some slight transposition has been made in the chapters, in order to improve the connection between the subjects which they treat. The orthography of the manuscript has been kept, except in a few well-known names : hence the proper names are to be read as in Italian.

It cannot be necessary to enumerate the difficulties experienced in conducting a large English work through a foreign press. Independently of the great labour of correction, it required some courage to think of imitating the beauty of typography which distinguishes the works printed by the parent committee in London. We flatter ourselves that we have done as much as circumstances would allow us, and that our present attempt will be indulgently received, as an earnest of our desire to forward the useful and noble objects of the Fund.

N. WISEMAN.

Rome, *June* 1, 1833.

DESCRIPTION

BURMESE EMPIRE

THE Burmese Empire comprises the tract of territory bounded on the south by the Indian Ocean, on the east by the Kingdom of Siam, on the west by Bengal, and on the north by the Kingdom of Azen [Assam] and the Chinese Empire. It includes not only the Kingdom of Ava, but likewise those of Pegù and Aracan, together with the petty States of Martaban, Tavai [Tavoy], and Merghi [Mergui]. Before proceeding to give an ample and detailed description of the manners, religion, and laws of this empire, it is not only expedient but necessary to premise some account of the system of the world according to the Burmese, or, in other words, of their cosmography. By this explanation various points relating to their religion and manners, to their theogony and ethics, will be rendered intelligible, which otherwise would be very obscure and difficult to comprehend.

A

BURMESE COSMOGRAPHY

CHAPTER I

OF THE MEASURES AND DIVISIONS OF TIME COMMONLY USED IN THE SACRED BURMESE BOOKS [1]

ACCORDING to these books there are five species of atoms. The first consists of that fluid by which all bodies are penetrated, and which, though invisible to man, is yet visible to the Nat,[2] superior genii of whom we shall speak hereafter. The second species is that very fine dust which is seen dancing in the air when the sun's rays penetrate through any aperture into a chamber. The third species consists of the dust raised from the earth by the motion of animals or vehicles. The fourth comprises those grosser particles which, unable to rise in the air on account of their natural gravity, remain fixed to the ground. Lastly, the fifth species consists of those little particles which fall when writing with an iron pen upon a

[1] For a full account of measures and the divisions of time the reader is referred to *The Burman, his Life and Notions*, by Shway Yoe, London, 1882, c. 30. The scales in common use differ from those of the books. ' For astronomical purposes, such as the casting of the horoscope, and the calculations for fortunate days and the like, an exceedingly elaborate scale exists, but it is never made use of in ordinary life.' There are twelve months with an intercalation every third year ; and, as among the Hindus, the month is divided into the dark and bright halves. The year begins in April. The seven days of the week are named after the planets. The people define time and distance by terms like the following :—When the sun was as high as a toddy palm, when monks go a-begging, children's go-to-bed time, the time it takes to boil a pot of rice, a stone's throw, a musket's sound.

[2] These Nats are the Dewas of the six lower heavens. In Burmah the belief in good and bad demons, also called Nats, existed before the spread of Buddhism. They are still as numerous as the fairies and elves were among the Saxons of old, every tree, stream, and town having its guardian Nat. Of the evil Nats, Burmans and other tribes have an extreme dread.—Bigandet's *Legend of the Burmese Buddha*, i. 18, 77 ; ii. 324.

palm-leaf. Thirty-six atoms of the first class make one atom of the second, thirty-six of the second make one of the third, and so in progression. Seven atoms of the fifth and last species are equal in size to the head of a louse; seven such heads equal a grain of rice; seven grains of rice make an inch, twelve inches a palm, and two palms a cubit; seven cubits give one *ta*, twenty *ta* one *ussabà*, eighty *ussabà* one *gaut*, and four *gaut* a *juzenà* [yojana]. Finally, a juzenà contains about six Burmese leagues, or 28,000 cubits.

Again, twelve hairs are equal to the size of a grain of rice, four grains of rice make a finger, twelve fingers a foot; the ordinary stature of a man is seven feet.

The following is the measure of time: that instant in which the fore or the middle finger withheld by the thumb darts from it to give a fillip is called a *carasi*: ten *carasi* make a *pian*, and six *pian* a *bizanà*. A quarter of an hour is composed of fifteen *bizanà*; four quarters make an hour, the day consists of sixty hours, the month contains thirty days, and twelve months form a year.

CHAPTER II

1. THE world is called logha, a word which signifies alternate destruction and reproduction. The Burmese admit a world, not everlasting, but having a beginning and an end; and this beginning and end they do not attribute to the power and will of a superior being, but merely to fate, which they call Dammatà [Dharma]. The world is divided into three parts, the superior, the inferior, and the middle. In the superior part is situated the seat of the Nat, in the inferior are the infernal regions, and in the middle is the seat or abode of men and animals. Of these beings and their abodes we shall treat lower down. The middle part is conceived to be flat and circular, though somewhat elevated in the centre, and bounded by a chain of very high mountains called Zacchiavalà [Sakwala], which gird it all round and form an impenetrable barrier. These mountains rise 82,000 juzenà [yojana, reckoned at 10 miles by Hardy] above the surface of the sea, and have an equal depth in the sea itself. The diameter of this middle part is 1,203,400 juzenà, and its circumference is three times the diameter. Its depth is 240,000 juzenà. The half of this depth entirely consists of dust; the other half, or the lower part, is a hard, compact

---

[1] For fuller information on the subjects of this and the next two chapters, the reader may consult Spence Hardy's *Manual of Buddhism*, ch. i., and his *Legends and Theories of the Buddhists*, p. 80, which are used by Dr. Kern of Leyden as the most complete review of the mystic cosmology of the Southern Buddhists. *Geschiednis van Het Buddhisme in Indie*, p. 289, Haarlem, 1882. The Buddhist system of the universe is fundamentally that of the Hindus, as is remarked by Yule in his *Narrative of the Mission to Ava*, London, 1858, p. 237, in a learned note.

stone called Silapatavi. This enormous volume of dust and stone is supported by a double volume of water, under which is placed a double volume of air; and beyond this there is nothing but vacuity.

2. In the centre of this middle part, above the level of the sea, the largest of the mountains, called Miemmò,[1] rises to the height of 84,000 juzenà, having an equal depth within the sea. Two truncated cones, united at their bases, may give an idea of the figure of this mountain. The diameter of the superior plane of Miemmò is 48,000 juzenà, and its circumference three times the diameter. Three enormous rubies, 3000 juzenà in height, serve as feet to this immense mass, and connect it with the great stone Silapatavi. The part of the mountain looking to the east is of silver, that looking to the west of glass, the side exposed to the north is of gold, and finally that to the south of dark ruby. Seven concentric chains of mountains enclose within them this celebrated eminence, and in their intermediate spaces run seven great rivers called Sità [Sidanta], whose waters are transparent and clear as crystal, and so very light that the feather of the smallest bird, if thrown into them, will sink to the bottom. These mountains are not of an equal height, nor are their rivers of equal breadth and depth. While the first range, called Jugantò, is 84,000 juzenà high, and the first river as many juzenà wide and deep, the second chain has half that height, that is to say, 42,000 juzenà, and just so wide and deep is the second river.

3. At the four cardinal points of Mount Miemmò, between the Zacchiavalà mountains and the last enclosure of Jugantò, in the midst of an immense sea, are situated four great islands, the abodes of men and animals. The eastern island has the form of a half-moon, and is 21,000 juzenà in circumference. The western island bears a circular figure like the full moon, and has likewise 21,000 juzenà in circumference. The northern island has 24,000, and is of a square figure; and lastly, the southern one, which is lozenge-shaped, is called Zabudibà [Jambudwipa], and is 30,000 juzenà in circumference. In this

---

[1] The Mount Myen-Mo of the Burmans is the Mount Meru of the Hindu cosmogony.

island the Burmese doctors place their kingdom, those of Siam and China, the coast of Coromandel, the island of Ceylon, and other parts with which they are acquainted. They likewise say that this island, with 500 smaller ones which belong to it and will be mentioned in the next paragraph, is inhabited by a hundred and one nations. Excepting, however, the Chinese, Tartars, Siamese, Cassè [Manipur], and Aracan, the names by which they denominate these nations do not correspond to those known in our geography. These four great islands take their names from certain large trees which grow in them and are considered their sacred emblems. For example, because its sacred tree is the Zabù, the southern island is called Zabudibà, or the Island of Zabù.

4. Besides these four great islands, they admit likewise 2000 of smaller dimensions (allotting 500 to each of the great ones) scattered here and there, but not widely apart, and bearing respectively the same figure as the larger islands. We have observed in sec. 2 that the eastern side of Mount Miemmò is of silver, the western of glass, the northern of gold, and the southern of dark ruby. Now, these four sides communicate their colour to the great and small islands and their inhabitants, as well as to the sea that surrounds them ; and consequently the eastern island and its inhabitants will be of a silver colour ; the southern, together with its inhabitants, rivers, trees, etc., will have the colour of the dark ruby ; and the same is to be said of the other islands. In like manner the great ocean is divided into four seas, that is to say, the white, the green, the yellow, and the dark red. These seas, however, are not everywhere of the same depth : that which is interposed between the small islands is shallow and almost always quiet, so that ships may conveniently sail in it ; but the seas in the midst of which the great islands lie have a depth of even 84,000 juzenà, and their waves rise to the height of 60 or 70 juzenà. Terrible whirlpools are here to be met, capable of swallowing up large ships. These seas abound with monstrous fishes of the length of 500 and even 1000 juzenà. When these merely move in the waters they agitate them to a considerable degree, but when they shake their whole body they excite a horrible tempest to the distance of even 500 and 800 juzenà.

Hence it follows that there can be no communication whatever between the inhabitants of the different great islands ; and the European ships that arrive in the Indies are supposed by the Burmese to come from some of the 500 small islets which surround the great southern island of Zabudibà. Hence they generally style them inhabitants of the small islands.

CHAPTER III

5. ALL living beings are divided by the sacred Burmese books into three classes : Chamà, or generating beings ; Rupà, or corporeal but ungenerated ; lastly Arupà, or incorporeal beings. And these three classes are again subdivided into thirty species, each of which has its Bon, or proper seat. The first class, or that of the Chamà, contains eleven species, or regions, or states of beings, seven of which are happy and four unhappy. The first of the happy states is that of man, and the other six are those of the Nat, who are corporeal beings, but in every respect superior to man, as will be shown just now. The four unhappy are the infernal states, in which beings, by the painful torments they suffer, pay the forfeit of the crimes committed by them in their antecedent life. The second class, called Rupà, contains sixteen regions or states, and the third, or the Arupà, contains only four.

6. Before we speak of the happiness or unhappiness of these beings, and of the places which they occupy, it is necessary to premise a few general observations. First, the Burmese, like many other nations of India, admit a metempsychosis or transmigration after death, but in a very different sense from that of Pythagoras, who taught that the soul, after the death of one body, occupied and animated another. The Burmese, on the contrary, say that at the death of a man, animal, or other living being, the soul perishes together with the body ; but then, from this complete dissolution another individual springs, which will be man, or beast, or Nat, according to the merits or demerits of the actions done by its predecessor during its life. Through this successive series of dissolutions and regenerations all beings go on for the duration of one or more

worlds till at length they have performed such works as render them worthy of the state of Niban [Nirvâna, Neibban], which is the most perfect of all states. This consists in an almost perpetual ecstasy, in which those who attain it are not only free from the troubles and miseries of life, from death, illness, and old age, but are abstracted from all sensation ; they have no longer either a thought or a desire. Secondly, we must premise that the Burmese books admit not only one but many or rather an infinite number of worlds. And this is to be understood in two senses. First, besides this world of ours, there are co-existent 10,100,000 others of the same shape and figure that mutually touch each other on three points, thus forming so many equilateral spaces, filled with very cold water impenetrable to the rays of the sun. Each side of these spaces is 3000 juzenà in length. Secondly, in force of that general law called Dammatà [Dharma], one world succeeds another, and no sooner is one destroyed than another is reproduced of the same form and figure. Nobody, not even the Divinity Godama himself, ever knew which was the first world and which will be the last : and hence the Burmese doctors deduce that this series of successive dissolutions and reproductions never had a beginning and will have no end, and they compare the system to a large wheel, to whose circumference it is impossible to assign any beginning or end.

7. Before we speak of the duration of life enjoyed by different classes of beings, it is further necessary to give an idea of the duration of a world, which is something truly portentous. The inhabitants of the southern island, and of the 500 smaller islets attached to it, are said perpetually to vary the duration of their life, which increases or diminishes according to the deserts of their good or bad conduct. We speak here merely of the inhabitants of the southern island ; for, as to those of the others, they have and ever will have the same length of life, as will be said in the sequel. The lives of the first inhabitants of the Zabudibà [Jambudwipa] island lasted an *assenchiè* [asankhya]. To give an idea of the pro-digious number of years which compose an assenchiè, it is said that, if it should rain continually for the space of three years over the whole world, which is 1,203,430 juzenà in diameter,

the number of drops of rain fallen in this time would express the number of years that compose an assenchiè. The sons and grandchildren of those primitive men fell off from the perfection of their ancestors, and abandoning virtue gave themselves up to vice, and hence the length of their life began gradually to diminish until it was reduced to ten years, the term allotted to some very wicked men. But afterwards their descendants, reflecting on the cause of this diminution, began to correct their morals and practise virtue. By this means they merited a new prolongation of their lives, first to thirty, then to eighty, a hundred, and a thousand years, and thus progressively, till they reached the term of an assenchiè, as was the case with the primitive inhabitants. Now these progressive variations from an assenchiè to ten years, and from ten years to an assenchiè, in successive generations, will take place sixty-four times before the final destruction of the world.

8. We may now proceed to treat of the happiness and misery of living beings and of the Bon, or regions which they occupy, in the three parts of the world : and we will begin by the happy beings, whose first species is man, as was observed in sec. 6. The diameter of the southern island, Zabudibà, is 10,000 juzenà. Subtracting from this number 3000, which are occupied by forests and deserts, and 4000 covered with water, the residue, or 3000 juzenà, contain the Bon, or region occupied by man. The longest term of life which a man can at present enjoy is eighty years. Among the inhabitants of the Zabudibà island some are observed to be rich, others poor; some learned, others ignorant ; some vile and abject, and others noble and elevated to the rank of kings, princes, or mandarins ; some are handsome and others deformed ; finally, some enjoy a long life and others a short one. All these diversities of condition are effects of the merit or demerit gained by each individual in his preceding life.

9. The inhabitants of the other three islands are not subject to the successive variation of the term of their lives mentioned above ; nor are they exposed to those troubles and that variety of condition which affect the inhabitants of the southern island Zabudibà. The term of life of the inhabitants of the

eastern and western islands is constantly 500 years. Their faces in shape resemble the figure of the island to which they belong; so that the eastern islanders have their faces of a semi-lunar form, and the western have theirs round like the full moon. Their stature is likewise different from that prevailing in the island Zabudibà, as the eastern islanders are nine cubits high and the western six. As to the state of society, sciences, agriculture, etc., these eastern and western islanders are perfectly similar to the southern. Both these islands have their sacred trees, which, by the power of fate, last from the beginning to the end of the world. They are a hundred juzenà high, and the spread of their branches is fifty juzenà.

10. But the inhabitants of the northern island differ in every respect from those of the other three islands because they make no use of agriculture or any other art or profession. A tree named Padesà grows in that fortunate island on which, instead of fruit, are seen hanging precious garments of various colours, whereof the natives take whatever pleases them best. In like manner they need not cultivate the soil, nor sow, nor reap; neither do they fish, nor hunt; because the same tree naturally produces them an excellent kind of rice without any husk. Whenever they wish to take nourishment, they have only to place this rice upon a certain great stone, from which a flame instantly issues, dresses their food, and then goes out of itself. While they eat their rice, various kinds of exquisite meats, ready dressed, appear upon the leaves of some trees, from which every one takes at will. The meal over, the remains immediately disappear. This food is, moreover, so very substantial, that what appears prepared for only one person is sufficient for many; and so nourishing, that those who partake of it can fast the seven following days without repeating their meal. These islanders are never subject to any kind of illness, nor to the troubles of old age, but live a thousand years, in continual youth. The manner in which they bring up their children, and contract marriage, is very singular. As the women there are not subject to menses nor the pains of labour, when their time arrives, they are delivered without any pain or difficulty, and abandon their newborn babe on the spot, without its running any risk of dying. For those that pass that way, putting their

finger in their mouth, extract from it a sweet liquor like nectar, which, wonderful to say, supports the child for seven days. Nourished and brought up in this manner, they are of course unable to ascertain who are their parents; the more so as in that island all the inhabitants are of the same shape and figure, and of the same golden colour. Hence it is provided, that when a couple, moved by reciprocal affection, wish to unite in wedlock, they should withdraw themselves under a certain beautiful tree. If this lowers its branches, and covers them round with its leaves, it is a sign that they are not near relations, and consequently the marriage is completed. If, on the contrary, the tree does not lower its branches, they consider it a proof of their consanguinity, and abstain from proceeding any further. In general, these islanders have no illicit inclinations, and the conjugal act is only exercised by them ten times during their whole life. Some of them live in a state of celibacy, as perfect and holy men, who have bridled the passions and inclinations of their hearts. Sorrow and all kinds of trouble or pain are strangers to this fortunate island, in which there is no cold nor heat, no winds nor storms, no lightning, thunder, nor rain. No ferocious animals nor venomous serpents threaten the lives of men. They have no need of houses for shelter; the island is full of pleasant, gold-coloured trees, which are ever covered with delicious fruit or flowers, of the most grateful odour, or which yield a fragrant liquor, with which the inhabitants are wont to anoint their bodies. Here and there are little rivulets of odoriferous sandal or other aromatic waters, in which they bathe and disport themselves. Although these islanders have a stature of thirteen cubits, they are still proportioned and well made, especially the women, who are endowed with singular beauty and possess great agility, softness, and symmetry of form. After having spent their life of 1000 years, amidst continual enjoyments and delights, they tranquilly expire; and their bodies are immediately transported to the other side of the island by some large birds, ordained by fate to this office.

11. The inhabitants of the eastern, western, and northern islands do not pass after death into the superior state of Nat, nor to the inferior, infernal state, as happens to those of the

southern island; but they are always born again inhabitants of the same island. And although this seems to be a desirable thing, especially with regard to the northern islanders, on account of their felicity, nevertheless the Burmese doctors say that if the inhabitants of the southern island are endowed with judgment and reason, they should not envy this lot: because in this southern island alone may one rise by the merit of good deeds, not only to the superior states of Nat, Rupà, and Arupà, but, moreover, to the most perfect of all, that of the Niban; and, for this reason, the Burmese poets call the southern island the Niban's ferry.

12. After man come the six states of the Nat, happy beings who are superior to man.[1] The first seat or Bon is called Zatumaharit, the second Tavateinsà, the third Jamà, the fourth Tussità, etc. These seats are disposed in order, beginning from the centre of Miemmò, and continuing along the Jugantò mountains, so as to form the first enclosure of the Miemmò, as far as the last barrier of the world, called Zacchiavalà. Here the first seat of the Nat, called Zatumaharit, is situated; and to this seat the sun, moon, planets, and stars belong. For, according to the sacred Burmese books, these are all so many houses or habitations of the Nat. The second seat, called Tavateinsà, extends from the summit of Mount Miemmò to the Zacchiavalà. The other seats are placed, one above the other, at a distance of about 42,000 juzenà. Above the seats of the Nat come those of the Rupà as follows:—558,000 juzenà above the last seat of the Nat are placed the three seats of the Rupà, called the first Zian, in form like a tripod. Although they are on the same level, one does not touch the other; but they are distant from each other 558,000 juzenà. At an equal distance above are placed the other three, bearing likewise the same figure. These are called the second Zian; and above them again are other three, of the same shape and distance, called the third Zian. At a similar distance succeed the other two seats of the Rupà, called the fourth Zian, which are placed on the same level. The five remaining abodes of the Rupà lie one above the other at the same distance of 558,000 juzenà from

---

[1] The six dewa-lokas.

one another.[1] And in the same manner and order are placed, one over the other, the four dwellings of the Arupà. This last abode is so far distant from the southern island, that should a stone be dropt from it, according to the Burmese doctors, it would not reach its destination till four years after.

13. We have now to speak of the happiness of the Nat, and of the length of their life. In the first place, the seat called Zatumaharit is divided among four great princes or kings of the Nat, each of whom possesses, at one of the four cardinal points of Miemmò, a vast city of 1000 square juzenà. These cities are all of the same form, and in the midst of each its prince has his large palace of twenty-five square juzenà, the columns, beams, and boards of which are of silver. For the magnificence of these cities we must refer the reader to what we shall say later, when we describe the second seat called Tavateinsà. The famous Padesà trees grow over the whole of this region ; and from them, in place of fruit, rich garments and exquisite food are seen hanging, with all that can contribute to the splendour and delight of the Nat who inhabit the place. Small rivulets and lakes of the clearest water, delightful orchards and gardens, are everywhere to be found. The length of life of these Nat is 500 years, which are equal to 9,000,000 of ours. Their height is half a juzenà. Both in this and in the superior seats there are males and females, who exercise the duties of matrimony, but whose fecundating principle is only wind or air ; and the children produced are brought to light, not like infants, but as if they were fifteen years of age. Other Nat of an inferior condition, such as giants, great birds, dragons, and other evil genii, who inhabit the declivity of the Jugantò mountains, or the forests and rivers, are subjected to the Nat of this seat.

14. It has been noticed above that to this seat belong those Nat that inhabit the sun, moon, and stars, ordained by fate to illuminate the world, to divide day from night, to distinguish the seasons, and to indicate good and evil to mankind. Hence it will be proper to give a short essay of Burmese Astronomy.

---

[1] The above sixteen regions are the Rupa-brahma-lokas, where the senses do not exist.   In the four Arupà worlds there is no bodily form.

The Burmese admit eight planets, the sun, the moon, Mercury, Venus, Mars, Jupiter, and Saturn. From these the days of the week take their denomination; for the Burmese call the first day the day of the sun; the second, the day of the moon, etc. Besides these seven planets they suppose an eighth invisible one, by them called Rahù, of which we shall speak just now. The sun, or the abode of the Nat called sun, has fifty juzenà in diameter, and 150 in circumference. This habitation is of gold within, and without of crystal; and as gold and crystal are naturally warm, therefore the rays of the sun always excite a sense of heat. The moon has forty-nine juzenà in diameter and thrice that measure in circumference; it is of silver without and ruby within; and silver and ruby being naturally cold, so the moon's light causes a cold sensation. Mars has twelve juzenà in diameter, Mercury fifteen, Jupiter seventeen, Venus nineteen, and Saturn thirteen. Of the stars they give no kind of measure, but merely say in general that they are the habitations of many Nat. The sun, moon, and stars all revolve round the great Mount Miemmò, but disposed in parallel orbits, so that, for example, the sun, in one diurnal revolution, illuminates successively the four great islands; and night is caused by the interposition of Miemmò between it and them.[1] When it is midday in the southern island, in the northern it is midnight; and when the sun sets to the eastern island, it rises to the western. Besides the diurnal motion common to the planets and stars, they allow the planets another periodical movement, and say, that from the north they pass to the south, and then return again to the north, passing always through the twelve constellations of the zodiac, Aries, Taurus, etc. Hence the sun returns, after a year, to the same point in the heavens whence it set out; while the moon accomplishes the same revolution in the space of a month. And although they seem to admit that the sun, moon,

---

[1] 'Major Phayre endeavoured to explain the solar system; but as the Burmese theory is that of a central mountain called Myen-Mo, several millions of miles high, around which are firmly fixed four great islands, on the southern of which Asia and Europe are situated, the sun which lights them revolving round the central mountain, the Envoy of course did not succeed in convincing the Minister of the truth of our view of the case.'—*Yule*, p. 67.

and other heavenly bodies have a gradual declination, alternately to north and south, yet they account for the variety of seasons upon a totally different hypothesis. And here we must notice that the Burmese divide the year, not into four, but into three seasons—the hot, the rainy, and the cold. To account for these, they have imagined three distinct paths in the heavens—the inner, the middle, and the outward. The inner path is nearest to Mount Miemmò, and when the sun is upon it, it is the season of rain; when in the middle path it is that of heat; and when in the outward one that of cold. The inner path nearly answers to our summer solstice; the middle one to our equinox; and the exterior to the winter solstice. Besides these they admit three other paths, one elevated above the other; for the Burmese doctors consider the sun to be sometimes nearer and sometimes more distant from us. These three paths, commencing from the highest, they call respectively the paths of the elephant, the ox, and the goat. For, as the goat loves to feed in warm and dry places, and the sun, when nearest to us, or moving along the lower path, causes the greatest heat and dryness, they have given to this path the appellation of the goat's. On the contrary, great cold is felt when the sun is distant, and the highest path, through which it then passes, is called the elephant's; because this quadruped delights in cold and damp places. The sun is determined to one of these paths by the bad or good conduct of man. Is he good and obedient, it chooses the middle one, which is the most temperate; is he, on the contrary, wicked and disobedient to the laws, it revolves through the higher or lower path, which is always the occasion of injury to the crops, and is detrimental to the health of man. The sun's motion in all three paths is far swifter than that of the moon. In the inner path it travels more than a million of juzenà a day; in the middle one, more than two millions; and in the outer one, more than three. Lastly, the sun, moon, and all the other heavenly bodies, although they appear spherical, are in reality acuminated like the flame of a candle. It is their distance which gives them a spherical figure.

15. We must now speak of the eclipses of the sun and moon, of the phases of the latter, and the causes that produce them.

It has been mentioned above that the Burmese, besides the seven principal planets, admit of an eighth, called Rahù, which is opaque and dark, and, for this reason, invisible to us. The size of this aërial monster is 4800 juzenà. Its body measures 600 juzenà, its breast twelve, its head 900, its forehead, nose, and mouth 300. The size of the feet and hands is 200 juzenà, and that of the fingers fifty. When this monstrous planet is instigated by envy towards the sun and moon, probably on account of their clearness and splendour, he descends into their respective paths, and, opening his horrible mouth, devours them. Should he, however, retain them for any length of time, his head would burst, as both the sun and moon irresistibly tend to prosecute their course; he is therefore obliged, after a short time, to vomit them up. Sometimes he places them under his chin, at others he licks them with his tongue, and sometimes covers them with his hand; and thus are explained the total and partial eclipses of the sun and moon, together with their immersion and emersion. Every three years Rahù goes thus to meet the sun, and every six months the moon. The eclipses are not, however, always visible in the southern island; but whenever they are, the same is the case in all the others. The phases of the moon are accounted for by the following hypothesis. It is supposed that, when this planet is in conjunction with the sun, the latter is suspended perpendicularly over it, and consequently it can produce no light : in the same manner as a house at midday has no shadow. But the moon recedes from the sun 100,000 juzenà every day; and, as it thus frees itself from the overshadowing disk of the sun, it increases in light and splendour; as the shadow of a house increases in proportion to the approach of sunset.

The cause of cold and heat, at the different seasons of the year, is the following. The Burmese doctors say that the sun, from the vernal equinox to the autumnal, is always in the northern portion of its path, and the moon, on the contrary, in the southern. Hence the rays of the sun, which are by nature warm, prevailing over those of the moon, which are cold, necessarily produce a high degree of heat. The contrary happens from the autumnal to the vernal equinox; for then,

the sun being in the south, and the moon describing the
northern part of its orbit, the cold rays of the latter prevail
over the warmth of its rival, and thus occasion cold. Lastly,
the causes of rain are, first, the influence of the dragons; the
second that of the Galons, a species of enormous birds. Both
of these creatures may be classed with the Nat. The third
cause is the virtue of Sizzà, a word that signifies the faith observed in contracts and promises. The fourth that of Silà,
which signifies the observance of the laws. The fifth is the
power of religious men. The sixth cause is, that it is the
time of rain; the seventh the gathering of the clouds; and
the eighth and last is the influence of those Nat that preside over rain, and who, when they leave their habitations, and
go running and playing about through the air, dispose the
weather for rain. When the sun is in the path of the goat,
the Nat do not leave their respective habitations on account
of the excessive heat, and therefore no rain falls. For this
reason, when the inhabitants of the Burmese empire are in want
of rain, they usually flock together in the public streets, and
take a great and long rope which they earnestly pull from
one side to the other, at the same time sending up loud cries
to heaven, to invite the Nat to come forth and play about
through the air. The thunder and lightning, that ordinarily
precede rain, are supposed to be nothing but the sports of
the Nat, as they play with their spears and other weapons.
Besides these, they admit of other Nat that preside over the
clouds and winds.

16. After Zatumaharit we have the seat called Tavateinsà,
which extends from the summit of Miemmò to Zacchiavalà.
The supreme prince or emperor of the Nat of this seat has
thirty-two other princes subject to him. He resides in a vast
city of a square form, the streets and squares of which are
paved with gold and silver. Its wall forms a perfect square,
each side of which is 10,000 juzenà long; it is 150 juzenà
high, and one and a half thick. Its gates, the height of
which is 40 juzenà, are covered with plates of gold and
silver, and adorned with precious stones. Seven wide ditches,
one juzenà distant from each other, surround these superb
walls; and beyond the last ditch, at a juzenà and half distance,

follows a range of marble columns, wonderfully enamelled with gold and precious stones. Then follow, at the same distance, seven rows of palm-trees, shining in every part with gold and pearls; and, in the space between the palm-trees and columns, lakes of the clearest water are scattered up and down, where are boats of gold and silver, in which the Nat of both sexes, with drums and other musical instruments, roam, singing and dancing, through these delightful regions. Sometimes they stop, to contemplate the beautiful birds that fly among the trees on the banks of the lakes, sometimes to gather delicious fruits or beautiful and fragrant flowers. Beyond the seven rows of palm-trees, the Padesà tree grows on every side; upon which, instead of fruit, precious garments and rich ornaments are suspended. At the distance of twenty juzenà north of the great city is the orchard called Nandà, 100 juzenà in length and breadth; in the midst of which is a lake of the same name. It takes its appellation from the crowds of Nat that flock to it, to gather the celebrated flower with which they adorn their heads. It grows in this place alone, and is reported to be as large as the wheel of a chariot. Twenty juzenà to the east of the city is situated another orchard of the same size and beauty as the first, in which grows that celebrated species of ivy which, every thousand years, yields fruit of such an exquisite flavour, that, to eat of it, for a hundred years before, multitudes flock towards the garden, and there, amid music, singing, and dancing, await the ripening of the wished-for fruit; and having tasted it, they remain for four whole months in a state of intoxication. Two other orchards of a similar size are situated to the south and west of the city. To the north-west is a most superb portico or terrace, 300 juzenà square and 450 high. The pavement is of pure crystal, and a row of 100 columns adorns each range of the building. Gold and silver bells hang from every part of the roof, and the staircase, the walls, and every other part of the building shine with a profusion of gold and precious stones. The street that leads to it is 20 juzenà long and one wide; it is shaded on both sides by delightful trees always covered with fruit and flowers of every kind. When the great emperor visits this magnificent

palace, the Nat that preside over the winds shake down from
the trees such a quantity of flowers as to reach to the knees
of those who pass; the trees all the time putting forth new
flowers to supply for what have fallen. In the centre of the
portico is raised the great emperor's throne, which far excels every other part of the edifice in richness, gold, and
precious stones. This superb throne is surrounded by thirty-
two smaller ones for the princes of the Nat, and then come
all the other Nat, each in the seat and place appointed for
him. At this assembly are also present the four princes of
Zatumaharit, the seat above mentioned. While the Nat
around the great emperor strive to pay him their court, and
to amuse him by the sound of musical instruments, by dancing
and feasting, the four princes just mentioned, assembling the
Nat of their own seat, order them to go and inform themselves
whether or no the men in the southern island of Zabudibà
observe the laws and holidays, and exercise charity. At this
command the Nat, swifter than the wind, transport themselves in an instant to the island; and after having written
in a golden book all the good and evil deeds of men, they
immediately return to the grand assembly, and present the
book to the great emperor, who opens and reads it before
them all. Even when he talks or reads with a low and soft
voice, he is heard at a distance of 22 juzenà; but when he
raises his voice and reads in a louder tone, the sound is heard
throughout the whole seat of Tavateinsà. If the report presented to the emperor shows that the number is great of those
who observe the law and attend to charitable deeds, then do
the Nat rejoice, exclaiming, 'Now indeed will the infernal
abodes be desert and empty, and ours filled with inhabitants.'
But if it be reported that the observers of the law are few,
'Oh miserable creatures!' do they say, 'foolish men! who, for
a life of short duration, for a body merely four cubits long,
for a stomach the length of a palm, neglect charitable deeds, to
indulge in luxury and pleasure; and thus treasure up demerits,
which will be the cause of their unhappiness after death.'
Then the great emperor with a loud voice will exclaim, 'Verily,
I say, if men are observers of the law, if they bestow alms, they
shall become after death great emperors of Nat, as I am.'

At the conclusion of the assembly, the great emperor, accompanied by above thirty-six millions of Nat, returns to his great city.

17. In the centre of this superb city stands the great imperial palace, which is 500 juzenà in height. No description can do justice to its beauty and magnificence, nor tell of the abundance of gold and silver, the inestimable treasures of jewels and precious stones, contained therein. The chariot upon which the emperor is drawn is 150 juzenà large; and from its centre the great throne rises to the height of three juzenà. The throne is covered by a white umbrella, and the whole is drawn by 2000 horses. The great flag, 150 juzenà high, is planted in the forepart, and when it waves to and fro in the wind, yields a grateful and sweet murmur. Twenty juzenà to the north-east of the great city grows the celebrated tree, the sacred ensign of this seat of the Nat, which vegetates for the whole duration of a world. Under it is placed a great stone, sixty juzenà long, fifty wide, and fifteen high, which is exquisitely polished, and at the same time as soft as wool. Whenever the great emperor desires to mount upon it, it lowers itself, and afterwards returns to its natural height. While everything goes on quietly and prosperously in the southern island, half of the great emperor's body sinks into this stone; but if the contrary be the case, the stone then will remain firm and drawn tight like a drum. Many Padesà trees and other species of fruits and flowers surround the great sacred tree; and the road that leads to it is twenty juzenà wide. By this road the Nat of this region pass every year to visit the sacred tree; and when they see the old leaves falling off and the new ones budding forth, they communicate the joyful intelligence to each other with mutual congratulations. The red colour of the flowers of this tree is spread on every side to a distance even of 100 juzenà. As soon as the tree is in blossom, the keepers of it give notice to the great emperor, who, desiring to go thither immediately, speaks as follows:—'It would afford me infinite pleasure, if in this moment an elephant should appear:' and no sooner has he uttered the words than an enormous elephant does appear. For, it must be observed, that animals in the abodes of Nat are ideal, and created by

the Nat themselves, for a given space of time. This elephant has thirty-three heads: a large one, destined to carry the great emperor, and thirty-two lesser ones for the thirty-two minor princes. Each head has seven teeth, fifty juzenà in length; in each tooth there are seven lakes, and in each lake seven flower trees; each tree has seven flowers, and each flower seven leaves; in each leaf there are seven rooms; in each room seven beds, and in each bed there are seven female Nat dancing. The size of the head on which the great emperor sits is thirty juzenà, that of the others only three. A pavilion, three juzenà in size, is situated in the great head; under which a throne of ruby is raised for the emperor. This elephant, whose name is Eraum, approaches the great emperor, who mounts upon the greatest head, and then all the other princes take their places upon the remaining thirty-two heads.

The elephant is followed by all the other Nat in order, each in his proper seat. When this innumerable company arrives at the great tree, all descend from the elephant and from their seats, and place themselves around the great emperor, who is placed upon the great stone, which we have already mentioned. Music, dancing, and feastings immediately commence, and continue four entire months. When these are past, they begin to gather the flowers; for which purpose there is no need of climbing the tree, for the winds, or the Nat that preside over them, shake the tree, so that the flowers fall off; but, at the same time, that they may not touch the ground, other winds support their weight, and hold them suspended in the air. Then the entire body of the Nat is seen covered with the fragrant dust blown from the stamina of the flowers. The stature of the Nat of this region is three-quarters of a juzenà, and the duration of their life is four times as long as in the inferior region, that is, 36,000,000 of our years. The Nat of this, as likewise those of the superior regions, need not the sun's light, as they themselves shine like so many suns.

18. In sec. 2 we have shown how the immense mountain Miemmò is supported by three feet of ruby. In the space between these three feet there is situated another abode of the Nat, called Assurà, of the same species as those of Tavateinsà, from which region they were turned out by fraud. The

Burmese sacred books relate the event in the following manner. Godama, while yet a mere man in the southern island of Zabudibà, with other thirty-two persons of a certain village, performed many good works, among which was that of sweeping the streets. By these they deserved after death to become Nat of the region Tavateinsà; and the name of Godama was changed for that of Maja. In the course of time Maja became ambitious, and, desiring with his companions to occupy the first places in this region, resolved to expel its old inhabitants. With this view, he and his associates drank plentifully of a liquor which they called wine, but which really was not such : the old Nat, hearing of this and wishing to taste the beverage themselves, drank real wine and were intoxicated. Maja immediately assembled his companions, who, taking advantage of the feeble state of their rivals, dragged them by the feet to the sea, and easily precipitated them into it. But as the term of their reward was not yet finished, another abode was formed for them, among the foundations of Mount Miemmò, between the three feet of ruby. Here the banished Nat betook themselves, and their new abode was called Assurà, from the wine they had drunk. It is similar to the one they had left in all respects, except in its sacred tree.

Besides the violence just described, the Nat of Assurà had to suffer another injury from the new inhabitants of Tavateinsà, whose emperor once ravished the daughter of their king. Mindful of these injuries, the Assurà Nat vowed a perpetual war with those of Tavateinsà; and, whenever they see that their holy tree does not produce the same flowers as that of their enemies, they furiously ascend the high mount Miemmò, and drive away the guard stationed there by the emperor of Tavateinsà, which is composed of giants, dragons, and enormous birds.

The emperor, roused by the noise, immediately mounts his great elephant, and calling to his assistance the Nat of the sun, moon, and stars, together with those of the clouds and winds, goes out from the great city to resist his enemies. At first their ardour prevails, and he is compelled to retreat; but when the fury of the Assurà is somewhat abated, the great emperor unites his forces, drives the enemy from the walls, and finally compels them to take to flight. The Assurà, thus seeing themselves unable to overcome, beat their great drum, which is formed from the foot of a large crab, and retreat to their own abode. In these conflicts no lives are lost, only the Nat are oppressed by fatigue and lassitude.

According to the doctrines of the god Godama, all who honour their relations and reverence old age, all who have veneration and respect for the three excellent things, God, the law, and the priests, and all who are averse to quarrels and dissensions, will pass after death to the state of the Tavateinsà Nat.

19. The sacred books of the Burmese are silent with regard to the happiness of the Nat, whether superior or inferior to these. With respect to the duration of their life, they make it four times longer than with the inferior Nat ; according to which those of the highest region will live 576,000,000 years. The duration of the life of the Rupà and Arupà differs according to their order. Of the three orders of Rupà, known by the name of the first Zian (see sec. 12), those of the first live twenty-one durations of worlds, those of the second thirty-one, and those of the third sixty-four; of the Rupà called second Zian, those of the first order live two Mahakap, each Mahakap comprising four times sixty-four durations of worlds; and in the same proportion is lengthened the life of the Rupà and Arupà of the higher orders.

Since happiness and the duration of life increase proportionably to the elevation of each class, a corresponding degree of merit from almsdeeds and good works here below determines to which we shall belong after death.

20. HAVING thus explained all that regards the blessed and their habitations, we must now proceed to speak of the damned, of the regions they inhabit, of their states of suffering and the duration of their lives.[1] In sec. 5 it has been said that there are four classes of the unhappy. The first comprehends animals that live on the earth or in the waters, or fly through the air. The second is that of the Preittà, the third that of the Assurichè, and lastly, the fourth includes those who are punished in the Niria, or what is properly called hell. And first with regard to animals. Some Burmese doctors affirm that the domestic ones, in the duration of their life, follow the lot of the persons to whom they belong; so that when the latter are long-lived, their animals are so likewise. Such animals as are not domesticated have a long or a short life according to the number of sins for which they have to do penance.

It has been ascertained that the elephant lives sixty years, the horse thirty, the ox twenty, and the dog ten. They assert that the louse and other similar insects live only seven days; and they argue this from a circumstance related in their books. A certain priest or Talapoin conceived an inordinate affection for a garment of an elegant shape, which he possessed, and which he diligently preserved to prevent its wearing out. He died without correcting his irregular affection, and, immediately becoming a louse, took up his abode in his favourite garment. According to custom, the other Talapoins divided the effects of

---

[1] For the common notions of the Burmans about future punishment, see the Abstract of the work called *Nemi*, Bigandet, ii. p. 162, where a virtuous prince is conducted by a heavenly guide through the regions of hell and paradise.

the deceased; and would have cut the garment in pieces, had not the louse, running frequently backwards and forwards, showed, by his extraordinary movements, that such a division was displeasing to him. The astonished Talapoins consulted their god Godama, who desired them to wait seven days before they proceeded to the division; and when they inquired the cause of this delay, he manifested to them the sin in which that Talapoin had died; and said, that as he knew that seven days after the louse would be dead, he had ordered them to wait six days more, lest, should they proceed to the division before that period, the louse might perhaps allow some expression of anger to escape him, for which he would be condemned to pass into some worse state of punishment.

Those who do not keep a guard upon their tongue, those who do not repress the inordinate affections of the heart or the vicious tendencies of the body, and those who neglect to give alms pass after death into the state of animals.

21. The second state of punishment is that of the Preittà, and of these there are various species. Some there are who live upon spittle, ordure, and other filth, and inhabit the common sewers, cisterns, and tombs. Others wander naked through the deserts and forests, continually sobbing and groaning, and are consumed by hunger and thirst. Others for the whole duration of a world are constrained to turn up the earth with a fiery plough: some feed upon their own flesh and blood, and with their own hands tear themselves with hooks : others, although they are a quarter of a juzenà in stature, have a mouth as small as the eye of a needle; for which reason, they are ever tormented by cruel hunger : and lastly, there are some who are tormented inwardly and outwardly by fire.

All those who give alms to the Talapoins that do not wear the proper habit, all who do violence to Talapoins, whether male or female, or who injure the observers of the law, as well as all misers, will pass after death into the state of the Preittà.

22. The third infernal state is that of the Assurichè. Their habitation is in the base of a certain mountain, situated far remote from the abodes of men. They inhabit likewise the forests and desert sea-shores. Their sufferings are almost the same as those of the Preittà. There is another species called

Assurichè-preittà, that have a body three-quarters of a juzenà in height, and are so squalid and lean that they resemble skeletons. Their eyes project outwards like those of a crab, and they have a mouth in the upper part of the head, as small as the eye of a needle, and are therefore consumed by hunger.

All such as make use of clubs or arms in their quarrels will become Assurichè-preittà. Those also who offend or despise the observers of the law, or who, on the contrary, honour and advance the violaters of it, will pass to the condition of Preittà. In the states of punishment just described, as well as in the fourth called Niria, there is no fixed or determinate duration of suffering, as this depends on the species of the bad works committed by men in their lifetime. For, if it be heavy and weighty, according to the expression of the Burmese doctors, they will be made to suffer for a longer time. That is to say, according to the greater or lesser enormity of the crimes committed and the bad habits acquired, the punishment will last for a longer or shorter period.

23. The fourth state of suffering is called Niria, and this is properly the hell of the Burmese. It is situated in the deepest recesses of the southern island Zabudibà, in the centre of the great stone called Silapatavi, and is divided into eight great hells. Each of them has four gates, at the four sides; and in each gate there are four smaller hells; and besides these, other 40,040 smaller hells surround each great hell, being disposed above, below, on the right hand, and on the left. Every such group of hells has an extension of 10,000 juzenà.

The infernal judges are seated before the gates of the greater hells, and are called Jamamen. These are Nat of the Assurà species, as described in sec. 18, and both they and their satellites enjoy the felicity of the Nat. They do not, however, take cognisance of very heinous crimes, because the mere weight of these hurls the wicked down to hell, but only of those of lesser enormity.

It is a custom with the Burmese, when they give an alms, to pour out a vessel of water upon the earth, by which ceremony they think they make all their fellow-creatures participators in the merit of the action. If in performing this ceremony men do not forget the Jamamen, these will be propitious to them should they chance to be thrown after death into the infernal regions, and will do everything in their power to procure their release. But if, on the contrary, in pouring out the water they did not intend to share with them the fruit of the good work, they will be received with a terrible aspect, their bad deeds will be, not only not excused or diminished, but rather exaggerated ; and as they are unable to adduce anything in their justification, they will be given over to the infernal ministers to be tormented.

24. It has been noticed above that, according to the species of their bad works, the wicked are condemned to punishment. These species are four, according to the Burmese sacred books. One is called grievous, the other three are venial.

To kill one's own mother or father, to kill a priest or Talapoin, to strike or wound any God, as Beodat [Devadat, the relative and opponent of Gaudama] did who threw a stone against Godama, and to sow discord among Talapoins, are the five sins that constitute the grievous class ; for which the wicked will have to suffer fire and other dreadful torments, in one of the greater hells, the whole duration of a world.

This species of sins is called the first, because it is the first to produce its effect: for although the individual who has committed one of these five sins may have done many good deeds, yet he cannot receive the reward till after the first species is expiated by his having paid the penalty of that great sin.

Still more grievous than these are the sins of the Deitti,[1] or of those impious men who give no faith to the revelations of Godama, who deny the Niban, the transmigration of men into animals, or into other superior beings, and teach that there is no merit in doing charity or other good works, and who adore the Nat or Genii presiding over the woods and mountains. All these, should they die obstinate in such wickedness and irreligion, will be tormented not merely for the duration of a world, but eternally.

Among the minor species of sins, the first merely comprises every offence committed in the last moment of life, and this

---

[1] See Chap. XIV. sec. 4.

holds the first rank, as it is the first to take effect. All such sins are punished in one of the greater hells.

After this class come all sins of habit; which, although in themselves light, are nevertheless, on account of the evil habit, considered as punishable in the greater hells. The fourth and last species comprises all evil desires, and these are expiated, not in the greater hells, but in the minor ones that surround them.

25. Before speaking of the punishments inflicted in these, we must remark that, of the eight greater hells, four are called Avizi [Awichi], that is, hot, because there the punishment is by fire, and four Loghantreh, or cold, because sinners are there tormented by cold. It is necessary also to premise that the infernal days and years are not of the same length as ours, for a thousand of our years make but one day in the greater hells. In the smaller ones a day is equal to 500, 700, or even 800 of our years.

I. All passionate, quarrelsome, fraudulent, and cruel men, all who in their deeds, words, or desires are either dishonest or lascivious, will be cut to pieces after death in one of the greater hells, with instruments of burning iron, and afterwards exposed to the most severe cold ; and the parts cut off, returning again to their former state, will be a second time cut off, and exposed to the same cold ; and in these alternate torments they will pass 500 infernal years.

II. All those who by signs or words insult their relatives or masters, priests, old men, or observers of the law, and all who with nets or snares kill animals, will be condemned to one of the greater hells, there to be tormented upon a fiery bed by continual lacerations with red-hot wire, and by being sawn with fiery scythes into eight or sixteen pieces, for the course of 1000 infernal years.

III. Those who kill oxen, swine, goats, and such other animals, all hunters by profession, warlike kings, and ministers who cause culprits to be tormented or executed, will after death be pressed and squeezed by four fiery mountains in one of the greater hells, for the space of 2000 infernal years.

IV. Whoever does not assist his fellow-creatures, those who are accustomed to pluck animals or kill them by putting them alive into the frying-pan, those who in a state of intoxication commit unlawful and indecent actions, they who dishonour or ill-treat others, will have their bowels burnt 'up by a flame entering through their mouths ; and this punishment will last 4000 infernal years.

V. Whoever takes away furtively, or by deception, fraud, or open force, the property of others, such ministers and judges as receive bribes for deciding suits unjustly, mandarins and generals that desolate the enemy's lands, all who cheat by false scales, weights, or measures, or who in any way appropriate to themselves the goods of others, as well as all who steal or damage things belonging to priests and to pagodas, etc., all such will be tormented in one of the greater hells by fire and smoke, which, penetrating through the eyes and mouth and all the other inlets of the body, will burn them alive for the course of 8000 infernal years.

VI. Those who, after having slain deer, swine, and other similar animals, do skin them, pluck off their hair, or roast their flesh, the makers of arms, those who sell pork or turkeys, those likewise who sell wines or poisons, or set fire to villages, cities, or woods in order to destroy animals, those who with poison, or arms, or enchantments cause men to perish : all these after death, being hurled headlong from a very high mountain, will be received on the point of a red-hot spit, and cut in pieces by the infernal ministers with swords and spears : and this punishment will last 16,000 infernal years.

VII. The Deitti, or unbelievers, of whom we have spoken above, will be impaled with the head downwards, on a great red-hot spit, without being able to move on either side, in the greatest of all the hells.

VIII. Lastly, parricides, and those guilty of the sins that are comprised in the first or grievous class, will have to endure dreadful sufferings, for the whole duration of a world, in the midst of smoke, scorching flames, and other horrible torments, in the hell called the great Avizì, the pavement of which is formed of red-hot iron to the depth of nine juzenà.

26. We must now speak of the minor hells which surround the greater ones. Among these we must specify the hell of ordure, in which immense worms as large as elephants swim and bite the sinners who are there immersed ; that of burning

coals ; that of swords and other sharp weapons ; that of knives, sabres, and other arms, with which the bodies of the condemned are cut to pieces; that in which the lungs, liver, and other viscera are torn out from the bodies of the guilty by iron hooks ; that where they are cruelly beaten with fiery hammers ; that in which melted lead is poured down their throats ; that of thorns and briers ; that of biting dogs ; that of ravens and vultures, which tear the flesh with their bills and talons. Again, there is a place in which the condemned are compelled to ascend and descend the Leppan tree covered all over with the sharpest thorns ; and another, in which sinners are forced to drink blood or purulent matter. All who honour not their parents, masters, and old men ; all who drink wine or other inebriating liquors ; all who corrupt the waters of lakes or wells, or break up the roads; all dishonest dealers ; they who speak bitterly and impatiently, or beat with their hands or with sticks ; those who despise the counsel of honest men, and afflict their neighbour ; evil speakers, detractors, the passionate and envious ; such as injure others, or torment them by putting them in chains ; all who in word, deed, or desire are guilty of evil ; lastly, those who afflict the sick with harsh words will be condemned to these minor places of punishment, to be there tortured, in proportion to the heinousness of their offences and evil habits. Besides these hells, there is another consisting of an immense caldron full of melted copper, to ascend and descend which, from one surface to the other, requires 3000 years. To this task are condemned the lascivious, that is to say, those who violate the wives, daughters, or sons of others ; and those who through life, despising acts of charity and the observance of holidays, give themselves up to drunkenness and excess. Those equilateral spaces full of very cold water (sec. 6) are also, according to the Burmese books, so many hells, to which are condemned all who offend or insult their parents or the observers of the law. These after death are born anew, three-quarters of a juzenà in height, with hooked nails on their hands and feet, and are compelled to climb, like so many bats, through the obscure caverns of the mountains. Here they annoy and ill-treat each other, and, instigated by cruel hunger, tear each other's flesh, which, falling into those cold waters, is first dissolved like salt, and then, by a fatality attending on their wicked deeds, reunites itself to the body, so to suffer new torments.

27. Before we pass to other matters, we must observe that not only in the southern island, but also in all these places of torment, beings may gain merit or demerit, according to their works, and so pass to a superior or inferior situation. It is, however, only in this island that the perfect state of Niban can be attained: because for this it is requisite to see some God, and listen to his exhortations and revelations; which can happen in this island alone. In sec. 6 we have explained what the state of the Niban is: this cannot be said to have any specific seat; for it is a perfectly incorporeal and spiritual state of being, and deserves the name of annihilation rather than of existence.

CHAPTER V

28. To conclude this treatise on Burmese cosmography we have only to describe the way in which their sacred books explain the end of one world and the commencement of another.[1] They suppose the remote and moral causes of the world's destruction to be three—lust, anger, and ignorance ; from which, by the power of fate, spring three other immediate and physical causes—fire, water, and wind. When lust prevails in the world, it will be destroyed by fire ; when anger, by water ; and when ignorance, by wind. They suppose also that this destruction and reproduction does not take place in a moment, but very slowly ; so that for the world to be entirely destroyed an assenchiè will pass, and another before it be reproduced : and there will be the same interval of time between the total end of the old and the beginning of the new world.

29. Before describing the destruction of the world, it is

---

[1] Once a world is constituted, the law of merit and demerit is the sole principle that regulates both physical and moral things.—Bigandet, i. p. 23, where the subject of this chapter is treated. Similar ideas lie at the roots of earlier Indian philosophies, of which a list will be found in Sykes' *Notes on the State of India before the Mahomedan Invasion*, pp. 20, 21, London, 1841.

' Buddhism does not attempt to solve the problem of the primary origin of all things. . . . Buddhism takes as its ultimate fact the existence of the material world and of conscious beings living within it ; and it holds that everything is subject to the law of cause and effect, and that everything is constantly, though imperceptibly, changing. There is no place where this law does not operate ; no heaven nor hell, therefore, in the ordinary sense. There are worlds where *devas* live, whose existence is more or less material, according as their previous lives were more or less good ; but the *devas* die, and the worlds they inhabit pass away. . . . The whole Kosmos, earth and heavens and hells—is always tending to renovation or destruction.'—*Buddhism*, by Dr. Rhys Davids, p. 87.

C

necessary to refer to what we have said in sec. 7, that in each world there are sixty-four successive diminutions and augmentations of age in the generations of men ; and hence the life of man will be sixty-four times reduced to the term of only ten years. At these periods there will be a general scourge and extermination. Should lust be predominant, then will men, worn away by hunger, thirst, and misery, to so many moving corpses, almost all perish. Should anger be the reigning vice, then men will turn their weapons against each other, and in furious combats labour for their mutual destruction. If, in fine, ignorance, as is generally the case, prevails over the world, then will a horrible consumption waste mankind away to mere skeletons ; and thus will they die. After this almost universal mortality a heavy rain will fall, which, carrying off all the impurities of the earth, together with the unburied corpses, will discharge them into the rivers ; and this will be succeeded by a shower of sandal, flowers, and every kind of garments. Then shall the few men who have escaped the extermination we have just described come forth from the caverns into which they had retired, then shall they begin to do penance for the sins they have committed, and thus deserve a prolongation of their life beyond the period of ten years.

30. A hundred thousand years before the world's destruction, some Nat of the superior seats, descending to this southern island with a sad and lugubrious countenance, with their locks dishevelled and dressed in mourning, will proclaim in all the public streets and squares with a loud and lamentable voice that the destruction of the world is approaching. They foresee it in the same way that the birds of the air and the fishes of the sea, by a certain natural instinct, foresee the approaching storm. After this they will admonish and strive to excite mankind to the observance of the laws, and to those works which may elevate them after death to the abodes of the Rupà and Arupà. The good works on which they will principally insist are alms-deeds, the honouring parents and old men, the observance of justice, and the mutual love of each other. They are earnest in exhorting men to these works that they may be raised to the state of Rupà and Arupà ; because these abodes will remain untouched when the world is destroyed by fire.

Upon hearing this terrible presage, all will be struck with fear, and will use every endeavour to practise the four good works recommended to them. The Nat inhabiting Mount Miemmò, and those of the mountains, rivers, and forests, will then be transported to the states of Zian and Rupà. The infernal beings also, having now expiated the species of sin for which they had been condemned, will again become men, and strive to practise the same good deeds in order to deserve, together with the others, the state of Zian. For the impious alone and for the unbelievers there is no chance of relief, as they will be eternally tormented in the equilateral spaces full of the coldest water, which are placed without the world. The irrational animals likewise must perish with the world.

31. When the world is to be destroyed by fire, as soon as the Nat have finished their proclamation, a heavy rain will fall from heaven, by which all the lakes and torrents will be over-flowed; and men, conceiving strong hopes of an abundant crop, will sow their richest seeds. But this rain will be the last to descend upon the earth; and from this time, for the space of 100,000 years, not a single drop of water will fall from heaven. All plants and vegetables will now perish through the long drought; and men, dying with hunger, will be transported to the abodes of the Nat, or the Zian. The sun and moon having lost their Nat, who have become Zian, will cease to shine; and in their stead two other suns, not inhabited by Nat, will per-petually succeed each other; so that there can be no longer any night; and hence the heat will be such that the small rivers, lakes, and torrents will be dried up, and no vestige of plants will be seen on the surface of the earth. After some time a third sun will appear; and then the Ganges, with the other four great rivers, will dry up. After many ages a fourth sun will make its appearance, by whose heat will be drained the seven great lakes which, as the Burmese books relate, lie to the north of the southern island, and give rise to five great rivers, whereof the Ganges is one. After another long period a fifth sun will rise, and then all the seas will be laid dry. At the appearance of a sixth sun, all the islands of this and of every other world, to the number of 10,100,000, will open; and from the apertures smoke and flames will burst forth.

Finally, after a lengthened term of years, at the appearance of the seventh and last sun, Mount Miemmò, with all the abodes of the Nat, will be consumed by fire. And, as in a lamp when the oil and wick are consumed, the flame goes out of itself, so when the fire shall have devoured all that exists in this or any other world, it will spontaneously cease. The whole time occupied by these events, from the last rain that fell to the final ceasing of the fire, will fill up the interval of an assenchiè.

32. When the world is to be destroyed by water, at the beginning a small shower of rain will fall, which, increasing by degrees, will become so heavy and horrible that each drop of it will be of the size of a thousand juzenà ; and thus the abodes of men and the Nat, together with some of those of the Zian and the 10,100,000 worlds, will be dissolved and destroyed. So likewise when the world is to be destroyed by wind, as soon as the Nat have finished their admonitions, the heavy rain will fall ; and 100,000 years after, a wind will begin to blow, which, increasing by degrees, will at first raise the sands and small pebbles, and afterwards the heavy stones, the tops of mountains and the trees, and then shaking and breaking up all the earth, with all the abodes of the Nat and many of those of the Zian, will disperse everything in the immense vacuum of heaven. The annexed table shows the order and method of the destruction of the world, by fire, water, and wind :—

From this scheme it appears that the world will be destroyed fifty-six times by fire, seven by water, and only once by wind. The smaller lines serve to show the different heights to which the fire will ascend. When it reaches that indicated by No. 1, it will destroy the five inferior regions of the Zian. No. 2 shows how high the water must ascend to dissolve the world, when it will also destroy the eight inferior regions of the Zian. And No. 3 shows the intensity of the wind in the same circumstances, when the nine regions of the Zian will be destroyed. After the world has thus been destroyed sixty-four times, the series will begin again. Fire was the agent in the destruction of the last world, and it ascended to the height indicated by the line No. 4 in the table.

33. Having now shown how the world will be destroyed, we must speak of its reproduction. Fire, water, and wind are the three agents in its dissolution, but water or rain alone acts in reproducing it. An assenchiè after the end of the world, this begins to fall, at first slowly, but increasing by degrees till its drops successively reach the size of one, two, a hundred and a thousand juzenà. Yet it still continues falling without intermission, while the wind, by which it is continually beaten about and compressed, condenses it precisely in the place where the preceding world was situated. On the surface of this condensed body of water, by the action of the sun, a kind of crust or greasy scum is formed, from which those abodes of Nat and Zian that have been destroyed will be reproduced. Afterwards Mount Miemmò and the other seats of the Nat placed in its vicinity, will be formed ; and as the water successively decreases, from its sediment will arise the four great islands, Mount Zacchiavalà and all the 10,100,000 worlds, in the same order and symmetry as before.

34. The new world is then repeopled in the following manner. Immediately after the formation of the islands, a kind of crust appears on their surface, having the smell and taste of butter. The odour of this substance ascending up to the abodes of the Rupà fills their inhabitants, who before the destruction of the last world had become Zian, with the desire of eating it. For this purpose they assume human bodies, endowed with great agility and splendour, and so descend upon the island which we inhabit. At first they pass their lives happily and quietly with this supernatural food for their only sustenance ; but avarice and the thirst for private gain springing up amongst them, give birth to quarrels and disputes. Thence it happens that in punishment of their sin, the nectareous crust that had nourished them disappears, and their bodies, losing their original splendour, become dark and opaque. This loss is instantly succeeded by darkness and black night, for the sun and moon have not yet shone out: which fills them with the greatest consternation. But the sun now rising in the east, dispels their fear, and fills them with satisfaction by its unhoped for appearance. Yet is this universal joy and content succeeded by a new cause of perturbation and trouble, when the

sun, after its diurnal revolution is hidden by Mount Miemmô. Then do men in affliction and consternation begin to lament and exclaim 'Oh! how soon has the light which came to illumi- nate us disappeared.' Whilst they are thus ardently desiring a new luminary, behold, in the same quarter of the heavens, at the beginning of the night, the moon and stars shine forth. At the appearance they are greatly comforted and exultingly exclaim: ''Truly this is a welcome sight.' It is on a Sunday, in the month of Tabaun, which corresponds to our March, that the sun, moon and stars first give light.

As in preparing rice, some grains are perfectly cooked and others remain raw or half-dressed: so the Burmese Doctors say, that by the power of fate part of the earth remains flat, part is elevated into mountains, and part is depressed into valleys.

35. The crust of butter, which, as we have said, had dis- appeared on account of the sins of mankind, having penetrated into the bowels of the earth, is changed into a large stone called Silapatavi : and instead of that crust a kind of ivy-tree springs up having likewise the flavour of butter. Men feed upon this for some time, until avarice arising again among them, this plant also disappears; and in its place a kind of rice with- out husk, of an excellent quality, grows up from the bowels of the earth. At the same time earthen vessels appear, which they fill with the rice; and having placed them upon stones, fire spontaneously comes out from them by which the rice is instantly cooked. Different kinds of food also present them- selves, according to each one's desire. In the beginning, when their nourishment is the crust and ivy which we have described, as this food is all converted into blood and flesh, men have no need of the different organs and channels, for the excretion of that part of their food, which contributes nothing to their nutriment. But now that they have begun to feed upon rice, these various organs are formed in the human body to suit the coarser quality of the new food. This nourishment also pro- duces the first sensations of passion, which are instantly followed by the division of mankind into the two sexes, each individual being in this respect as he was before the destruction of the world. This distinction, at first, gives rise to illicit

desires, but ends in establishing the matrimonial state. A
great many, however, preserving their virginity, become men of
great virtue and holiness, and are called Manussa-Biammà.
These do not exercise commerce, agriculture, or any other
mechanical art, but solely employ themselves in the sublime
ministry of making oblations and giving alms. For a length
of time they preserve their celibacy; but afterwards seeing
their race diminish considerably, many contract marriages in
order to perpetuate it. Upon hearing this, the other Manussa-
Biammà are highly scandalised; and detesting their deprava-
tion, declare hatred against those who have contracted such
marriages, and separate themselves from their society. And
hence the Burmese Doctors derive the custom of the modern
Bramins, who pretend to be descendants of the Manussa-
Biammà, of not bathing, eating, nor cohabiting with persons of
a different caste. Although, according to the law of the god
Godama, matrimony is lawful, yet still, as the Niban cannot be
obtained without the observance of celibacy, the men learned
in this law repute marriage as a less perfect state. Those
Biammà who have entered into the married state begin to
build houses, villages and cities; and the more they multiply,
the greater and more frequent are the quarrels and ruptures
among them; because, through the predomination of avarice,
every one attends to his own interest and convenience. In
order to remedy these disorders and put an end to quarrels,
in which the most powerful always prevails, they agree by
common consent to elect a king, who may administer justice
and bestow rewards or punishments according to desert.
Having found one among them who excels the others in stature
and graceful shape, as also in the observance of the natural law,
they choose him for prince of the earth, and call him Mahasamatà, as also Cattia, which signifies Lord of the earth, and
Hazù, because he has the power of rewarding and punishing
according to merit. From this first king forty-four others
descend, the tenth of whom is named Godama.

Thus is the human species renewed, and from these different
orders the four castes or races of men descend. The descendants of Mahasamatà constitute the royal race. The other
castes, that of the Bramins, of the rich, and of the Suchoiè, in

which are comprised merchants, artisans, and husbandmen, are
derived from those Biammà who contract matrimony.

36. In the supposition that all mankind are descended from
the same stock, a Burmese Doctor asks why the languages of
men, their customs and religion, the shape and colour of their
bodies, are so various. To this question he answers, that the
primitive inhabitants of the world, having greatly increased in
number, were obliged to disperse themselves into various countries and regions, in which the difference of climate, water and
products gave rise to different customs, languages, and religions.
And as children born from the same parents are not all called
by the same, but by different names, so, among the descendants
of the Biammà, some were called Burmese, some Peguans,
others Sciam [Shan], etc. The same Doctor also derives the
difference of name from the fact that a person may be considered in different lights, as Godama takes various names,
according to the different divine attributes and properties with
which he is endowed. Again, our author inquires what gave
rise to the various species of herbs and trees ; and answers that
they sprung from the seeds of the preceding world, which had
been deposited by the reproducing rain. The same cannot be
said of the mines of gold, silver, and precious stones; which were
not to be found at the beginning of the world, and were only
produced by the merits and good works of men. He then adds,
that when just and upright princes reign in the southern island,
or when men illustrious for holiness and virtue flourish there,
then Padesà trees will grow ; and the showers of gold, silver,
and precious stones will fall from heaven: the sea also will
deposit on its shores various kinds of treasures: and whatever is sown will wonderfully fructify. On the contrary, when
the princes are unjust, and men observe not the law, not only
will riches not increase, but rather diminish : the ancient gold
and silver mines will disappear ; and for want of moisture the
sown lands will be dried up, or yield fruit of a pernicious
quality.

CHAPTER VI

37. THE extensive territories which constitute the Burmese empire are not inhabited by one nation alone, but by many, differing essentially in language, manners, and customs. The principal of these are the Burmese, who occupy the tract of land called the kingdom of Ava, which extends from the city of Piè or Pron [Prome], in 19° north latitude, as far as 24°, and from 112° to 116° east longitude, from the meridian of the island of Ferro.

38. Next in importance are the Peguans [Talaings, Mons, Muns], anciently their competitors. They once formed a powerful monarchy, whose sovereigns were for a length of time masters of the kingdom of Ava. They inhabit the country called Pegù, extending, from west to east, from the island of Negraglià [Negrais] to the kingdom of Siam ; and from north to south, from the city of Pron to that of Martaban. The Peguan language is totally different from the Burmese.

39. The third nation is that of the Aracanese. Not many years ago, this likewise was an independent state, under the name of the kingdom of Aracan. The language of this country likewise differs entirely from that of the other two.

40. Beyond the point of Negraglià, as far as Azen [Assam], and even farther, there is a small chain of mountains that divides Aracan and Cassè [Manipur] from the Burmese. All these mountains are inhabited by a nation called Chien [Chin, Khyeng], part of which is independent, and part subject to the Burmese emperor. In the latter, besides a particular language and a peculiar manner of dress, there prevails a strange custom which deserves to be mentioned. It is that of tatooing with black the faces of the women. The origin of this custom is as follows. During the time that the residence of the Burmese

kings was in the city of Pagan, they were accustomed frequently to despatch their soldiers into the country of the Chien to carry off the most beautiful women and girls. It was in order to free themselves from this disgraceful oppression that the Chien adopted the practice of thus disfiguring the features of their women.[1]

41. To the east of the Chien mountains, between 20° 30′ and 21° 30′ north latitude, is a petty nation called Jò [Yaw]. They are supposed to have been Chien, who in progress of time have become Burmese, speaking their language, although very corruptly, and adopting all their customs. These Jò generally pass for necromancers and sorcerers, and are for this reason feared by the Burmese, who dare not ill-treat them for fear of their revenging themselves by some enchantment.

42. All that tract of land which extends from 25° to 20° north latitude, between the Chinese province of Junan [Yunnan], Siam and the kingdom of Ava, is inhabited by a numerous nation called Sciam [Shan], who are the same as the Laos. Their kingdom is divided into small districts under different chiefs called Zaboà [Sawbwa], or petty princes. From the time of Alomprà, the present king's father, till the beginning of the present reign, all these Zaboà were subjects and tributaries of the Burmese ; but the cruel despotism, the continual vexations and oppressions of their masters have forced many of them to rebel ; all of whom have leagued themselves with the Siamese, as we shall have occasion hereafter to relate. In language, manners, and customs these Sciam bear a nearer resemblance to the Siamese than to the Burmese.[2] Other tribes of the Sciam inhabit the forest to the north of the city of Miedù, and are otherwise called Konjen. These, although situated within the kingdom of Ava, still retain their own language, together with customs peculiar to themselves.

43. Casting our eyes upon the map of the Burmese empire, we shall see, that besides the nations already mentioned, there

---

[1] The practice existed in Arakan and Thayetmyu when I was in Burma.

[2] The form Siam is nothing but a corruption of the French method of writing Shan or ' Sciam.'—Census Report, 1891, p. 201.

are also included in it the Cadù [Kadu or Kudo], the Palaun [Palaung], the Koes and the Cachien [Kachin, Kakhyeng],— who are descended from the real Chien,—nations, all of whom speak a peculiar language, and have customs different from the Burmese.

44. We must not omit here the Carian [Karen], a good and peaceable people who live, dispersed through the forests of Pegù, in small villages consisting of four or five houses. These villages, upon the death of any inhabitant, are thrown down and destroyed in a moment by the survivors, who suppose the devil to have taken possession of the place. It is worthy of observation that, although residing in the midst of the Burmese and Peguans, they not only retain their own language, but even in their dress, houses, and everything else are distinguished from them; and what is more remarkable, they have a different religion. This indeed only consists in adoring, or rather fearing, an evil genius whom they suppose to inhabit their forests, and to whom they offer rice and other food, when they are sick, or apprehend any misfortune. They are totally dependent upon the despotic government of the Burmese.

45. But it is not so with the other Carian who inhabit the neighbourhood of Taunù [Toungoo, Toung-ngoo, Taun-gu], and are called Red Carian [Karenni], to distinguish them from the former. These, retired in their mountains and inaccessible forests, have very often defied the Burmese, to whose yoke they have never submitted. The Red Carian, who live to the east of Canton about 24° north latitude, consider themselves as descended from these; because, when the Burmese seized upon the country of Taunù, many of the inhabitants took to flight.[1]

---

[1] See Appendix I. for more recent classifications of the peoples and languages of Burma.

BURMESE HISTORY

CHAPTER VII

ORIGIN OF THE BURMESE NATION AND MONARCHY

1. WHEN I enumerated the nations subject to the Burmese dominion, it was not my intention to convey to my reader any idea of their origin, of the country whence they came, nor the time and manner of their emigration to their present position. Not to say that this would be irrelevant to my present design, which is to treat only of the Burmese and their kingdom, it would be truly a difficult or rather impossible task, not only because the different languages of those nations are unknown, but also because they have no historical books nor authentic traditions, from which any true records might be gleaned.   In fact, some of them have no knowledge of writing or of books, especially the Carian and Chien.   I shall therefore confine myself to the origin of the Burmese, as they are the ruling nation, and have consequently introduced their customs and laws into Pegù, Aracan, and other countries which they have subdued, and will commence with a brief sketch of the origin and subsequent history of their monarchy.   Even on this the reader must not flatter himself that he will receive accurate information, since the Burmese histories and traditions are filled with strange hyperbolical accounts and fabulous narratives.

If you ask the Burmese what was their origin, they will reply :—' Our name alone demonstrates at once the antiquity and nobility of our race, and our celestial origin.'   In fact, in their own language their name is not Burmese, which we have borrowed from the Portuguese, but Biammà, the very name, as we have seen above,* borne by the descendants of those

---

* See Cosmography, sec. 34, 35.

beings who once occupied the blessed regions of the Rupà.[1] Nevertheless if we notice many peculiarities of the Burmese, and especially a certain fierceness of character not possessed by other Indian nations, we shall be led to conclude that they are of Tartar origin, being probably descendants of some tribe of Tartars, who, as we are informed by history, spread themselves over every part of Asia, especially in the expeditions of the famous Gengis-Khan.

Even on the origin and progress of the Burmese monarchy, the reader must be prepared to meet nothing in their annals but marvellous tales, mixed up with a very little truth. Before my arrival in India, some missionaries made it their particular study to compose a faithful history of the Burmese kings, but in vain. I myself, while residing in the kingdom of Ava, asked one of the wisest and most learned of the natives, whose intimate friendship I enjoyed, whether there were any book from which I might learn the true history of the founder and perpetuators of their monarchy. He candidly answered, that the task was difficult, or rather impossible; and endeavoured to persuade me to give up the study as useless. To satisfy the curiosity of my readers, I have, therefore, nothing better to offer them on this subject than an abridgment of the Mahara-zaven, that is, the great history or annals of the kings. It is only towards the conclusion of this work that anything like a glimpse of truth appears.

---

[1] 'Only a few of the names by which the indigenous tribes were called in the remote past are now known; but the Indian settlers gave to them, and adopted themselves, the name of Brahmâ, which is that used in Buddhist sacred books for the first inhabitants of the world. This term, when used to designate the existing people, is now written Mrâmmâ, and generally pronounced Bamâ. Hence have been derived the words used by Europeans for this people.'— *History of Burma*, by Sir Arthur P. Phayre, p. 2.

Bigandet, however, derives Mrâmmâ from Mian, meaning man; and this view is adopted in the Census Report, 1891, p. 194.

2. DURING the period that the age of man is increasing from ten years to an assenchiè, there is no king in the world; but when, on the contrary, it is on the wane, then there are kings, and the first that reigns during this diminution of age, is always called Mahasamatà. In every world the ages decrease sixty-four times, so that in each there must be sixty-four kings of the name of Mahasamatà.

In the present world there have existed only eleven. Beginning to count, therefore, from the eleventh, the Burmese reckon 252,256 kings to Uggagarit; 8210 from him to Zejasena, the grandfather of Godama; and twenty-nine from Azadasat his son, to Siridamasoga. This is the series of kings that have flourished in the kingdom called Engà, Meggada [Magadha], etc. We must next speak of those who have reigned in Baranasì [Benares], Sautti [Thawattie, Sravasti], etc.

Whilst the god Godama was living upon the earth, he received an assurance that his laws would be observed in these kingdoms for the space of 5000 years. This induced him to accept of a magnificent convent of sandal wood, which a celebrated rich man named Maunzalà had built for him in these regions. During his residence there, and whilst for seven whole days he was practising every virtue, he obtained as a reward for Maunzalà, that he should acquire great sanctity, should be free from the passions of anger, covetousness, and lust, and should, moreover, have a title to the Niban after his death.

One day that Godama had ascended a mountain, and was looking towards the sea, he beheld some cow-dung floating upon the waters; and at the same time a Poè, which is a species of mole living under ground, approached, and to show him respect, took in its mouth a small quantity of earth and presented it to him. Seeing it, Godama smiled; and being asked the reason of his smiling by one of his disciples, by name Anandà, replied prophetically: 'Know that 110 years after I shall have obtained the Niban, five great prodigies will happen in this place; and a great kingdom will here be established, of which this little mole, having assumed the name of Duttabaumen, will be a king.' We must now see how this prediction was fulfilled. But first it may be well to pre-mise that this kingdom, as well as those of Engà, Meggadà [Magadha], etc., have no existence, save in the fancy of the compilers of these annals.

3. Twenty years after Godama had obtained the Niban, the mighty monarch of the great Kingdom of Tagaun [Tagaung], lord of the white and red elephant, died, and his son suc-ceeded to the throne. He gathered together a numerous army, and marched against his own brother-in-law; whom having conquered, he pursued to the place where the Kingdom of Sarekittrà [Tharêkhettara] was to be founded, and there killed.[1]

After the death of his adversary, the king did not return to his realm of Tagaun, but having laid aside his royal ornaments,

---

[1] For a more critical account of the early dynasties, the reader is referred to Sir Arthur Phayre's *History of Burma*, and his Appendix, containing the lists of kings taken from the Great History of Kings or Mahâ Râjâweng, the work used by Sangermano. Phayre holds that the Burman nation was formed many ages ago by the union of Mongoloid tribes, under the influence of Aryan immigrants, chiefly Kshatriyas from Gangetic India, who introduced the softening influences of the Buddhist religion in its simplest form, probably 2000 years ago. The Mahâ Râjâweng knows not the kinship of the Burmese with the Indo-Chinese people; but as the Buddhist religion has led the people to link their line of descent with that of their first teachers, or those referred to in the legends concerning Sakya Muni, so these annals open with an account of the first formation of the earth according to Buddhist cosmogony. The Mahâ Râjâweng then 'describes the small states of the Sâkya Râjâs in Northern India. Prince Siddhârtha, destined to become Buddha, was the son of a Râjâ of one of those States. Long before his birth, in conse-quence of wars among the Sâkya clans and between them and their neighbours, a chief to whom tradition gives the name of Abhî Râjâ, left Kâpilavâstu, and came with an army to the country of the Middle Irâwadi; there he established himself and built the city of Tagaung, the ruins of which still exist.' —*History of Burma*, by Sir A. Phayre, p. 7.

devoted himself to a solitary life in this place; and was renowned for sanctity and virtue in the village of Piudì [Prome],[1]
where he had fixed his abode. This holy hermit having one
day made water, a hind drank of it, and shortly after conceived and brought forth a female called Bedarì, who was
afterwards carried home by her father the hermit. About the
same time, in the year 40, the queen of the kingdom of
Tagaun brought forth two blind sons, whose names were
Mahasambavà and Zulasambavà. In the year 59, she exposed
them both in a small boat upon the river, the current of which
carried them to the exact place where the kingdom of Sarekittrà was to be founded. Hence the hermit-king having
carried the two blind boys to his abode, educated them, and
in due time married one of them, Mahasambavà, to his own
daughter; in consequence of which he became prince of the
village Piudì. Shortly after Bedarì conceived the renowned
king Duttabaun. Three months later Mahasambavà died, at
the age of twenty-six. He was born on a Monday, and at his
death were heard seven horrible noises.

4. In the same year Mahasambavà's younger brother Zulasambavà, marrying his deceased brother's wife, became prince
of Piudì. He lived sixty-one years, of which he reigned
thirty-five. He was born on a Monday, and at his death the
sun was eclipsed for seven whole days, during which time it
seemed a continual night.

After the death of Zulasambavà, a hermit and six Nat met
in a vast plain, and there built a most magnificent city, similar
to one of the capitals of the abodes of the Nat, with walls,
gates, ditches, battlements, and everything necessary for its
ornament or defence. This city was built in the following
manner:—The king of the Nat ordered a Nagà or Dragon to
take a rope a juzenà in length, and therewith describe a circle;
and in this circular plain was the city built, having thirty-two
great gates and as many smaller ones, with a very superb
palace of gold in the centre. This magnificent work was
finished in only seven days, and the city called Sarekittrà.

---

[1] Tharêkhettara or Shrikshatra is a ruined place a few miles east of Prome,
and still called the town of the hermit.

D

After this the king of the Nat, taking the celebrated Dutta-baun by the hand, placed him on the throne, and gave to him a portentous spear which had the power to wound and kill any of his enemies. He gave him likewise a prodigious wand, which, being thrown from his hand, would beat and lacerate those it was aimed at. To these he added a white elephant and a horse, a drum and a great bell, with seven Nat to serve him as satellites; wherefore Duttabaun became absolute lord of all the great southern island Zabudibà. This king had two wives, one was the daughter of his father Mahasambavà, and was named Zandaderì, and the other was the daughter of a certain Nagà or Dragon, and was named Bezandì. The first was the prior wife, and had a son called Duttran. Finally Duttabaun, after having reigned seventy years, died in the hundred and fifth year of his age. He was born on a Tuesday, and at the time of his death the water of the rivers changed their natural course, and ran upwards to their source; the shade of the sun being towards the north, was instantly turned to the south; and seven great noises were heard in the heavens.

5. In the year 171 Duttabaun was succeeded on the throne by his first-born, named Duttran, who reigned twenty-two years, and died in the fifty-seventh year of his age. He was born on a Wednesday, and at his death seven thunderbolts fell. From the year 193 to 637 there were eighteen kings; but in these annals no mention is made of any memorable adventure of any of them, but merely the day of their birth and the prodigy that was seen at their death are recorded. From this it appears, as well as from what we shall relate hereafter, that on the day of each king's death some prodigy must happen in heaven or on earth.

The king who reigned in the year 637 was the son of Samandà; his reign lasted only seven years. Under this king, as something unlucky was apprehended, the prince of the Nat struck out of the era 642 years, and ordered that the 644th year should now be called the second. Ever since this time it has been the custom of the Burmese monarchs to order similar corrections whenever, according to the prejudices of their judicial astrology, any year was considered as ominous of misfortune. The present king has once made this abbreviation of the era.

6. In the second year of the new era, Ahiedià son of the preceding king began his reign. It lasted three years, and in the year 5, he had for successor his brother, who reigned eleven years, and died in the fortieth year of his age. On the day of his death it happened that a countryman's corn-sieve was carried away by an impetuous wind. The countryman followed it, crying out, 'Oh! my corn-sieve! oh! my corn-sieve!' The citizens, disturbed by this clamour, and not knowing what had happened, began likewise to cry: 'Army of the corn-sieve, soldiers of the corn-sieve.' A great confusion consequently arose, and all the citizens divided themselves into three parties, who afterwards formed three different nations, the Biù, the Charan, and the Burmese.[1] The first took up arms against the second and was victorious; but afterwards, being agitated by intestine discord, was again divided into three parties; one of which put itself under the government of the prince Samudritmen. He led them to a place called Mungnò, from whence the Peguans expelled him three years after. He then took shelter in Menton, but was driven thence also by the Aracanese; upon which he passed into the great kingdom of Pagan, which contained nineteen cities. Pagan still retains its name, and is situated at the distance of four days' journey from the capital. While he there reigned, as he was destitute of virtue and power, he was compelled to feed swine, tigers, great birds, and other animals of the forest, which had rebelled against him. In progress of time the daughter of a prince of Dragons, having married the son of the Sun, bore him a child called Biumentì [Pyu-mengti], who lent his assistance to the king of Pagan, and tamed all his rebellious animals. After this he took in marriage the daughter of Samudrit [Thammudarit], and succeeded him in his kingdom. Samudrit, after having reigned forty-five years, died in the seventy-seventh year of his age. He was born on a

---

[1] Phayre calls these tribes the Pyû, Kânrân, and Mrâmmâ. He takes the story to mean that Tharé-Khettarâ was conquered by the Talaings of Thahtun, where an Indian dynasty from Telingana reigned in the first centuries of our era. —Phayre, pp. 18, 19.

Sunday, and at his death a great fiery globe, of the diameter of a large waggon-wheel, fell from heaven.

In the year 89 a hermit succeeded to Biumenti; between whose reign and the year 535 there were eighteen kings. No action of theirs of any note has been recorded; the day of their birth and the prodigy at their death are alone mentioned.

In the year 535 the reigning king was Poppozorahen [Puppá-tsau-Rahan],[1] who was famous for his skill in the Beden, a book on judicial astrology. Having from this derived information of some impending calamity, he struck off all but two years from the era 535. He reigned twenty-seven years, and died the same year in which he had altered the era. He was born on a Sunday, and on the day of his death seven enormous vultures alighted on the great roof of the royal palace, a circumstance ever looked upon as a bad omen.

7. From the second year of the corrected era to 450, twenty-two kings reigned.[2] In this year Alaunzisù succeeded his grandfather on the throne. On the day of his birth the great drum which is kept in the royal palace beat of itself; also the great palace door of itself flew open. This king, on board a most superb ship belonging to the Nat, and accompanied by 80,000 smaller vessels, sailed to the place where grows the sacred tree of this island, Zabudibà, and there for seven entire months held high festivity. The prince of the Nat went to the same place, and in the following manner saluted Alaunzisù:—'Oh king! most powerful, most wise, most excellent, oh king of kings! etc.' He then made him a present of the statues of two ancient Deities. This most puissant prince died in the eighty-fifth year of his age, after having reigned seventy years. He was born on a Thursday, and at his death Jupiter fought with Saturn. From the year

---

[1] This is the Thenga Raja who reformed the calendar. 'The common era which he established commenced in A.D. 639, on the day when the sun is supposed to enter the first sign of the Zodiac. This era is now observed in Burma. The reformation of the calendar was probably brought about by the assistance of Indian astronomers. The Burmese systems of astronomy and method of computing time are essentially those of the Hindus.'—Phayre, p. 21.

[2] Our author omits to notice Anoarahta, in whose reign in the first half of the eleventh century, the territories taken by the Shans were recovered, and the Talaing King of Pegu conquered. Anoarahta restored orthodox Buddhism.

520, in which the last mentioned king ended his reign, to the year 682, eleven kings are numbered. At this year we find the throne occupied by a king called Zunit,[1] whose reign lasted forty-three years. With him the series of the princes of Pagan ends, there having been fifty-five in all.

8. In the year 662, three brothers of the true stock of the kings of Pagan disputed among themselves the possession of that kingdom. After several intestine wars, the eldest brother obtained the quiet possession of the province called Mienzain [Myinsaing], in the vicinity of Pagan. The second brother made himself king of Maccari; and the third established himself in Penlè, a city existing at the present day.

In the year 666, the king of Mienzain built a palace of gold and became very powerful; but, fifteen years afterwards, was poisoned by his younger brother. Three years before his death he had built the city of Panjà [Panya], which is at present three days' journey from that of Ava, which latter he had four times in vain attempted to rebuild. His wife was a daughter of the Emperor of China called Poazò, by whom he had a son named Uzzanà, who was the founder of seven great convents of Talapoins. He had also another son named Chiozoà, lord of five white elephants. By another queen, the daughter of a musician, he had a son, who was afterwards lord of Chegain [Sagaing], and two daughters. After having reigned twenty-two years, he died in the fiftieth year of his age. He was born on a Monday, and on the day of his death the planet Jupiter was seen in the lunar circle, and the Pagoda worked many miracles.

In the year 685, Uzzanà succeeded his father, and reigned twenty years; after which his younger brother Chiozoà, having bought five white elephants, dethroned him, and in 704 began to reign in his stead. He had, by his queen, sister of the king of Peniè, a son named Uzzanabiaun, who succeeded to the throne in the year 726; and with him finishes the series of the five kings that reigned in Panjà.

---

[1] Zunit appears to be the King Tarukpyèmeng, in whose time the army of the Mongol Emperor of China, Kublai Khan, defeated the Burmese and took Pagan, A.D. 1284, as related by Phayre. After the fall of Pagan kings of Shan race reigned at Myinsaing and Pánya and at Sagaing.—Phayre, ch. vi.

9. Zajan, who was lord of Chegain in the year 680, having converted that place into a city, by surrounding it with brick walls and ditches, established there a new kingdom, in which he concentrated the best forces of the country. This city is situated opposite Ava, on the western side of the river. Zajan had three sons and a daughter, of whom the eldest was named Chiozoà. After having reigned eight years he died at the age of twenty-eight. At his death Saturn fought with Venus.

After Zajan's death his brother Trabià seized the reins of government, but three years afterwards was surprised and imprisoned by his own son, Sciocdantek, who, however, did not long enjoy the fruit of his perfidy ; for his body-guards killed him in a mutiny, after he had reigned only three years. The throne was restored to Trabià ; but he also enjoyed his re-acquired dignity but a few days, being unexpectedly murdered by one of his prime ministers, who placed Chiozoà, eldest son of Zajan, on the throne in his stead. This prince reigned five years, and died at the age of twenty-one. He was succeeded in the year 714 by his brother Trabià, lord of the white elephant, who reigned two years, and died in the twenty-fourth year of his age. He was born on a Monday, and the day of his death was remarkable for the appearance of a comet.

In the year 716, Menpiauk, grandson of the Emperor of China's daughter, succeeded Trabià in the kingdom of Chegain ; and at the same time his step-son Satomenchin [Thadomengbya], held the government in the kingdom of Tagaun. Narassù king of Panjà, having conceived the desire of conquering these two kingdoms, sent ambassadors to Sokim-puà, lord of Mogaun, a district in the country of the Sciam, demanding assistance in his enterprise. Sokimpuà accordingly despatched a great army against Tagaun, by which Satomen-chin was conquered and made prisoner. But afterwards escaping, he fled to Menpiauk his step-father, who received him with reproaches for his cowardice, and banished him into a forest. From the conquest of Tagaun, the army of the Sciam advanced and laid siege to Chegain. The resistance was short, the town was given up to the enemy, and Menpiauk constrained to take refuge in the same forest to which he had sent his step-son. From Chegain the Sciam passed on to

Panjà, where they spent some days. During this time, taking advantage of the false security of Narassù, they one day forced an entrance into the palace, made themselves masters of the person of the king, and carried him away prisoner into their own country. After their departure, the chief ministers placed upon the throne Uzzanabiaun, the brother of Narassù. In the third year of his reign, Satomenchin, having first put to death his step-father Menpiauk, invaded Panjà with a powerful army : and having killed Uzzanabiaun, possessed himself of the kingdom. He reigned there for the space of a month.

The following is the order of the events just narrated. In the month of May of the year 726 Chegain was destroyed, and in June the same was the fate of Panjà ; in the following month Uzzanabiaun ascended the throne, and in September lost it, giving place to Satomenchin.[1] In October this king, in his progress through Navarà, founded the city of Ava, and on the sixth day of the moon of March gave to it the name of Radanapura, that is, the city of gold and precious stones. Thus was he at the same time master of three kingdoms, Panjà, Chegain, and Ava. He died at the age of twenty-five, having reigned in Panjà seven months, and three in Ava.

10. To him succeeded, in the year 729, his brother-in-law Aminmenchokè, who, after a reign of thirty-three years, died in the seventieth year of his age, and had for successor his son Tarabià, called the lord of the white elephant, because one of that colour was born on the same day with him. He died at the age of thirty-two, having been betrayed and murdered by his own tutor. At the time of his death a comet was seen.

His brother succeeded him on the throne, and, after reigning twenty-one years, bequeathed the kingdom to his son Siahassù. His reign lasted but three years, when he was killed by the Sciam. His successor was Menlanè, his son, who ascended the throne in 787, but was shortly afterwards poisoned by his wife. To him succeeded a stranger, whose name and pedigree are unknown. But after him, in the year 788, Saddamarazà obtained the crown ; under whom the era was abbreviated, and only three years of the old computation

---

[1] Satomenchin is the King Thadomengbya, who in A.D. 1364 founded a new city at Ava.

retained, on account of some omen portending misfortune. He reigned twenty-three years and expired in the sixtieth year of his age.

11. In the third year of the new era, Menrekiozoà, son of the preceding, mounted the throne; and to him succeeded Sciassù, his brother, who assigned to his numerous sons and daughters by various queens the revenues of many cities and provinces, together with a number of elephants; and raised them to the rank of princes and princesses. In the sixty-fourth year of his age he was murdered by his own nephew. At his death many Pagodas fell down, and a large fissure opening in the breast of the statue of Godama, sent out a stream of water.

In the room of Menrekiozoà, his son Mahasihassu was placed upon the throne; and he was succeeded, in the twelfth year of his reign and fifty-fourth of his age, by his first-born son; to whom again succeeded his son. The last-mentioned prince, after a reign of twenty-five years, was taken prisoner, and put to death by the Sciam of Zemme [Zimmé, Chiengmai, spelt Iamahey or Jangomai by Fitch and other old travellers]; and with him finishes the series of the kings of Ava, who were in all fourteen.

12. After the death of this king, in the ninetieth year of the new, but the 888th of the true era, a certain Sohansuà, a Sciam by birth, obtained the kingdom of Ava, and kept possession of it for fifteen years, when he was killed by the illustrious Ranaon. He, however, did not seize upon the crown, but made it over to another, whose reign lasted but four years. This king upon his death in the year 908 of the true era was succeeded on the throne by his son Pinarapatì; but he, after having reigned five years, was taken prisoner by the lord of Chegain, who, assuming the name of Narapatizisà, ascended the throne of Ava in the year 953. He rebuilt the city of Chegain and surrounded it with a wall of brick, and reigned there for six years, when he was killed by the lord of many white elephants, Barasinmendraghiprà. He had likewise reigned three years in Ava, and his death took place in the sixtieth year of his age. His throne was given by Barasinmendraghiprà to his son-in-law Sadomenzò. This prince, after a reign of thirty-two years, hearing that his brother-in-law, the lord of

Taunu, was coming against him with a numerous army, fled towards China, but died on the way in the fifty-second year of his age.

13. Having now to speak of the origin and progress of the kingdom of Taunu,[1] we must turn back to the year 614, when one of the royal family of Pagan, of the name of Saun, built this city. From the year 614 to 872 twenty-nine kings reigned here, and in the last-mentioned year, the one who then occupied the throne, built the city anew, and surrounded it with a wall. Having reigned forty-five years, this prince died, leaving his crown to his son Mentrasvedi, who, after the space of twenty years, was killed by Zotut, lord of Cittaun, a city lying to the south of Taunu.

In the year 900 flourished a great and powerful king, lord of the white and red elephants. He had many queens and many children, to whom he gave cities, villages, and provinces for their maintenance. His eldest son having taken a wife, had a son, who was afterwards king of Martaban. Of his other

---

[1] Many Burmese families of high rank, unwilling to remain under the Shan King, settled in Taungu under a dynasty destined before long to become supreme in the land of the Irâwadi. Tabeng Shwèhti, King of Taungu, in A.D. 1538-39, took the city of Pegù, and annexed the kingdom, of which it was the capital, defeating Takârwutbî, the son of the Pegùan King, Binya Ran, who died A.D. 1526, and whose magnificence impressed two of the Italian travellers. Phayre, pp. 83, 89, 94. 'For the first time Europeans now took part in the wars of Burma. The Portugese Viceroy had sent from Goa a galliot, commanded by Ferdinand de Morales, to trade in Pegù. A battle was fought between the Burmese and the Talaing flotillas, in which the former were victorious, and the Portuguese commander, who had fought with the Talaings, was slain. The capital then surrendered.' For the reigns of Tabeng Shwèti's successors Bureng Naung and his son Ngyaung Ram Meng, who died A.D. 1581 and 1599 respectively, see chap. xiii. and xiv. of Phayre's History. In chap. xv. the capture of Syriam, near Rangoon, by the Arakan King, Meng Râjâgyi, *alias* Salim Shah, with the aid of the Portuguese adventurer Philip de Brito is described. The latter held this port for about ten years on account of the Portuguese Viceroy of Goa, until it was retaken in A.D. 1613 by the Burmese King Mahâ Dhammâ Râjâ when 'De Brito, the sacreligious wretch who destroyed Pagodas, as is remarked in the Burmese history when his punishment is related, was impaled on a high stake before his own house, and so lived for three days in dreadful agony. Most of the leading Portuguese were executed, and the remainder, as well as de Brito's wife, and many of mixed race, were sent as slaves to Ava.'— Phayre, p. 129. See also the account in *The Portugese in India*, by Manuel de Faria de Sousa, translated by Stevens. London, 1695.

children, one became king of Chegain, another of Ava, and a
fourth of Pron. Among his wives may be reckoned the
daughters of the king of Pegù, of the prince of Mochaun, of
the lord of Lezan, of the prince of Bamò, and of the prince of
Seimè. Finally, after a reign of thirty-one years, in the sixty-
sixth year of his age, he died, and was immediately transported
to the happy abodes of the Nat. He was born on a Wednesday, and on the day of his death the great Pagoda fell into
ruins, an inundation covered the whole city, and a shower of
rubies fell from heaven. His son Mahauparazà succeeded him,
and reigned seventeen years, dying in the sixty-third year of
his age.

In the year 961 the kingdom of Pegù was destroyed, and
laid waste; upon which the king Mahasihasurà gathered together the people, who had been scattered over the country,
into the city of Taunu, where, after a reign of some years, he
died at the age of fifty-eight. To him succeeded his son, with
whom finishes the race of the kings of Taunu.

14. In 959 Gnaunjan, son of the lord of the red and white
elephants, was king in Ava. His principal queen was his own
sister, and besides her he had twelve inferior ones, all daughters
of kings or princes, by whom he had ten sons and twelve
daughters. He was transported to the abodes of the Nat, in
the eighth year of his reign, and the fiftieth of his age. On the
day of his death a thunderbolt set fire to the gate of the
palace.

In the year 967 his first-born son Mahauparazà succeeded to
his throne. He took for wife his own sister, but had besides
many inferior queens. After a reign of twenty-four years, he
perished by the hand of his own son Menredeippà, in the fifty-
first year of his age.

The parricide followed up his crime by making himself king,
and establishing his throne in Hansavedi [Hansâwadi] or Pegu.
But Dammaranzà [Thado Dhammâ Râjâ] [1] and Menrekiozoà,
two brothers of the late king, had no sooner heard of his

---

[1] For Dhammaranza or Thado Dhammâ Râjâ's reign, see Phayre, ch. xvi.,
where an incursion of Chinese, A.D. 1659-62, and succeeding events are related
up to the taking of Ava by the Talaings of Pegu, and the fall of the Burmese
monarchy, A.D. 1752.

tragical death, than they collected a numerous army in the kingdoms of Tampi and Kianzi, and immediately marched towards Ava, making, however, a halt at Panjà. At this news the ministers of the parricide deprived him of his dignity, and despatched an embassy to Dammaranzà, inviting him to take possession of his deceased brother's throne. Accordingly he marched with all his army into Hansavedi, and in the year 995 was proclaimed king. The next year he went with an immense army to Ava, where he built a golden palace, and in the year 997 took the title of king. He had many sons and daughters by his various queens, and after a reign of nineteen years, in the sixty-fourth year of his age, passed to the happy state of the Nat.

15. In the year 1010 his eldest son, Menrerandameit, mounted the paternal throne. After a reign of thirteen years, in the fifty-fourth year of his age, he was put to death by his own brother, the king of Pron, who succeeded to his crown. The son of this prince, having rebelled against him, was by his orders enclosed in a sack and thrown into the river ; for this is the punishment of the princes of the blood-royal when guilty of any crime. His reign lasted ten years, and he passed to the happy abodes of the Nat in the fifty-third year of his age. His eldest son and successor reigned sixteen years, and was followed by his brother, who, in the year 1035, washed his head and assumed the title of king. He died in the fortieth year of his age, after a reign of sixteen years.

In the year 1076, his son Sirimahasihasurà took possession of the golden palace. There were borne to him by different queens many sons and daughters. His death happened in the sixteenth year of his reign and fortieth of his age ; the day of his departure was signalised by a violent earthquake, which overthrew several Pagodas.

In the same manner that the Nat wait with impatience for the flowering of their sacred tree, which takes place every hundredth year, that they may gather its blossoms; so did men expect and desire the birth of that great king, whom fate was to bestow on the southern island, for the greater good of both God and man. This monarch at length appeared in the person of Mahauparazà, the son of the preceding king. He was a Pralaun [Phra-alaong], or aspirant to divine honours, which epithet is given by the Burmese to all their kings, as an augury of their apotheosis, as in the case of Godama. This great king was adorned with wisdom, prudence, and fortitude ; and in the whole course of his reign ever had nearest to his heart the advancement of his kingdom, the happiness of his subjects, and the observance of the divine law.   His life and his reign lasted for the space of a hundred years.

16. The source from which the foregoing narration has been drawn is the Maharazaven, or history of the kings ; what follows I have in part received from the oldest inhabitants of the country, and in part have myself witnessed during my long residence in the Burmese empire.

From Mahauparazà to Alompra [Alaungh-pra—embryo Buddha], the restorer of the kingdom, there are reckoned six kings, the last of whom was called Chioekmen.   Under him the Peguans made an irruption into the Burmese empire, and took by siege the city of Ava.   The king and queen with all the great officers of the court were made prisoners and carried to Bagò or Pegù, then the capital of the enemy's kingdom.   At first the captive king met with humane treatment, but being afterwards detected in divers conspiracies, was made a spectator of the cruel murder of all his wives, and then, being tied up in a sack, was thrown into a river.

CHAPTER IX

17. THE first who ventured to make any resistance to the Peguans, after they had taken and sacked Ava, was a countryman of the village of Mozzobò [Moksobo, Shwebo], who, after having assumed the title of king, was known by the name of Alomprà. He put himself first at the head of a few friends ; but having in a short time formed a powerful army from the people that flocked to him, he speedily drove the Peguans, not only from the city of Ava, but out of the whole territory of the Burmese. Peace being thus restored, and all disturbances quieted, he caused himself to be proclaimed king in Mozzobò, which place he surrounded with fortifications, and raised to the dignity of capital of his kingdom. It is situated to the northwest of Ava, at the distance of about twenty leagues. His next care was to take vengeance on the Peguans by carrying the war into their own kingdom, where he overcame them, and dispersed their army over the neighbouring countries. He then laid siege to Siriam, the principal sea-port of the kingdom, and took it, as well as the capital city Bagò [Pegù]. Here an end was put to the war by the capture of the king. At the same time he made himself master of the two districts of Tavai and Martaban, which had hitherto been subject to the king of Pegù. Alomprà now determined to undertake a war against the Siamese, whose king had refused him his daughter in marriage. He was soon in full march against this monarch, but on the way was seized with a mortal distemper which forced him to return to Pegù. There it quickly put an end to his life, after he had reigned six years in the midst of a continual war. Before his death he declared his will to his nobles, that his seven sons should successively occupy the throne after

his decease—a most fatal disposition, as it was the cause of the many troubles and civil wars that shortly arose.

18. According to this regulation, the eldest of the brothers, Anaundoprà ascended the throne, which he held but for three years. Yet in this short space he had to contend with two formidable rebellions. The first had for its author one of the generals of the deceased Alomprà, by name Nattun, who, returning from Siam with the army, made himself master of the city of Ava, and maintained himself in it for some time. An uncle of the king was the leader of the other rebellion. He attempted to make himself king in Taunu [Toungoo], a city lying about forty leagues to the north-east of Rangoon, but was taken prisoner, and paid with his head the forfeit of his crime.

19. To Anaundoprà succeeded the second brother Zempiuscien [Hsengbyusheng, Sinbyushin], that is to say, lord of of the white elephant; his reign lasted twelve years. In the first and second years of his government he carried his arms against the Cassè, a barbarous nation occupying the country to the north-west of Ava. This he did to revenge the frequent irruptions they had made into the Burmese empire, previous to the coming of the Peguans. Their country was devastated with fire and sword, and numbers of the inhabitants carried prisoners to Ava; but they were never entirely subdued, on account of the secure retreats which their mountains and forests afforded them. In the third year of his reign, Zempiuscien abandoned the new city of Mozzobò, and transported the court to Ava, the ancient residence of the Burmese kings. At the same time he despatched his army against the Siamese, who had refused to pay the tribute promised to his father Alomprà. Jodià [Ayuthia, Ayodhia, and in Fitch's Voyage Odia], the usual residence of their kings was taken and sacked; more perhaps through the cowardice of the Siamese, or rather the dissensions that distracted the court, than by any valour on the part of the Burmese. After a short time, the conquerors abandoned the city, carrying with them an inestimable booty, together with an innumerable multitude of slaves, among whom were most of the members of the royal family. In this expedition the Burmese also obtained possession of Merghi [Mergui], and its district on the coast of Tenasserim. Besides these exploits, Zempiuscien

had twice to oppose the Chinese, who from Zunan [Yunnan] had poured down upon his territories, with the design of subjecting them to a tribute. He discomfited their numerous armies; principally perhaps by the aid of his heavy artillery, served by the Christians who had established themselves in these parts.

The prince of Zandapori [Chandapuri, Viang-chang], a province situated near the country of Laos, having been attacked by Patajac [Phayâ Tak], the new king of the Siamese, implored the protection of Zempiuscien, sending, with many other presents, one of his daughters as a concubine. The Burmese monarch immediately despatched a large army against Siam, which speedily so reduced its king that the city of Bancok alone remained in his possession. This too he would have lost, had not the unexpected news of the death of their emperor recalled the invading army to their own country.

After the storming of Jodià in Siam, and the expedition against the Chinese, King Zempiuscien resolved to declare his eldest son the heir to his throne, although this arrangement was expressly contrary to his father's will. The lord of Amiens, younger brother to the king, finding himself thus excluded from the succession, conspired against his life. The plot was discovered, and he was doomed to die; but the tears of their mother, who yet lived, saved him from his fate. Besides this conspiracy there were two rebellions, which, but that they were speedily suppressed, would truly have wrought much turbulence and harm. Of these one was raised by those Cassè whom Zempiuscien had brought prisoners into Ava; the second by the inhabitants of Martaban, of whom many served in the royal armies. For these, while absent from home on the king's service, heard that their families were vexed and oppressed by the governor: whereupon they mutinied, and having elected a chief, came to lay seige to Rangoon. The city could have made no long resistance, but a Dutch vessel, which chanced to be there, beat off the assailants with its guns, and discomfited them utterly.

Then did Zempiuscien hasten hither, and place on the great Pagoda its crown of massive gold, the weight whereof is eighty of our pounds. While this great ceremony was performed with much pomp and rejoicing, the last king of Pegù was beheaded, in order, by this bloody execution, to crush entirely the power of that realm.

20. Upon the death of Zempiuscien, the nobles of the kingdom raised to the throne his eldest son, whose name was Zinguzà. His uncle, the lord of Amiens, to whom, as we have said, the succession of right belonged, remained a quiet spectator of his elevation, because at the moment he was destitute of a party and of sufficient forces: but the lord of Salem, his younger brother, made an attempt to grasp the crown. But the conspiracy was discovered, and its author paid the penalty of his rashness by being enclosed in a sack of red cloth and thrown into the river. The lord of Amiens underwent a similar fate, upon attempting, eighteen months later, to dethrone his nephew. After this Zinguzà banished from the royal city all his uncles and near relations: and, thinking himself thus secure, he passed all his time in hunting and fishing, almost always intoxicated, so that he was called by the opprobrious name of the drunkard or the fisher king. But this conduct led to his final ruin. For his cousin, the only son of Anaundoprà, taking advantage of his absence, advanced by night to Ava, in company with about forty inhabitants of a village called Paongà, and, without experiencing any resistance, made himself master of the palace. Upon which the youth of Ava and the neighbouring places came eagerly to be enrolled, and take up arms in favour of the new king, who, in the space of five days, was in possession of the person and kingdom of Zinguzà. But the usurper, whose name was Paongozà, from the long abode he had made in Paongà, by these rapid and successful advances, only served as a means to Badonsachen, the reigning sovereign, to mount upon the throne. For, scarcely had he taken possession of the palace, than he called together his uncles, and made them an offer of the kingdom; saying, that according to the dispositions of Alomprà, to them it of right belonged. But they suspected this ingenious declaration of Paongozà to be nothing more than a malicious contrivance to pry into their secret thoughts, and, upon their accepting his offer, to give him a pretence for their destruction: and, therefore, not only declined to receive it, but declared themselves, by

drinking the water of the oath, his subjects and vassals. And here we may observe that the oath of fidelity is taken by drinking certain water upon which have been pronounced sundry false incantations, and which the king gives to drink to the mandarins, ministers, generals, and military officers, and to all others from whom he exacts an oath of fealty. Paongozà then raised them to their former state, and restored all the honours whereof they had been deprived by Zinguzà. But they a few days later took that by force which, when peacefully offered, they had not dared to accept. For on the 10th of February 1782, they suddenly entered the palace, seized Paongozà and placed on the throne Badonsachen,[1] third son of Alomprà. He, according to custom, caused the deposed monarch to be thrown into the river, calling him in scorn the king of seven days. Paongozà at the time of his death had only reached his twentieth year. On the following day the unfortunate Zinguzà underwent the same fate in his twenty-sixth year ; and all his queens and concubines, holding their babes in their arms, were burnt alive.

21. No sooner had Badonsachen ascended the throne, than he had to defeat two great conspiracies, by which he stood in no small jeopardy of losing his kingdom and his life. Of the first was head a certain Nassà, first a famous general under king Zempiuscien, then deprived of his command by Zinguzà and afterwards restored by Badonsachen to his former rank, and by him graced with many honours and dignities. Yet he repaid with ingratitude the kindness of his benefactor ; for he attempted to thrust into his place an illegitimate son of Alomprà, intending so to open a way for his own accession to the throne. The conspiracy was, however, brought to light ; and so terrified and troubled therewith was the new king Badonsachen, that never after did he put trust in man, no, not though he were his nearest of kin. Then also did he begin his practice of changing daily his chamber and bed.

Still more dangerous was the other conspiracy, headed by Miappon, son of the last king of Ava, who was taken prisoner by the Pegùans and thrown into the river. In consideration of

---

[1] Badonsachen, the Badun Meng, now usually known as Bodoahpra or Bhodawbhoora, reigned from A.D. 1781 to 1819. For this reign see Phayre, ch. xx.

his tender age, his son was fortunately saved from this miserable doom, and lived an unknown wanderer until the time of Zinguzà. Having then retired into the territories of a tributary to the king of Ava, he began to form designs upon the crown. Upon being informed of this, Zinguzà despatched an armed force to apprehend him, from which he fled into concealment. One of the principal inhabitants of Paongà, who had been mainly useful in elevating Paongozà to the throne, finding that all his hopes had been foiled by his death, resolved to make a second attempt by abetting the well-known pretensions of Miappon. To him therefore he repaired, accompanied by a friend, and easily persuaded him to place himself at the head of their party. This proposal exactly tallied with his long-cherished plan ; so, without loss of time, followed by fifty men, mostly natives of the same village, and twenty others who joined him on the road, he set forward towards Ava. After midnight of the 4th of December 1782, he scaled with his party the city and the palace without meeting with any resistance ; when his friends raised the following cry, ' Behold the true branch of the royal stock ! ' Of the royal guards, who were alarmed by this clamour, some fled from their posts and concealed themselves, others feigned themselves asleep. Meanwhile the king and his more immediate attendants, awakened by the uproar, closed the doors and guarded the avenues to the interior of the palace. Although the conspirators had possessed themselves of the cannon and powder, yet could they not effect their purpose from want of balls : notwithstanding which, they obliged the Christian cannoneers to discharge blank cartridge against the palace, and hereby caused their own destruction. For the noise of the cannonade brought together the Mandarins with their guards, who, lighting immense fires, encamped without the palace. As soon as it was day, Badonsachen having discovered that the number of conspirators was only about sixty, and these mostly without arms, had them all seized by his guards, and cruelly put to death. Three also of the cannoneers were beheaded for their conduct. Miappon alone escaped, but was the same evening dragged from his concealment, and paid with his life the forfeit of his audacity. Still was the fury of the king unsatisfied, for he now gave full scope to that cruel and inhuman disposition, of which he had already discovered sufficient signs. Notwithstanding the innocence of the great majority of the inhabitants of Paongà, he caused them all to be dragged from their dwellings, not excepting even the old men or tender infants, nor respecting the character of the priests and Talapoins, and then to be burnt alive upon an immense pile of wood which had been erected for the purpose. The village was afterwards razed to the ground, the trees and plants in its gardens cut up and consumed by fire, its very soil was turned up with the ploughshare, and a stone erected on the spot as a mark of perpetual malediction.

This cruel execution done, Badonsachen next turned his attention to securing the succession to the crown in his family, after the example of his brother Zempiuscien. And judging that to set himself up as the founder of a new dynasty would be one of the best means to accomplish his purpose, he resolved to abandon his present capital and to build another, thus the more easily to obliterate the memory of his predecessors, and fix the eyes of the multitude upon himself alone. Pretexts were not wanting to give a colour to this proceeding. It was said that the city and palace had been defiled by the human blood shed within its precincts, and therefore it no longer became the monarch to inhabit it ; and hence it was ordained that a new imperial residence should immediately be constructed. To this proposal none dared to object, and all the Mandarins and royal ministers strove who should best give effect to the orders of the king. As in this country all is regulated by the opinions of the Brahmins, so that not even the king shall presume to take any step without their advice, therefore was counsel taken of them, and thereupon a site selected for the new city, on an uneven spot three leagues from Ava, upon the right or eastern bank of the river. Here the work was commenced by the erection of the walls. These form a perfect quadrangle, each side a mile long, within which is another line of fortification somewhat inferior in height. In the centre was raised the royal palace, almost entirely of teakwood. The walls are built wholly of brick, cemented with an argillaceous earth tempered with water. They are protected on the north by the river, and on the south by an extensive pool; on the other two sides was sunk a deep fosse. When the work was completed, the king went in solemn state to take possession of the city and palace, on the 10th of May 1783, observing many superstitious rites and ceremonies prescribed by the Brahmins. After seven days he returned to Ava, in order personally to urge the removal of all his subjects to the new capital, which he effected on the 14th of the next month. Thus were these miserable inhabitants compelled to quit their home with all its comforts, and exchange a delightful situation, salubrious in its air and its waters, for a spot infected with fevers and other complaints, from the stagnant waters that surround it. Badonsachen gave to his new metropolis the name of Amarapura, that is, city of security and peace. Of the new inhabitants some took up their abode within the walls; and these were for the most part Burmese and persons attached to the royal family or to the Mandarins: to others were allotted dwellings without the city, whence arose various suburbs, or, as they are called by the Portuguese, *campos*. Besides the Burmese, the principal foreign nations who occupy special districts are the Siamese and Cassè, who were brought captives to this country in the wars of Zempiuscien, and have greatly multiplied in number. Perhaps still more populous is the suburb of the Mohammedan Moors, who have settled in the Burmese capital, as in every other part of India. Their profession is mostly traffic, and they enjoy the free exercise of their religion, having many mosques. To these must be added the suburb of the Chinese, whose industry is peculiarly remarkable, and that wherein the Christians dwell. The entire number of the inhabitants of Amarapura amounts to about 200,000. Vain would it be to describe the sufferings and fatigues, the oppressions and exactions, which this transmigration caused, to those whose eyes have not witnessed the extreme rigour with which the royal orders are here executed. No sooner was Amarapura inhabited, than Ava, famed not only as the residence of so many kings, but also for its pleasant and convenient situation and the magnificence of its public buildings, was instantly abandoned. Indeed Badonsachen caused its total destruction, by giving general permission to overthrow at will the superb Baò, or convents of Talapoins, some of which were gilt all over, within and without, with the finest gold, the magnificent wooden bridges, the public halls and porticos. All the cocoa-trees, which, planted along the interior of the walls, overtopped them with their green shadowy branches, and gave the city a cheerful and sweet prospect, were cut down and given to the elephants for food. In fine, part of the walls was torn down by order of the king, and the river, being sluiced in, reduced the whole to an uninhabitable pool.

In the meantime, the king was also busied with having his eldest son publicly recognised as his legitimate successor. He conferred upon him the title and rank of Einyè or crown-prince; and as he was born of the second queen, in order to strengthen his claims still further, he was married to his own sister, the daughter of the first. It needs not be told how little pleased with these arrangements were the two surviving sons of Alomprà. Of these the younger, called Pandelisachen, being a youth ardent and courageous, protested loudly against the violation of his father's will; and not content with words, proceeded to actions, attempting many times to seize upon the kingdom. But his plots and devices were ever discovered, and his brother, wearied with repeated pardonings, at length put him to the usual death of drowning in a red-cloth sack. The other brother was still alive when I left the country, and led an obscure and miserable life, supported by the labour of his hands.

All things being thus set in order at Amarapura, and all conspiracies thus foiled, the king resolved, in emulation of his brother Zempiuscien, to undertake some glorious achievement. As early as the last year of Zinguzà, ambassadors had come to Ava from the son of the king of Aracan, to beg assistance against the author of a rebellion. Zinguzà, ever more inclined to diversion and debauchery than to feats of arms, refused to interfere in the concerns of that kingdom. New troubles had thence risen, and new dissensions, which king Badonsachen resolved to use as a means of seizing on a new crown. Already was the general of his army appointed, and arms and warlike stores prepared, and nought was wanting to undertake the expedition except the conclusion of the great three-months' fast, when a mighty rebellion, breaking out in Pegù, diverted him from his purpose. The occasion thereof was as follows. A certain Pegùan of great authority dreamed one night that the kingdom of Pegù should shortly be restored; whence, upon its being reported abroad among the Pegùans, about three hundred of them made consultation among themselves, and resolved to make themselves masters of Rangoon, and thereafter raise the dreamer to the throne. Hereupon, at eight in the evening, they marched into the city without opposition, and proceeded to murder its governor. The Mandarins and people, scared by the tumult of the assailants and the conflagration which they raised, abandoned the city and fled to the neighbouring woods. In the meantime the conspirators divided into two bodies, two hundred remaining in garrison, while the other hundred proceeded in haste to the neighbouring towns and villages, to collect as many Pegùans as possible. The Burmese, who had fled in the night ignorant of the enemy's true numbers, having now discovered that only two hundred men kept guard over the city, placed at their head the Mandarin next in command to the governor, and returned to the town; of which being easily possessed, they put to the sword the two hundred conspirators. Meanwhile a vast concourse of Pegùans, collected by those who had gone forth, approached in small barks to the city, fearless and rejoicing, nothing doubting but that it was still in the possession of their friends: but scarcely had their boats reached the land than the Burmese, assisted and directed by the Europeans, made of them with their cannon a cruel slaughter. Great numbers were drowned, and the rest fell beneath the spears and swords of their enemies.

The expedition to Aracan took place in the following year, 1784. The army, which is said to have consisted of forty thousand men, was under the command of the king's eldest son. Part thereof was sent by land, and part by sea, but all arrived nearly at the same time at Aracan; and the city, being badly provided with men and munition, and governed by a weak effeminate prince, in an instant fell into the hands of the Burmese. By some Aracanese prisoners, of whom many were brought slaves into the empire, it was reported that the inhabitants were grossly deceived by the Burmese: for they said that upon the approach of the army, heralds were sent forth to ask the cause of their coming; whereunto answer was made that they came to worship and honour with due solemnity the great idol venerated in their city. This was a colossal statue of bronze representing Godama, as the Aracanese and Burmese have the same religion; which statue, after the taking of the city, the king brought to Amarapura and placed in a stately and sumptuous Pagoda built for the purpose.

The glory acquired by the prince his son in this rapid conquest of Aracan, inspired Badonsachen with the desire of consulting his own fame, by the subjection of the richer and more powerful kingdom of Siam. Such was the pride with which his good fortune, whether in overcoming the enemies of his kingdom, or in discovering the numerous conspiracies which had been formed against him, had filled his heart, that he began to think himself the most powerful monarch in the world, and to form vast plans of ambition. In a great assembly of the Mandarins of his empire he declared it to be his intention, first to take and destroy the chief city of the Siamese, then to turn his victorious arms against the Emperor of China, and to make him his tributary; thence he would bend his course towards the west, possess himself of the British colonies, attack the Great Mogul in his empire,[1] and, in fine, make himself undisputed master of the whole of the southern island, Zabudibà [Jambudwipa]. But the folly of his pride was soon made manifest to the ruin of all his mighty projects, in his first expedition against Siam. He had set out towards this country with an army amounting to 100,000 men, accompanied by all his sons and concubines. But he had no sooner

---

[1] In chapter xx. Phayre mentions the entry of Burmese troops into British territory in 1794 and 1797, and the despatch of several missions between 1807 and 1813 to the native courts of India, on the pretext of procuring religious books, but with the aim of intriguing against the British Government. They visited Lakhnow, Delhi, Bhartpur, the Punjab, and probably Cashmir, and even Poona. 'The direct object of these secret negotiations did not appear until later. The conquest of Arakan had brought Burmese officers into more immediate contact with India than at any previous period, and the ambitious king was inspired with the desire of acquiring the districts of Eastern Bengal, at least as far as Dacca, which had once belonged to Arakan. Even a claim to Murshedabad was some years afterwards openly made.'

reached the confines, than he was struck with a sudden panic, upon a rumour being spread that the king of Siam was advancing with a large body of troops to oppose him. It was the general opinion of his officers, that through the superiority of his forces, he might easily have overwhelmed his enemies; but he refused all advice, and betook himself to a shameful flight, leaving his elephants, arms, and military stores a prey to the Siamese. Such was his apprehension that he did not think himself safe till he found himself in the vicinity of Rangoon; yet such at the same time was the insanity of his pride, that he caused himself to be proclaimed, in all the places through which he passed, as the conqueror of the empire of Siam. This disgraceful retreat put an end to all his fine projects against the Emperor of China and the Great Mogul, for the Siamese gave him sufficient employment nearer home, and it was with difficulty he could defend his kingdom against their attacks. In these they were assisted by many of the Zaboà or petty princes of the Sciam [Shans], subject to the Burmese, who, wearied by the oppressions and exactions of the Burmese Mandarins and generals, had revolted and made common cause with the enemies of their cruel masters. The Zaboà of Zemmè [Zimme] seems to have been the most considerable amongst them. The war which the Burmese had to sustain with these enemies was long and disastrous. During a period of nine or ten years, did Badonsachen annually send out his armies against them. But the united forces of the rebels and Siamese defied all his efforts, though supported by numerous troops, and directed by his bravest generals; he was always beaten back, and, instead of overcoming the Sciam, only lost day by day the territories they inhabited, and saw their princes range themselves, one after another, under the protection of the king of Siam. Indeed nothing but the peaceful disposition of the last-mentioned monarch has saved the Burmese empire from total subjection, as few can doubt, that had he, in conjunction with the revolted Sciam, made a general attack upon Badonsachen, he would have forced him to yield up his crown, or become a tributary to Siam.

CONSTITUTION OF THE BURMESE EMPIRE

CHAPTER X

OF THE EMPEROR, AND OF HIS WHITE ELEPHANTS

1. I SUPPOSE that there is not in the whole world a monarch so despotic as the Burmese Emperor. He is considered by himself and others absolute lord of the lives, properties, and personal services of his subjects; he exalts and depresses, confers and takes away honour and rank ; and, without any process of law, can put to death not only criminals guilty of capital offences, but any individual who happens to incur his displeasure. It is here a perilous thing for a person to become distinguished for wealth and possessions ; for the day may easily come when he will be charged with some supposed crime, and so put to death, in order that his property may be confiscated. Every subject is the Emperor's born slave ; and when he calls any one his slave he thinks thereby to do him honour. To express their sense of this subjection, all who approach him are obliged to prostrate themselves before him, holding their hands joined above their heads. Hence, also, he considers himself entitled to employ his subjects in any work or service, without salary or pay, and if he makes them any recompense, it is done, not from a sense of justice, but as an act of bounty. Their goods likewise, and even their persons, are reputed his property, and on this ground it is that he selects for his concubine any female that may chance to please his eye. It is, however, sanctioned by custom that no married woman can be seized for the king, as there has never been an instance of it.; and, indeed, so sacred is this usage, that a son

of the present Emperor, having violated a married woman, was apprehended, and condemned to death by his father, and only escaped through the prayers of the queen his mother and of the crown-prince. The Burmese make use of this privilege to save their daughters from the hands of the king's ministers, by engaging them, while young, in real or fictitious marriages. The possessions of all who die without heirs belong to the king, as do those of foreigners who have not married in the country; for they are not allowed to dispose of them, not even in favour of their illegitimate children. In case of ship-wreck upon any of the coasts of the empire, the effects and persons saved are the property of the king, who regards them as a present sent to him by the ocean. The exaction of the two last-mentioned rights has, however, been enforced with a less rigour of late, in consequence of the urgent representations made by the foreigners resident at Rangoon. To the king it belongs to declare war or to conclude peace; and he may in any moment call upon the whole population of his empire to enlist themselves in his army, and can impose upon them at pleasure any labour or service.

2. Although despotism in its worst form constitute, as it were, the very essence of the Burmese monarchy, so that to be called its king is equivalent to being called a tyrant; still has Badonsachen, the despot who for the last twenty-seven years has governed this kingdom, so far outstripped his predecessors in barbarity and pride, that whoso but hears it must shudder with horror. His very countenance is the index of a mind ferocious and inhuman in the highest degree, and what has above been related of him, as well as some more facts to be brought forward, will show that it does not deceive. Immense is the number of those whom he has sacrificed to his ambition upon the most trivial offences; and it would not be an exag-geration to assert that, during his reign, more victims have fallen by the hand of the executioner than by the sword of the common enemy. To this atrocious cruelty he has united a pride at once intolerable and impious. The good fortune which has attended him in discovering and defeating the numerous conspiracies which have been formed against him, has inspired him with the idea that he is something more than mortal, and

that this privilege has been granted him on account of his numerous good works. Hence has he for some years laid aside the title of king and assumed that of Pondoghì, which signifies great and exalted virtue ; nor was he content with this, for but a few years since he thought to make himself a God. With this view, and in imitation of Godama, who, before being advanced to the rank of a divinity, had abandoned the royal palace, together with all his wives and concubines, and had retired into solitude, Badonsachen withdrew himself from the palace to Menton, where for many years he had been employed in constructing a Pagoda, the largest in the empire. Here he held various conferences with the most considerable and learned Talapoins, in which he endeavoured to persuade them that the 5000 years assigned for the observance of the law of Godama were elapsed, and that he himself was the God who was to appear after that period, and to abolish the ancient law in substituting his own. But to his great mortification many of the Talapoins undertook to demonstrate the contrary ; and this, combined with his love of power and his impatience under the denial of the luxuries of the seraglio, quickly disabused him of his Godhead, and drove him back to his palace.

As a specimen of the veneration which this king exacts from his subjects, I shall here subjoin the form of address which, on occasion of an embassy from the British Governor-General of India, was presented to the ambassador, to be by him pronounced before the Burmese Emperor. 'Placing above our heads the golden majesty of the mighty lord, the possessor of the mines of rubies, amber, gold, silver, and all kinds of metals ; of the lord under whose command are innumerable soldiers, generals, and captains ; of the lord who is king of many countries and provinces, and emperor over many rulers and princes, who wait round his throne with the badges of his authority ; of the lord who is adorned with the greatest power, wisdom, knowledge, prudence, foresight, etc. ; of the lord who is rich in the possession of elephants, and horses, and in particular is the lord of many white elephants ; of the lord who is the greatest of kings, the most just and the most religious, the master of life and death ; we his slaves, the Governor of Bengal, the officers and administrators of the

Company, bowing and lowering our heads under the sole of his royal golden foot, do present to him, with the greatest veneration, this our humble petition.'

3. Nothing was now wanting to the pride of the Burmese monarch but the possession of a white elephant; and in this he was gratified in the year 1805, by the taking of a female one in the forests of Pegù. This anxiety to be master of a white elephant arises from the idea of the Burmese, which attaches to these animals some supernatural excellence, which is communicated to their possessors.[1] Hence do the kings or princes, who may have one, esteem themselves most happy, as thus they are made powerful and invincible; and the country where one may be found is thought rich and not liable to change. The Burmese kings have therefore been ever solicitous for the possession of one of these animals, and consider it as their chiefest honour to be called lords of the white elephant. To excite their subjects to seek for them, they have also decreed to raise to the rank of Mandarin anybody who may have the good fortune to take one, besides exempting him from all taxes or other burthens. Not only white elephants, but also those of a red colour, spotted ones, and such as are perfectly black, are greatly prized, though not equally with the former; and hence have the Burmese kings assumed in their proclamations the title of lords of the red and spotted elephants, etc.

To convey an idea of the superstitious veneration with which the white elephant is regarded, I shall here give an account of the one taken whilst I resided in the country, and of the manner in which it was conducted to the imperial city. Imme-

---

[1] The notion is derived from the Hindu mythology, which treats the elephant as one of the signs of the Chakravarti, the great wheel-turning king or universal monarch. The dream of Queen Maya, the mother of Gaudama Buddha, about his entering her womb as a white elephant, thus invests with supreme sovereignty the supreme intelligence.

Senart and Kern trace these legends to the worship of the Sun, Vishnu, and Mahadev. The sun, representing regularity, next becomes the Dharma-raja, who utters religious law. Yule, p. 135, with his usual learning, quotes Ælian and Ibn Batuta about white elephants. Their stately caparisons are described by all the old travellers and by our envoys. Cæsar Fredericke, as well as the native traders, had to pay a tax for the privilege of seeing them

diately upon its being captured it was bound with cords covered with scarlet, and the most considerable of the Mandarins were deputed to attend it. A house, such as is occupied by the greatest ministers and generals, was built for its reception; and numerous servants were appointed to watch over its cleanliness, to carry to it every day the freshest herbs, which had first been washed with water, and to provide it with everything else that could contribute to its comfort. As the place where it was taken was infested by mosquitos, a beautiful net of silk was made to protect it from them ; and to preserve it from all harm, Mandarins and guards watched by it both day and night. No sooner was the news spread abroad that a white elephant had been taken than immense multitudes of every age, sex, and condition flocked to behold it, not only from the neighbouring parts, but even from the most remote provinces. And not content thus to show their respect, they also knelt down before it, with their hands joined over their heads, and adored it as they would a god, and this not once or twice, but again and again. Then they offered to it rice, fruit, and flowers, together with butter, sugar, and even money, and esteemed themselves most happy in having seen this sacred animal.

At length the king gave orders for its transportation to Amarapura, and immediately two boats of teak-wood were fastened together, and upon them was erected a superb pavilion, with a roof similar to that which covers the royal palaces. It was made perfectly impervious to the sun or rain, and draperies of silk embroidered in gold adorned it on every side. This splendid pavilion was towed up the river by three large and beautifully gilded vessels full of rowers, and was surrounded by innumerable other boats, some filled with every kind of provision, others carrying Mandarins, bands of music, or troops of dancing girls, and the whole was guarded by a troop of 500 soldiers. The towns and villages along the river, where the train reposed, were obliged to furnish fresh herbs and fruits for the animal, besides all sorts of provisions for the whole company. At each pause too it was met by crowds from every quarter, who flocked to adore the animal and offer it their presents. The king and the royal family frequently sent messengers to bring tidings of its health, and make it rich presents in their name.   Three days before its arrival, Badonsachen himself with all his court went out to meet it.   The king was the first to pay it his respects, and to adore it, presenting at the same time a large vase of gold, and after him all the princes of the blood, and all the Mandarins paid their homage, and offered their gifts.

To honour its arrival in the city, a most splendid festival was ordered, which continued for three days, and was celebrated with music, dancing, and fireworks.   A most magnificent house was assigned to the elephant for its residence, adorned after the manner of the royal palace ; a guard of 100 soldiers was given to it, together with 400 or 500 servants, whose duty it was always to wait upon it, to bring its food, and to wash it every day with odoriferous sandal water.   It was also distinguished with a most honourable title, such as is usually given to the princes of the royal family ; and for its maintenance were assigned several cities and villages, which were obliged to furnish everything necessary for it.   All the vessels and utensils employed in its service were of pure gold ; and it had besides two large gilt umbrellas, such as the king and his sons are alone permitted to make use of.   It was lulled to sleep by the sound of musical instruments and the songs of dancing girls. Whenever it went out it was accompanied by a long train of Mandarins, soldiers, and servants carrying gilt umbrellas, in the same manner as when attending the person of the king ; and the streets through which it was to pass were all cleaned and sprinkled with water.   The most costly presents continued daily to be brought to it by all the Mandarins of the kingdom, and one is said to have offered a vase of gold weighing 480 ounces.   But it is well known that these presents, and the eagerness shown in bestowing them, were owing more to the avaricious policy of the king than to the veneration of his subjects towards the elephant, for all these golden utensils and ornaments found their way at last into the royal treasury.

The possession of a white elephant filled Badonsachen with the most immoderate joy.   He seemed to think himself in some manner partaker of the divine nature through this animal, and could not imagine himself anything less than one of the great emperors of the Nat. Besides that he now expected to conquer all his enemies, he confidently supposed that he would enjoy at least 120 years more of life. As a symbol of this number the members of the royal family were making ready 120 glass lamps and other things to the same number, which, according to the advice of the Brahmins, were to be presented to the great Pagoda, when the elephant disclaimed all pretensions to divinity by a sudden death, caused by the immense quantity of fruit and sweetmeats which it had eaten from the hands of its adorers. It is impossible to describe the consternation of Badonsachen at this disaster; for as the possession of a white elephant is esteemed a pledge of certain good fortune to a king, so is its death a most inauspicious omen. So that he, who but lately was elated by the most presumptuous pride, was now overcome by the most abject fear, expecting every moment to be dethroned by his enemies, and imagining that there remained to him but a few days of life.

4. At the death of the elephant, as at that of an emperor, it is publicly forbidden, under heavy penalties, to assert that he is dead; it must only be said that he is departed, or has disappeared. As the one of which we have spoken was a female, its funeral was conducted in a form practised on the demise of a principal queen. The body was accordingly placed upon a funeral pile of sassafras, sandal, and other aromatic woods, then covered over with similar materials, and the pyre was set on fire with the aid of four immense gilt bellows placed at its angles. After three days, the principal Mandarins came to gather the ashes and remnants of the bones, which they enshrined in a gilt and well-closed urn, and buried in the royal cemetery. Over the tomb was subsequently raised a superb mausoleum of a pyramidal shape, built of brick, but richly painted and gilt. Had the elephant been a male, it would have been interred with the ceremonial used for the sovereign.

The consternation of Badonsachen on the loss of his elephant was not of long duration, for, a few months later, some white elephants were discovered in the forests of Pegù. Instantly, the most urgent orders were issued to give them chase; and after several unsuccessful efforts one was at length captured.

It was to arrive at Rangoon on the 1st of October 1806, the very day on which I sailed from that port for Europe ; and it was generally supposed that, being a male, it would receive greater honours than its female predecessor.[1]

---

[1] ' Bodoahprâ probably considered that the greatest glory of his reign was the possession of a perfect white male elephant. This animal, caught in the forests of Pegú, was received at court with honours due to an object of worship. He lived in captivity for more than fifty years.'—Phayre, p. 230. He was seen and described by Crawfurd and Yule.

CHAPTER XI

5. THE absolute authority of the Emperor is exercised
through various inferior magistrates and tribunals, having no
power to counsel or direct, but considered as the blind execu-
tors of his commands. The first and most respectable of the tribunals is that called
the Luttò,[1] composed of four presidents called Vunghì [Wungyi],
who are chosen by the sovereign from the oldest and most experienced Mandarins, of four assistants, and a great chancery.
Its sittings are held in a spacious hall or portico situated
within the precincts of the palace itself. All orders or favours
emanating from the Emperor, and even all capital sentences
must pass through this tribunal, not because it has power to
modify them, but in order to be registered and speedily put in
execution. Its grants and commands are written upon palm
leaves, in a most concise style ; and indeed, the more concise
this is, the more forcible and efficacious the sentence is considered. These leaves are cut at the ends, so as to bear the
figure of a sabre, probably to symbolise the respect and dread
with which the sentence of this tribunal should be received.

6. Next to the four Vunghì of the Luttò are the Attovun

The Hlut-daw (spelt otherwise Lotoo, Lwat-dhau, Hlwot-dau), the high
court and council of the Burmese monarchy, has been described by our different
envoys,—Symes, pp. 308, 385 ; Crawfurd, p. 401 ; Yule, p. 243.

Cæsar Fredericke, who was at Pegù about 1570, relates how Bureng Naung
sitteth every day in person to hear the suits of his subjects, up aloft in a great
hall, on a tribunal seat, with his barons round about.'—*Purchas' Pilgrims*,
ed. 1625, Book x. 1716. Ralph Fitch describes Nanda Bureng, king of Pegù
in 1586, as sitting as judge twice a day.—*Ibid.* p. 1738. The Hlut-dau was
retained under English supervision for some time after the taking of Mandalay.

[Atwinwun] or grandees of the interior,* who are also four
in number. They have the superintendence of the royal
palace, and are the privy counsellors of the Emperor; and
though inferior to the Vunghì in authority, yet by their
vicinity to his person they frequently procure advancement to
places of great dignity and influence. After them in rank
come the four general Prefects of the four parts of the empire,
the northern, southern, eastern, and western. The Governor
of Amarapura corresponds, in some respect, to a prefect of
police. His duty it is to maintain the peace of the city in
times of drought, and still more to have all fires extinguished
during the prevalence of high winds, as conflagrations are
extremely common in the cities of this empire, in consequence
of the houses being built of wood or bamboo.[1] He takes cognisance of thefts, quarrels, and other delinquencies, not only
in the city, but also in its neighbourhood, and makes report
thereof to the Emperor, who either pronounces sentence himself,
or refers the matter to the Luttò, to be judged and punished
according to custom. It would be useless to attempt an
enumeration of all the offices and situations which confer upon
their holders the title of Vun, President, or Men [Meng, Min],
that is, Mandarin. There is a Treasurer, a keeper of the
forests, another of the ordnance, a third of the concubines, etc.
All who are attached to the personal service of the sovereign,
his water-carrier, the bearer of his betel-box, his umbrella, and
sword, down to his very cook, have the title of Men or
Mandarin.

7. Besides these Mandarins and Vun who act as great
officers of State and of the household, all the sons and wives
of the Emperor have their particular courts. Among the
innumerable wives and concubines whom he keeps, four are
raised to the rank of queen, taking their titles from the four
cardinal points, according to the quarter of the palace which
they occupy. As these four consorts and their children,
particularly the eldest son, are most in favour with the
sovereign, and receive the greatest share of distinctions and

* Grandi di dentro.
[1] See Appendix, No. 2, about the punishment of a Minister for being absent
when a fire was going on.

attentions, they affect to copy, in their respective apartments, the form of the royal court in the great palace. They have their steward of the household, their counsellors and other attendant Mandarins. As the reigning monarch has had more than a hundred children by his numerous wives and concubines, they have swallowed up all the riches of the land; the cities, villages, and lakes have been almost all given them for their maintenance ; and the best situations, as of Vunghì of the Luttò, have been distributed among them.

8. Every great city in the Empire has a tribunal called Ion [Yôn], and by the Portuguese of India, Rondai. This is composed of the Governor, a Commissioner of the customs, one or two Auditors, and as many clerks or secretaries. Besides this court, the city of Rangoon has a Ieun [Yewun], or Inspector of the waters, who ranks next to the Governor, a Zicchè [Sitke], or military commander, and a Sciabandar, who has the inspection of the shipping and the exaction of port-dues. Merghi and Bassino [Bassein],[1] being likewise sea-ports, have their Sciabandar. The Governors of cities are invested by the sovereign with the right of the sword, as it is called, or the right of inflicting capital punishment, which is too often exercised not only against the guilty, but against private enemies. Smaller cities and villages have a chief, who in the former is styled Miodighì [Myothugyi], Grandee of the city, and in the latter Ioadighì [Yuathugyi], Grandee of the village. And as all these places are given by the Emperor to his children or other Mandarins for their maintenance, these feoffees or *eaters*, as they are called, have also a judge there on their own account. Under the present sovereign, as has been already observed, almost all the cities and villages of the em-pire are held in this manner by his sons, wives, or concubines.

9. With regard to the administration of justice, while all capital offences are brought before the Governors of cities, in civil causes the parties are at liberty to select their own judges. For, though ancient usage, confirmed by repeated sovereign orders, prescribe that all causes shall be heard by the Luttò in the capital, and by the Ion or Rondai in provincial towns, yet

---

[1] Older names of Bassein used by Europeans are Cosmin and Persaim.

this is so far from being observed, that any Mandarin can erect himself into a judge. Thus, when an individual is at difference with another, or has claims upon him for a debt, or for satisfaction of an injury, he goes to some Mandarin, whom he believes likely to favour him, and procures from him a summons against his adversary. It may be easily conceived to what injustice and inconvenience this practice must necessarily lead.

10.[1] The principal capital offences are rape, highway-

---

[1] The following passages from Crawfurd's Journal, pp. 407, 409, written in 1827, confirm Sangermano's statements.

'The Burman punishments are severe and cruel. The lowest in the scale is imprisonment and fetters ; the number of the latter varying, according to circumstances from one pair up to nine. Then follows mulcts, flogging, mutilation, condemnation to the perpetual slavery of the temples, and various forms of death, more or less cruel, according to circumstances. Decapitation is one of the most frequent of these ; but embowelling is also not uncommon. I shall give one or two authentic examples of these punishments. On the 26th January 1817, four persons were executed at Rangoon for robbing temples. Their abdomens were laid open ; huge gashes were cut in their sides and limbs, laying bare the bones ; and one individual, whose crime was deemed of a more aggravated nature than that of the rest, had a stake driven through his chest. The gentleman who related this to me was present at the execution. Another European gentleman, who had resided many years in Rangoon, informed me that for the same offence of sacrilege, he saw seven persons put to death at once. They were tied to stakes on the banks of the Irawadi at low water, and left to be drowned by the returning tide, which did not do its work for four hours. The Burmans commonly suffer death with the intrepidity or indifference of other Asiatic people. One gentleman told me that he had seen a deserter eat a banana with his bowels out, after the executioner had performed more than half his task : and another, also an eye-witness, stated that a woman condemned for murder to be thrown to a tiger, deliberately crept into the cage, made the savage a *shiko* or obeisance, was killed by a single blow of the animal's forefoot, and immediately dragged by him into the recess of his den.' These atrocities were however mitigated by bribery, which procured remission or reduction of nearly any sentence : and in cases of imprisonment or fetters, the executioner was bribed. Except in very extraordinary cases, the poor alone were sacrificed. The Judges took bribes from both sides, and passed decree in favour of the highest bidder. Litigation was looked on as a calamity by the people. After other instances, Crawfurd continues—' On the 7th February 1817, seven persons, found guilty of sacrilege, were conveyed to the place of execution near Rangoon, and secured in the usual way to the stake. The first of these, whom it was intended to execute, was fired at four successive times, by a marksman, without being hit. At every shot there was a loud peal of laughter from the spectators. The malefactor was taken down, declared to be invulnerable, pardoned, and moreover taken into a confidential employment by the Governor. It was after-

robbery, murder, and arson ; and under the present monarch, to drink wine, smoke opium, or kill any large animal, as an ox or buffalo. When one of these offences is committed in the metropolis or its neighbourhood, it is the duty of the Governor to seize the delinquent, try him, and then make report of his case to the Emperor, who sentences him through the Luttò. If the crime is committed in more distant parts, the Governors of the cities or provinces where they happen take cognisance of them, and pronounce judgment in the Emperor's name. Capital punishment is often commuted, through interest or bribery, for a term of imprisonment. Highway-robbery, however, when accompanied with murder, is never forgiven. Often the pain of death is changed into perpetual infamy ; the criminal is then branded on the face, his offence is written in indelible characters on his breast, and he is doomed to act as a satellite or executioner. Indeed it is persons of this class who generally do execution upon criminals, and each city is provided with them for this purpose. Although the crime of treason, and sometimes, in order to inspire terror, ordinary crimes are punished in a cruel manner, as by crucifying or burning alive, the ordinary means of putting to death is by decapitation. If it be not the season of the great fast, a cause is generally decided in a few days ; the culprit is then led from the prison to the place where corpses are burnt, with his hands tied behind his back ; he is placed upon his knees, his head is bent forward, and instantly cut off by a single blow. Women and the slaves of pagodas, who are considered infamous, are executed by a blow inflicted with a mallet upon the nape ; and this is done by a slave, and not by the public executioner. After execution, the body is left three days exposed to public view, and then buried or thrown into the river.

11. More cruel than death itself are the torments inflicted upon persons suspected of criminal offences, in order to extort from them a confession of their guilt ; for it is the custom not

wards ascertained that he had paid a large bribe. The second culprit was shot, and at the same moment the remaining five decapitated.' Crime was not repressed. 'The police is as bad as possible ; and it is notorious that, in all times of which we can speak with certainty, the country has been overrun with pirates and robbers.'

to execute any one unless he acknowledge his crime. I have no doubt but many, unable to bear the atrocity of these torments, have, in spite of their innocence, pronounced themselves guilty. These torments consist in tying the arms behind the back with fine cords, till these penetrate deep into the flesh, and the arms are made to touch ; in applying to different parts of the body heated iron plates ; in striking the legs and breast with iron hammers ; and in dipping the forefinger in melted lead or tin. Forgers of royal mandates, and sometimes thieves, suffer amputation of their right hand ; the wound is instantly cauterised by immersing the stump into a vessel of boiling oil. Adultery, petty larcenies, the transgression of orders issued by the police, in a word, all minor delinquencies, are punished by heavy fines, or by stretching the offender, for several hours on his back, in the scorching rays of the sun, or what is most common, by leading him bound through the city, and inflicting at the corner of each street five or six blows of a cane, while proclamation is made of the nature of his crime.

12. In civil causes, lawsuits are terminated much more expeditiously than is generally the case in our part of the world, provided always that the litigants are not rich ; for then the affair is extremely long, and sometimes never concluded at all. I was myself acquainted with two rich European merchants and shipmasters, who ruined themselves so completely by a lawsuit, that they became destitute of the common necessaries of life, and the lawsuit withal was not decided, nor ever will be.

Each of the parties provides himself with an advocate : and in this country every one can be an advocate, provided he know how to speak well and reason well, and has some slight notion of the laws of the country. The parties go with their advocates to plead their cause before the Mandarin, or his Chon, a species of judge, generally acquainted with the laws, and versed in the course of justice. Ordinarily, the cause is decided in one day ; if both the parties agree to the sentence pronounced by the Chon or Mandarin, a sort of coarse tea-leaves is presented to them, of which they take a pinch and chew it. Until this is done, the suit is not finished ; either party may appeal, and proceed before another Mandarin. But sometimes, the judge takes a summary means of enforcing his award, by obliging the litigants to masticate his tea against their will.

All causes and suits should be decided conformably to the code entitled Dammasat;[1] but gold too often prevails in procuring a contrary sentence. In causes relative to injuries in person or reputation, it is customary to call many witnesses and examine them upon oath. All are not admitted to act in this capacity, but only such as are qualified, by the regulations of the Dammasat. The ordinary form of taking an oath is by placing on the head a small book of palm-leaves, in which are inscribed many solemn imprecations, which the party is supposed to utter against himself, if he give false witness.[2] Strangers, however, are allowed to swear according to the forms usual in their respective countries and religions. Thus Christians are sent to take their oath in our churches upon the Gospels; and the Mohammedan Moors go to their mosques, there to conform to their own rites.

13. The Book of imprecation, or, as it is called by the Burmese, the Book of the oath, is as follows :—

' False witnesses, who assert anything from passion and not from love of truth, witnesses who affirm that they have heard or seen what they have neither seen nor heard ; may all such false witnesses be severely punished with death, by that God, who, through the duration of 400,100,000 worlds, has per-

---

[1] In chapter 24, Sangermano gives a full abstract of one of these Dharma-shasters or Codes. ' Their authority, however, is not appealed to in the Courts : and if they are read, it is only through curiosity.'—Crawfurd, p. 412. Captain Cox, who was sent to Rangoon in 1796, laughs at the translation made the year before of Sir William Jones' *Institutes of Manu* into Burmese, by an Armenian, at the King's order ; seeing that in these Dhammathats they had the Hindu laws of Manu already. Cox says, ' The Damasat is very little attended to, every prince framing a new code when he comes to the throne, and every petty magistrate innovating at will,' under the absolute monarch. *Tracts on Ava*, by Major William Francklin. London, 1811. *Account of Burman Empire and Kingdom of Assam.* Calcutta, 1839. How every new Prince made a new Code is explained by Forchhammer in his *Jardine Prize Essay*, p. 91.

[2] The oath here described is substantially that which is taken by Buddhists in the British Courts in Burmah. The concluding words are—' If I speak anything that is not the truth may I suffer the curses described in this book.' Those curious in imprecations will find the form of another Burmese oath in Crawfurd, p. 406, and appendix.

formed every species of good work, and exercised every virtue,
alms-deeds, chastity, charity, kindness, diligence, patience,
justice, magnanimity, love, and moderation, the ten fundamental virtues, with the twenty that spring from them,
making in all, thirty virtues. I say may God, who, after
having acquired all knowledge and justice, obtained divinity,
leaning upon the tree of Godama, may this God with the Nat
who guard him day and night, that is, the Assurà Nat and the
giants, slay these false witnesses. May the Nat who have in
keeping the seven parts of the writing of the all-knowing God,
and those who guard the divine deposit of his books and
writings, which amount to 84,000, slay these false witnesses.
May the Nat who keep the relics of the supreme God, the
conqueror of five enemies, consisting of his forty teeth whereof
four are grinders, of eight thousand of his hairs, of his cranium,
of his brow, of his cheek and breast bones, and of all his other
relics, slay these false witnesses. May the Nat, who guard the
84,000 pagodas all gilt, and ennobled by some divine relic,
slay these false witnesses. May the Nat who preside over the
period of 5000 years which the laws of Godama are to last,
and those who watch over the divine deposit of the statues and
figures of God, slay these false witnesses. May the dragons
and giants, the four greater Nat, guardians of the four great
islands, each whereof is surrounded by five hundred smaller
ones, and the Nat who guard the seven celebrated mountains,
the great forest, Heimmavuntò [Himâla-wana, the Himalaya],
and the great Mount Miemmò, slay these false witnesses.
May the Nat who watch and preside over the five great rivers
Gengà [Ganges], etc., and the five hundred smaller ones, over
lakes, rivulets and torrents, slay these false witnesses. May
the Nat who guard the woods and trees of the earth, the Nat
of the clouds and of the winds, slay these false witnesses. May
the Nat of the sun and stars, and of all the blessed seats,
moreover may all the 80,400 giants kill and devour piecemeal
the flesh of these false witnesses. May all those who, in
consequence of bribery from either party, do not speak the
truth, incur the eight dangers and the ten punishments; may
the ends of their fingers and toes be cut off, may all their
nerves be cut in sunder, may they suffer every sort of shameful

disease, leprosy, ringworm, etc. Moreover, may all these false witnesses, those who do not speak the truth, be infected with all putrid diseases and complaints which deform the body ; may they become fools and idiots, may they undergo every species of most grievous danger and illness ; may they send out from their mouths smoke and fire like that of hell. May they be tormented by all kinds of dirty and abominable complaints, the itch, scurvy, leprosy, white and red spots ; may they suffer dysury, ischury, strangury, gonorrhœa, aematury, diarrhœa, dysentery, tenesmus, asthma, deafness, blindness, and all other corporal miseries.'

'Moreover, may all sorts of elephants, male and female, kill them in an instant. May they also be bitten and slain by serpents, by the cerastes, the cobra-capello, etc. May the devils and giants, tigers and other ferocious animals of the forest, kill and devour them. Whoever asserts a falsehood, may the earth open beneath his feet and swallow him ; may he perish by sudden death, may a thunderbolt from heaven slay him, the thunderbolt which is one of the arms of the Nat Deva.'

'May all such as do not speak truth, die of inflammatory diseases, pains of the stomach, and bloody vomit. If they travel by water, whether in ships or in boats, may they sink, or may they be bitten and devoured by crocodiles. May their bodies be broken in pieces, may they lose all their goods, may they suffer putrid and ulcerous diseases, may they become lean, emaciated, impotent, and consumptive ; may their bodies be covered with pustules and buboes. May they incur the hatred and chastisements of the king and Mandarins ; may they have calumniating enemies ; may they ever be separated from their forefathers, parents, children, and descendants, may they become wretched; may fire burn their houses, and, although they escape the ten punishments, may the king, the Mandarins and every one else ill-treat them and raise lawsuits against them. May they be killed with swords, lances, and every sort of weapon ; and as soon as dead, may they be precipitated into the eight great hells and 120 smaller ones, may they fall with their feet upwards and their heads downwards, and may they be tormented for an immense time with fire and flame ; and after they shall have suffered in these hells every species of torment,

may they become anew Preittà-Assurichè, and then be changed
into animals, swine, dogs, etc. And finally, if again they shall
become men, may they be slaves of other men, a thousand and
ten thousand times.   May all their undertakings, thoughts, and
desires ever remain as worthless as a heap of cotton burnt by
the fire.'

14. In weighty causes touching injury or dishonour received,
as for instance in a case of rape, if witnesses are not to be had,
the principal parties are obliged to undergo an ordeal by water.[1]
Whether they be men or women, they are immersed in water,
and whoever comes out before the prescribed time is finished
and the signal given, loses his cause.   All must see how foolish
and insufficient such a proof must be : whoever is the more
expert in remaining under water is sure of victory ; and it must
be observed too, that it is allowed to undergo the trial by
proxy.   It is true that the presiding Mandarin or judge
endeavours to excite the fears of the parties, by assuring them
that the guilty will not be able to stay long overhead, without
some dreadful accident, as being devoured by alligators or
other aquatic monsters.   But these terrible denunciations do
not always take effect, and the innocent must often suffer condemnation.   To this ceremony it is usual to go with great
pomp and solemnity ; and the victorious party makes the
heavens ring with the news of his triumph, and returns home
surrounded by his friends and favourers, to the sound of martial
music.

There is another species of ordeal usual in criminal cases,
which consists in dipping the forefinger of the accused, covered
with a thin palm-leaf, into melted tin.   If the finger and leaf
remain uninjured, he is pronounced innocent ; otherwise he is
immediately condemned.

---

[1] For an account of the ordeal by water as witnessed by a European, see
Symes, p. 467.   For an ordeal by wax-candles, see the *Journal of Captain Hiram
Cox*, Edition of 1821, p. 14.   Writing in 1882 about the territory then under the
King of Burma, Mr. Pilcher of the Bengal Civil Service states that ordeal was
a recognised mode of determining disputes ; and that oaths were not used in the
courts on ordinary occasions.   The oath, he says, was taken with great solemnity,
as a sort of ordeal before the altar, the parties and their friends, going with a
band, in holiday attire, to the temple.—Jardine's *Notes on Buddhist Law*,
Note 3.

CHAPTER XII

15. The fixed revenues of the Burmese Emperor consist of a duty of ten per cent. on all merchandise brought by foreigners into Rangoon, or any others of the ports of Pegù; of the produce of the mines of silver, amber, and rubies; of certain contributions in rice, which several places are obliged to furnish for the use of the palace; and of the presents which on stated days are made by the Mandarins to the Emperor. These must not, however, be confounded with the presents, which are always necessary when any favour is asked for, as in this country nothing is ever obtained without them. But though the Burmese monarch has no fixed revenues besides these, still his means are far from being limited to them alone. For, as he considers the property of his subjects as in reality belonging to himself, he therefore exacts from them anything he pleases; so that it may be said with truth, that the unfortunate Burmese labour in acquiring riches, not for themselves or their children, but merely to gratify the avarice of the Emperor; as their possessions almost invariably find their way, sooner or later, into the royal treasury. The truth of this assertion will be made manifest by a short account of the oppressions, exactions, and injustices that the people are obliged to suffer at the hands of the king and his ministers.

Thus, whenever it pleases the Emperor to construct either a convent of Talapoins, a portico, a bridge, or a pagoda, the inhabitants of the capital are taxed to supply the funds. But the imposition is not limited by what is merely necessary, for the avarice of the minister and of the subalterns employed in the collection of the money must be satisfied; whence it ordinarily happens that twice or three times as much as is

---

[1] For further details, see Yule, p. 252, and Crawfurd, chap. xv.

requisite is exacted. By these means have all the buildings that adorn Amarapura, the walls, the palace, the convents of Talapoins, the pagodas, etc., been erected, during the reign of the present Emperor Badonsachen.[1] Besides this, several of the richest merchants in the city are obliged to furnish the court with any extraordinary aid that may be required.

16. The provincial governors do not fail, in their respective cities, to follow the example of the Emperor in his capital. And they are not content with burthening the people for the public works they may think necessary for the defence or ornament of their cities, but from the same source they draw funds for their own palaces, pleasure-boats, etc. But it is in Rangoon, perhaps, beyond every other city of the empire, that these exactions are carried to the greatest height. For besides the continual imposts for the repairs of the walls, etc., this city is exposed to numerous other taxes from its situation. Thus, should an ambassador arrive from a foreign court, the inhabitants must furnish everything necessary for his maintenance and that of his suite, and not only this, but must also defray all his expenses on his journey up the river to the capital ; again, whenever a white elephant is taken, to them it belongs to conduct it to Amarapura. The misery caused by these taxes is also increased by the unequal method of their distribution ; for it is not the possessions, but the number of persons in a family that is taken into consideration. Hence it will often happen, that a rich merchant and a poor artisan will have to furnish the same sum; and a fine house, built of wood, and containing, besides the family of the master, a great number of slaves, will be rated no higher than a miserable cabin of cane or bamboo, thatched with straw, and frequently not worth the money that is demanded.

17. The feudatories of the inferior cities, of whom we have spoken above under the name of *eaters*, again play their parts

---

[1] The first use made of his Doomsday book was to increase these extortions.— Phayre, p. 211. The amount levied appears to have been £600,000.—Crawfurd, p. 424. The privilege of entry into the Thootay or wealthy class, mentioned in sec. 3 of the *Wonnana Dhammathat*, was used as a means of pillaging merchants.—*Ibid.* p. 397.

as petty tyrants among the people under their jurisdiction. Their offices give them a right to a tenth of all the produce of the land, and they exact the half of the profits which the principal of each village, or the judges appointed by them, may derive from the decision of causes and lawsuits. This would suffice for their maintenance, but they are far from being satisfied with it. For whenever it pleases them to build a new house or repair their old one, or to erect a pagoda, or a convent of Talapoins, they have recourse to the most grievous extortions. And these evils have become almost insufferable during the present reign ; for as almost all these petty governments have been given to the wives, concubines, or children of the Emperor, greater oppressions have been practised by these members of the royal family than any simple Mandarin would have dared to have recourse to. Another imposition is likewise in use, in many of the towns lying along the course of the river, by which all boats are obliged to pay before being allowed to pass. Nor is this a trifling source of profit, considering that the want of roads obliges great numbers, whom their commercial or other interests draw to the capital and other great cities of the Empire, to make their journeys by water. In order to levy these duties, small houses, or rather open porticos, mostly of cane or bamboo, have been erected on elevated spots all along the course of the river, where a number of men watch day and night, that no vessel pass unobserved. At these places all boats are obliged to stop, to receive the visit of the inspectors, and pay the dues required. These consist of a tax according to the size of the vessel, and a present, which is regulated by the quantity and quality of the merchandise it carries. These buildings are called cioché [chauki]; and are very numerous between Rangoon and Amarapura. One or two belong to the Emperor, who employs them for the prevention of the introduction of contraband goods, and of the emigration of families from one place to another. The others belong to the different feudatories whose cities are on the banks of the river, and are said to amount at present to more than twenty-five. Sometimes those exactions are so oppressive that no one will venture to transport his goods to Amarapura, as any profit he might hope for, from their sale in that city, would be beforehand entirely absorbed by the payments at the ciochè. Foreigners in particular are exposed to the rapacity of the exactors, and unfortunate indeed is he who is so imprudent as to embark his goods for Amarapura. The visits of the inspectors resemble a robbery rather than a collection of dues; for besides the usual tax, so much is demanded under the name of presents, and so much is stolen, that the owner, after having passed two or three ciochè, will generally be glad to hasten back to Rangoon, rather than try the mercy of future plunderers. This in fact did happen a short time since to some foreign merchants.

18. But the extortions and oppressions, of which I have just spoken, are nothing in comparison to those practised by the Mandarins in the provincial cities, and above all in Rangoon. For this city, being situated at a great distance from the court, is more exposed to their rapacity; and being the principal seaport of the kingdom, where numbers of foreigners flock with their merchandise, the inhabitants have more opportunities of gain, and thus furnish a richer harvest for the avarice of their rulers. The Emperor gives no salary to the Mandarins; indeed before any one can obtain the dignity, he must spend large sums in presents; and in order to maintain himself in it, still larger ones are necessary, not only to the Emperor, but also to his queens and to all the principal personages about the court. To this must be added the expenses of these grandees in their houses, dress, and equipages, which must be proportionable to their dignity; and when we consider that the money for all this must be furnished by the people under their care, it will easily be imagined, what dreadful oppression is put in practice to draw it from them.

For this purpose, the Mandarins are always contriving means to elude the royal edicts, by which it is provided that all causes shall be tried in the Ion, or public portico, where the Mandarins are obliged to assemble every day excepting festivals. They seek to draw all causes to themselves and to decide them in their own houses, where there is no danger of their iniquitous proceedings being observed by the spies of the Government. In every lawsuit that is brought before them, they exact ten per cent. from both parties, besides the fees to the judge, to the scribe, and to the person who offers them the Lappech or tea. Should the litigants be rich, they will generally content themselves with requiring great presents, and leave the cause undecided. Thus if a creditor calls his debtor before a Mandarin and by his judgment recovers his debt, he must pay ten per cent. for the favour. But generally, cases of debt finish in a very different manner. The Mandarin will call the debtor before him, exact from him the ten per cent. and dismiss him. Before long, however, he will procure a second citation, when the same scene is reacted; and so a third and a fourth time, till the debtor has paid even more than the sum originally in litigation. Great numbers of spies and informers are also continually going about, searching out crimes and misdemeanours, often of the most trifling description, to report to their employers; who do not fail to draw from the offenders a sum of money as a reparation. And not only do they act the part of informers, but they are also employed to incite the people to lawsuits, and persuade them to have recourse to their respective masters.

Nor is it sufficient to avoid greater offences to escape the avidity of the Mandarins ; for an injurious word is enough to bring a man before them, and he can never escape but by the payment of a considerable fine. A few instances may serve to make more evident the excessive injustice which prevailed in Rangoon but a few years ago. Thieves had increased to such an extent that a night never went by without some robbery being committed. To remedy this, it was ordained that the master of every house should keep guard, to seize any thief who attempted a robbery, and deliver him up to justice. At this time it happened that a poor widow, having contracted a debt of about fifty crowns to pay the taxes, was obliged to sell her only daughter who had just attained the age of puberty, to satisfy her creditor. She put the money in a box in her house, intending the next morning to carry it to the creditor; but the same night some thieves entered her house, and carried off the fifty crowns, together with everything else they found in her box. The trouble of the poor woman may easily be conceived, upon finding in the morning that, besides the loss of her only daughter, she had now to grieve for that of her money.

She sat herself down before her door, and there gave full scope to her grief. Whilst this was going on, an emissary of one of the Mandarins passed by, and inquiring the cause of her tears was informed of the robbery. He hastened to his master to inform him of the circumstance; the poor woman was cited before him, and commanded to deliver up the thief; she was of course unable, but could only free herself from the demand by a considerable present. On another occasion as a woman was employed in cooking, a cat stole a half-roasted fish. The woman followed it, crying out, 'The cat has stolen my fish.' But what was her surprise, when a few days after she was called before a Mandarin, and commanded to produce the thief who had robbed her? It was to no purpose that she declared that the cat was the delinquent; she could not obtain her release but by the payment of a sum of money. Warned by these examples, the inhabitants of Rangoon are careful not to say anything of the thefts committed upon them, choosing rather to bear their loss in silence than run the risk of falling into the hands of a rapacious Mandarin.

19. By these means the greater part of the Mandarins acquire immense riches; but more it would seem for the Emperor than for themselves. For sooner or later the news of their conduct reaches the court, they are stripped of their dignity, and sometimes, if their crimes be great, are put to death, and their property is confiscated for the use of the Emperor. Generally, however, they save themselves at the expense of their riches, which are entirely consumed in presents to the wives, sons, and chief ministers of the Emperor; and then they are frequently sent back to the same governments where they had practised their extortions, to heap up new treasures for new confiscations. Hence it may justly be inferred, that the rapacity of the Emperor is not less than that of his Mandarins; and that he does not care for the spoliation of his subjects, but rather encourages it, that he may thus always have means in his power to replenish his treasury.

CHAPTER XIII

20. THE soldiery in the Burmese Empire is on a very different footing from ours : it does not consist of regiments of soldiers with various ensigns, who live separately from other members of society in barracks, castles and fortresses, without wives and children, and exercise no other trade but that of handling arms, and going through warlike exercises. Those who in this country perform military service are the whole Burmese nation, who in quality of slaves of the Emperor, and whenever he commands them, are obliged to take arms. But though all are bound to military service, yet all are not received and enrolled indistinctly and in the same manner. The population of this kingdom, which amounts to nearly two millions of souls, may be considered as divided into so many small corps, each of which has its own head who is called Sesaucchì, and corresponds to our sergeant. Some are employed in the service of fire-arms, some are armed with lances and sabres, some use the bow, and there are some corps of cavalry, who, mounted on horseback, fight with lances and sabres ; one corps alone, which is composed of Christians of the capital, is addressed to the management of cannon. In the time of Anaundoprà and Zempiuscien, the corps of Christian engineers, which then amounted to about two thousand, including their

---

[1] As to the Burmese army and war-boats, see Symes, ch. xiv. ; Crawfurd p. 413, and Yule p. 246. The Burman peasantry, according to all accounts, hated being called on for military service. Crawfurd writes, ' Europeans of respectability, who were present at Rangoon when expeditions were sent against the island of Junk Ceylon, and other portions of the Siamese coast, informed me that they had repeatedly seen the unwilling conscripts embarked in hundreds for that service, tied hands and legs, with as little ceremony as if they had been so many cattle.'

wives and children, was in great honour; they were descendants of those foreigners, chiefly Portuguese, whom the Burmese had transported as slaves from Siriam more than a century before.[1] As muskets and persons who knew how to use them were then rare, a greater importance was attached to them than in our own times ; when this sort of arms, imported in great quantities by the English and French ships, has become common. In the great cities there are still these corps of soldiers, but the greater part of their population are not enlisted, particularly the inhabitants of Amarapura and Rangoon, where the corporation of merchants, especially if they be foreigners or sons of foreigners, are exempted from military service. In compensation, however, for this, they are more heavily taxed for the support of the expenses of war. Each of these different corps has a Mandarin in the capital for protector.

21. When the Emperor orders any military expedition, either into hostile countries, or against rebels, he fixes at the same time the number of soldiers who are to march, and nominates immediately the general who is to command them. The Luttò in the capital, and the Ion or Rondai of the provincial cities then exact from the heads of the different places under jurisdiction, not only the number of men ordered by the Emperor, but also a certain quantity more. Those who are not fit for war, or who possess great riches, instead of personal service, furnish a certain contribution, of which the ordinary rate is a hundred dollars ; and this money, received from the surplus of the men required, serves to pay the expenses of the war, and provide the soldiers with necessaries. For the Emperor does not furnish anything but the arms, which must be well taken care of, and woe to the soldier who loses them. This money also serves to glut the greedy avarice of the Mandarins, many of whom, to enrich themselves, long for war as the farmer does for rain. The generals also, and the other inferior officers, are wont to appropriate a good part of the money which has been collected for the expenses of the expedition, besides which

---

[1] In 1613, after the Burmese King Mahâ Dhammâ Rajâ had taken Syriam from Philip de Brito. In 1554 Bureng Nyaung at the capture of Ava had a bodyguard of 400 Portugese, dressed in uniform and armed with arquebuses.— Phayre p. 107.

they often dismiss many of the soldiers who have enlisted, requiring money instead, and then say that they are ill or dead. This, however, is sometimes the cause of their own death, which is sure to ensue if the Emperor be informed of these extortions. All from the age of seventeen or eighteen to that of sixty are admitted to the ranks, but those are always preferred who have wives and children to serve as sureties and hostages, and be responsible for the desertion or rebellion of their fathers or husbands.

22. As soon as the order for marching arrives, the soldiers, leaving their sowing and reaping, and whatever occupation they may be engaged in, assemble instantly in different corps, and prepare themselves; and throwing their weapon over their shoulders like a lever, they hang from one end of it a mat, a blanket to cover them at night, a provision of powder, and a little vessel for cooking, and from the other end a provision of rice, of salt, and of napè, a species of half-putrid half-dried fish, pickled with salt. In this guise they travel to their place of destination without transport-waggons, without tents, in their ordinary dress, merely carrying on their heads a piece of red cloth, the only distinctive badge of a Burmese soldier. About nine o'clock in the morning they begin to march, after having taken a short sleep, and cooked and eaten their rice, and Carè, a sort of stew eaten with the rice, of which that kind which is used by soldiers and travellers is generally made of herbs or leaves of trees, cooked in plain water with a little napè. At night they bivouac on the bare ground, without any protection from the night air, the dew, or even the rain; merely construct-ing a palisade of branches of trees or thorns. Sometimes it happens that the expedition is deferred till the following year, and then the soldiers being arrived on the enemy's confines are made to work in the rice grounds, thus to furnish a store of that commodity for their provision.

23. It must not be imagined that battles in this country bear the slightest resemblance to those of Europe; for destitute as these people are of discipline and all knowledge of tactics, they never can be said to engage in a regular battle, but merely to skirmish under the protection of trees or palisades; or else they approach the hostile town or army under the cover of a mound

of earth, which they throw up as they advance. It may indeed sometimes happen that two parties will meet in the open plain, but then a strange scene of confusion ensues, and each side, without any method or order, endeavours either to surround the other or to gain its rear, and thus put it to flight. But it is when they enter without resistance an enemy's country that they show their true spirit; which, while it is most vile and dastardly in danger, is proportionably proud and cruel in victory. The crops, the houses, the convents of Talapoins are all burnt to the ground, the fruit trees are cut down, and all the unfortunate inhabitants, who may fall into their hands, murdered without distinction.

24. The great conquests of the Burmese under the Emperors Alomprà and Zempiuscien must not therefore be attributed to a native courage, which they are far from possessing, but to the rigorous discipline which keeps them in awe. Not merely the general, but even the officer of any corps which is separated from the main body, has the power of punishing with death, and this without any process, whatever soldier he may think deserving of it. The sword is always hanging over the head of the soldier, and the slightest disposition to flight, or reluctance to advance, will infallibly bring it down upon him. But what above all tends to hold the Burmese soldiery to their duty is the dreadful execution that is done on the wives and children of those who desert. The arms and legs of these miserable victims are bound together with no more feeling than if they were brute beasts, and in this state they are shut up in cabins made of bamboo, and filled with combustible materials, which are then set on fire by means of a train of gunpowder. The present Emperor in particular has rendered himself detestable by these dreadful barbarities; and on one occasion, about a year before I left the country, he put to death in this cruel manner, men, women, and children, to the number of a thousand persons.

25. But while the power of the generals and officers is so absolute over the common soldiers, the former are in like manner subject to the Emperor. Woe to the commander who suffers himself to be worsted. The least he can expect is the loss of all his honours and dignities; but if there has been the

slightest negligence on his part, his possessions and life must also be sacrificed to the anger of the Emperor.

26. From the time of Alomprà to the beginning of the present reign, the forces of the Burmese Empire were very great, as will appear from the numerous and important enterprises undertaken by the monarchs immediately preceding Badonsachen, as well as by his own expeditions into Siam and Aracan. But since this period they have fallen off not a little. For the continual wars with the rebel princes of the Sciam, and particularly with the one of Zemmè [Zimmè], which have since occupied the Burmese arms, together with the fatigues incident to them, and the diseases arising, partly from unwholesome food, partly from the malignant properties of the air in the countries where they have been engaged, have carried off vast numbers of the soldiers. Many also of the Burmese and Peguàns, unable any longer to bear the heavy oppressions and continual levies of men and money made upon them, have withdrawn themselves from their native soil with all their families; some retiring towards the east have taken refuge among the rebellious Sciam, others towards the west into Bengal, where they have established themselves in the vicinity of Sciatigan [Chittagong]. And thus, not merely the armies, but likewise the very population of his kingdom has been of late much diminished, through the tyranny of Badonsachen. When I first arrived in Pegù, each bank of the great river Ava presented a long-continued line of habitations; but, on my return, a very few villages were to be seen along the whole course of the stream. The Emperor is by no means ignorant of the pitiful state to which his subjects have been reduced by the calamities of war. A person of rank once ventured to point it out to him; his only reply was, 'We must hold the Burmese down by oppression, that thus they may not dare to think of rebellion.' To another who had represented to him that these continual wars were greatly diminishing the number of his subjects, he coldly replied, 'It would matter little if all the men were dead, for then we might enrol and arm the women.'

CHAPTER XIV

THE LAWS OF GODAMA

In order to fulfil this part of my undertaking, I think I cannot do better than present to the reader a short treatise on the religion of the Burmese, which a celebrated Talapoin, the tutor of the king, drew up at the request of one of our Bishops in the year 1763.

1. Four Gods have at different periods appeared in the present world, and have obtained the state of Niban [Nirvâna, Neibban], Chauchasan, Gonagon, Gaspà and Godama. It is the law of the last mentioned that is at present obligatory among men.

He obtained the privilege of divinity at the age of thirty-five, when he began to promulgate his laws, in which employment he spent forty-five years. Having thus lived to the age of eighty in the practice of every good work, and having conferred salvation on every living creature, he was assumed into the state of Niban. From that time to the year 1763, there have passed 2306 years.

2. Godama spoke and taught as follows. 'I, a God, after having departed out of this world, will preserve my laws and my disciples in it for the space of 5000 years.' Having likewise commanded that his statue and relics should be carefully kept and adored during this period, he thereby gave rise to the custom of adoring them.

When we say that Godama obtained the Niban, this is to be understood of a state exempt from the four following evils: conception, old age, sickness, and death. Nothing in this world nor any place can give us an idea of the Niban : but the exemption from the above-mentioned evils, and the possession of perfect safety, are the only things in which it consists. For example, a person is seized with a violent complaint, but by using the best remedies is cured; we say that such a one has recovered his health : but if it be asked how he recovered his health, the only answer we can give is, that to be free from infirmities is to recover one's health; and it is thus we say that a person has acquired the Niban. This is what Godama taught.

3. Is Godama the only true God in this world?

Yes, Godama is the only true and real God, who knows the laws of the four Sizzà, and in whose power it is to raise to the state of Niban. But as when a kingdom is overturned, numerous aspirants to the throne arise to claim the royal dignity, so did it happen when the period for the observance of the laws of Gaspà, the predecessor of Godama, had elapsed. For a thousand years beforehand, the approaching appearance of a new God was reported; but previous to his coming six different pretenders, each with 500 disciples, started up, and gave themselves out for Gods.[1]

4. Did these false Gods preach and teach any laws?

Yes, but what they taught is false and full of errors. One of them taught that the efficient cause of all good and evil in the world, of poverty and riches, of high and low birth, etc., was a certain Nat of the woods, who for this reason ought to be universally adored. A second taught that after death men did not pass into the state of animals, nor did animals become men; but men were born again as men, and animals as animals. A third denied the Niban; and asserted that all living

---

[1] One is often asked whether the Buddhists of Burma recognise any God. The question is, *teste* Bishop Bigandet, a difficult one to answer. The creed, examined by logic, excludes the idea of a supreme moral governor, the law of merit and demerit, by the action of Karma, controlling the whole Kosmos. Gaudama was a mere man, who attained the highest possible perfection, by means of virtue and science. But he is no more, and the creed admits no divine providence. 'No idea whatever of a supreme being is to be met in the genuine worship paid to Gaudama by his most enthusiastic adherents. It cannot be denied that in practice Buddhists of these parts betray often without perceiving it that they have some vague idea about a supreme being, who has a controlling power in the affairs of this world and the destiny of man.' Bigandet, i. p. 137; ii. p. 53.

creatures have their origin in the womb of their mother, and that with the death of the body they return to nothing; and that in this alone the Niban consists. Another affirmed that living beings have no beginning, and will have no end in acquiring the Niban. He denied the merit of good or bad actions, and made everything happen through the influence of chance. It was taught by another that the Niban merely consists in the length of life which some Nat and Biammà enjoy, who live for the whole duration of a world. He also said that it was a good work to honour one's parents, to suffer hunger and thirst, the heat of fire and of the sun; and that it is lawful to kill animals: that those who regulate their conduct by these doctrines will be rewarded in a future life, but they who neglect them will be punished. The last of these impostors taught that there exists a Supreme Being, the Creator of the world and of all things in it; and that he alone is worthy of adoration. All these doctrines of the six false Gods, are called the laws of the six Deittì.[1]

5. But when the true God Godama appeared, did these false Gods renounce their doctrines?

Some renounced and some did not; and many have remained obstinate to the present day. When Godama saw that many persisted in their errors, he gave a challenge to them all, who could work the greatest miracle under a mango tree. It was accepted, but Godama gained the victory, at which the chief of the Deittì was so vexed, that he threw himself into a river with an earthenware vessel tied about his neck. After the death of their leader many of his disciples abandoned his false doctrines, but others remained obstinate; for it is easy to draw a thorn out of the hand or foot by means of the nails or the megnac,* but it is very difficult to eradicate false doctrine from the hearts of the Deittì.

---

[1] The tenets of the six teachers are given in more precise language, out of a work written by a Catholic priest at Ava above a century ago. Bigandet, ii. pp. 62, 121. The early disputes raged round Gaudama's doctrines of Atheism and Neibban, and his principle of human equality. *Ibid.* i. p. 115. For lists of heretics out of Chinese books, see Sykes' *Notes*, pp. 20, 21.

* This is an instrument, like a pair of tweezers, which the Burmese make use of to pull out the beard.

6. But are there no means of doing it?

Yes, it may be done by the doctrine of Godama, and by the lessons of good men; which are like a megnac, of great excellence.

7. And what are these lessons and doctrines?

First, that all who kill animals or do anything contrary to the ten commandments, are subject to the punishments allotted to evil deeds. Then that those who give alms and practise the ten good deeds, adore God, the law, and the Talapoins, will enjoy the blessings attached to the performance of good works. Secondly, that these two kinds of works, the good and the bad, and these alone, accompany a man through his transmigrations in future worlds, in the same way as a shadow follows the body to which it belongs; and that these are the efficient causes of all the good and evil that happen to living beings, in this life or in the next, of high and low birth, of riches and poverty, of transportation to the seats of the Nat, and of condemnation to the state of animals or to hell. These are the revelations made by Godama; this is the true doctrine; this is the true megnac, alone able to tear out error from the hearts of the Deitti.

8. But what then are the doctrines, what the laws, that Godama gave to mankind?

They consist chiefly in the observance of the five commandments, and the avoiding the ten evil works. The five commandments are as follows. By the first we are forbidden to kill any living thing, even the smallest insect: by the second, to steal: by the third, to violate the wives or concubines of another: by the fourth, to tell lies or deceive; and lastly by the fifth is prohibited the use of wine, opium, or any intoxicating liquor. Whoever observes all these precepts, throughout his future transmigrations, will be either a man of high nobility or a great Nat; and will be exempt from poverty and all the other evils of life.

The ten evil deeds are divided into two classes. In the first class are comprised all works contrary to the three first commandments, that is, the killing of any animal, theft, and adultery. In the second are placed lying, sowing of discord, bitter and angry words, and useless and idle talk. And the third class consists of coveting our neighbour's goods, envy, and the wishing of misfortune or death to others, and finally adherence to the doctrines of the Deittì. Whoever abstains from all these evil deeds is said to observe the Silà, will after death become a great man or a great Nat, and be loaded with honours and riches; he will enjoy a long life, and in each successive transmigration will increase in virtue, till at length being thought worthy to see some God and listen to his discourses, he will thence obtain the perfect happiness of the Niban:[1] when he will be free from the four evils of which we have spoken above: conception, old age, sickness, and death.

9. Are there no good works but those just mentioned?

Yes, there are two others, known by the names of Danà, and Bavanà. The first consists in giving alms, particularly to the Talapoins. The second is practised in pronouncing and meditating upon these three words: Aneizzà, Docchà, Anattà [Change, pain, illusion]. In pronouncing the first, a man is supposed to consider in his mind that he is subject to the misfortunes of life: at the second, that he is obnoxious to its miseries; and at the third, that it is not in his power to free himself from them.

Whoever neglects all these good works, Silà, Danà, and Bavanà, will assuredly pass into one of the states of suffering, Niria, Preittà, Assurichè, or into animals. And he who dies without the merit of any good work, may be likened to a man setting out on a journey through a desert and uninhabited country, without taking any care for his necessary provisions; or venturing along a road beset with robbers and wild beasts, without providing himself with arms for his defence; or embarking in a small and worn-out bark upon a great river,

---

[1] One is constantly asked what the Burmans mean by Nirvāna. Is it annihilation, or absorption into deity or the universe, and does the soul remain individual? As to what the sacred books teach, I refer the reader to *Buddhism*, by Rhys Davids, p. 110. Bishop Bigandet thinks the metaphysic must, as a matter of logic, end in predicating complete annihilation. But for a long period the masses have revolted at this conclusion, and in some way, which they cannot very intelligibly explain, believe that the individual soul survives death and is found in new conditions of existence. The half-civilised Burman refrains from pushing his ontology too far.—Bigandet, ii. pp. 69, 98. See also in the same volume the abridgment of Buddhism called the 'Seven Ways to Neibban.'

agitated by hideous whirlpools, and tossing with a furious tempest. And every one, whether priest or secular, who gives himself up to the five works of the flesh, that is, to those which are committed by the five senses of the body, and thereby neglects the five commandments, and does not keep himself from the ten evil deeds, is likened to a butterfly that sports around the flame till it is burnt in it; or to a man who, seeing honey on the edge of a sword, cuts his tongue in licking it off, and dies; or to a bird that flies to seize the food, regardless of the net spread to entrap it; or to the stag who, running by the side of his beloved mate, falls unexpectedly into the toils of the hunters. Such are they who, unmindful of future dangers, abandon themselves to the five works of the flesh, and pass after death into hell. These are the precepts and the similitudes of Godama.

10. The Talapoin ends his summary by declaring, that out of the Burmese Empire and the island of Ceylon there are no true and legitimate priests of the laws of Godama, and by exhorting all strangers to embrace this law as alone containing the truth.

This treatise may give some idea of the laws of Godama regarding seculars; of those respecting the Talapoins, I shall speak further on. The sermons of Godama, as they are called, are all contained in a great book called Sout, and it must be confessed that they inculcate some fine morality, of which I will give some specimens in the next chapter.

11. The books which contain the history of Godama represent him as a king who, having laid aside the ensigns of royalty, withdrew himself into a solitary place, put on the habit of a Talapoin, and gave himself up to the study and practice of virtue. But Godama had even before this acquired great merits. For he had already lived in 400,100,000 worlds, having begun as a little bird, and passed through 550 transmigrations, some happy, some unhappy, so as once even to have been an elephant. These former merits, united to his present generous abdication, procured for him at the age of thirty-five the gift of divine wisdom. This consists in seeing into the thoughts of all living beings: in the foreknowledge of all future events, however distant they may be: in the knowledge

of the merits and demerits of all men : in the power of working miracles, particularly by causing fire and water to issue
from his eyes at the same time, or fire from one eye and water
from the other ; and finally in a tender love towards all things
living.   Among other prodigies related of him, we may notice
the one said to have happened at his birth ; for he was no
sooner born than he walked seven paces towards the north,
exclaiming : ' I am the noblest and greatest among men. This
is the last time that I shall be born ; never again shall I be
conceived in the womb.' In his stature also and the properties
of his body there was something extraordinary. His height
was more than nine cubits, his ears hung down to his
shoulders, his tongue being thrust out of his mouth reached
even to his nose, and his hands, when he stood upright,
touched his knees. In walking he always appeared elevated at
least a cubit from the ground ; his clothes did not touch his
body, but were always a palm distant from it ; and in the same
manner, anything he took up remained always at the distance
of a palm from his hands. During the forty-five years that he
spent on earth after becoming a God, he was continually
employed in the promulgation of his laws, and it is said that
through his preaching 2,400,000,000 persons obtained the
Niban. In the eightieth year of his age he died of a dysentery,
brought on by an excess in eating pork. Previous to his death
he recommended that his statue and relics should be preserved
and adored.

These have hence become objects of veneration to all the
Burmese, wherever they are met with ; but they are more
particularly worshipped with greater pomp and by greater
numbers in the Pagodas. These are pyramidal or conical
buildings made of brick, painted and gilded on the outside.
In these temples there is generally a niche in which is placed
the statue of Godama ; though in some both the niche and the
statue are wanting. These are the public places of adoration
for the Burmese, and are generally set apart from all other
buildings, and surrounded by a wall of the same materials as
the Pagoda itself.

12. Godama, upon his death, was immediately transported
to the Niban, where he remains in a sort of ecstasy, without

hearing, or seeing, or feeling, or having any sense of what goes
on in the world, and in this state he will remain for eternity;
and such will be the lot of all who have the good fortune to
obtain this reward. But the laws of Godama will be observed
upon earth for the space of 5000 years, reckoning from the
day of his death, from which year, therefore, the Burmese begin
their era. Of this period 2352 years have already elapsed.
As soon as it is at an end, the laws of Godama will cease to be
binding, another God must appear to promulgate a new code
for the government of mankind.

13. But the Burmese books do not confine themselves to the
narration of the past, they likewise pretend to tell of the
future. The God who will succeed Godama will be called
Arimatèa, and his stature will be eighty cubits; the size of his
breast will be four cubits, that of his face five, and the same
will be the size of his eyes, mouth and tongue, and even of the
hairs of his eye-brows. But this God will not make his
appearance as soon as the period for the observance of the laws
of Godama is expired; but many ages must previously elapse.
For between the appearance of each God the earth must
increase in height a whole juzenà; but as the rain which falls
every year only adds to its surface a crust of the thickness of a
tamarind-leaf, it is evident that more than 5000 years will be
required to fill up the period. Hence also it is not every
world that is honoured by a God. In the 400,100,000, during
which Godama has been going through his transmigrations,
only twenty-two have lived; and very few are in reserve for
succeeding worlds, for the total number of Gods that will
ever appear, comprising Godama, will be but twenty-eight.

14. The absurdity of this system will be manifest to my
readers at first sight; and indeed I have forced several learned
Talapoins partly to acknowledge it. In various conversations
with them I frequently urged against their system the vicious
circle in which it involved them. For, according to their
principles, before any one can become a God, he must have
acquired great merit in numerous transmigrations, which merit
consists in the faithful observance of the law. But, on the
other hand, the law is nothing else but the precepts and
revelations of God. I asked them, therefore, whether God or

the law were anterior? They all replied that the former was undoubtedly first, since the law is that which God reveals. 'But then,' I added, 'the observance of the law is necessary to become a God; therefore the law must exist before God.' They were overcome by the argument, and could not reply a word. I endeavoured further to convince them of the necessity of one Supreme Being, anterior not only to the law, but to everything else, by saying, that as speech cannot exist but in the mouth of some one speaking, so there could be no law, unless there had first existed a being to promulgate it, and command its observance, but who himself is totally independent of it.

15. If we except the nation of the Carian, who have before been noticed as adorers of an evil genius, who, as they suppose, inhabits the forests, and the Cassè,[1] who were brought prisoners into Ava by Zempiuscien, and who, after the manner of the ancient Egyptians, adore the basil, and other herbs and fruits, all the nations comprised in the Burmese Empire, the Pegùans, the Aracanese, the Sciam, etc., join in the adoration of Godama, and the observance of his laws. And not only here, but likewise in the kingdom of Siam this is the established religion. Godama is besides adored in China under the name of Fò, and in Thibet under that of Buttà. His worship also prevails in many places along the coast of Coromandel, and particularly in the island of Ceylon, which is the principal seat of the Talapoins. Hence do the Burmese and Siamese emperors from time to time send deputations of learned men to this island, either to bring over some sacred book which may be found wanting in their collections, or to consult with the Talapoins on the meaning of some passage in the writings of Godama, for they are composed in the Palì, the language commonly spoken in the interior of Ceylon.[2]

---

[1] A Burmese name for the people of Manipur.

[2] That high authority, Professor Childers, points out that Pali means the language of the sacred texts, and that the geographical name of the language is Magadha, from the region in Behar in India.

According to Dr. Rost, 'Pali is the name of the literary language of the Buddhists in Ceylon, Burma, Siam, and Cambodia. . . . When and where that language was formed is still a matter of controversy.' Professor Kuhn, following Westergaard, holds that Pali was the Sanskritic vernacular spoken at Ujjain, the

16. The Burmese Government allows to the Mohammedan Moors the free exercise of their religion, as likewise to about 2000 Christians who are scattered up and down the empire. But this toleration arises more from political and religious motives, for the Talapoins teach that there is no salvation out of the religion of Godama. Since the time that the Catholic missionaries have penetrated into these parts there have indeed been some conversions, but the number has not been so great as to excite the jealousy of the Talapoins or of the Government. Hence Christianity has hitherto experienced no persecutions in these parts, partly on account of the small number of the converts,* and partly through the prudence of the missionaries, who have been solicitous to preserve themselves and their disciples from observation. Otherwise it is probable they would have had to suffer much, as we may gather from the fate of the Zodì, who began by making a great stir throughout the whole kingdom, and thereby excited the zeal of the Emperor against them. It is believed that great numbers of them still exist in divers parts of the empire, but they are obliged to keep themselves concealed. They are of Burmese origin, but their religion is totally different from that of Godama. They reject metempsychosis, and believe that each one will receive the reward or punishment of his actions immediately after death, and that this state of punishment and reward will last for eternity. Instead of attributing every thing to fate, as the Burmese do, they acknowledge an omnipotent and omniscient Nat, the creator of the world; they despise the Pagodas, the Baos, or convents of Talapoins, and

capital of Mâlava, at the time that Mahendra, the son and successor of the great Asoka, took the sacred canon with him to Ceylon. 'On the other hand, Professor Oldenburg, rejecting that tradition, considers the naturalisation of the Pali language in Ceylon to have been the fruit of a period of long and continued intercourse between that island and the adjacent parts of India, more especially the Kalinga country. . . . Both scholars have discussed the question as to the Pali being identical with the Magadhi dialect, and have satisfactorily disposed of it.'—*Encyclopædia Britannica,* Art. Pali, by Dr. Rost. The Burmans give a wider meaning to the word Pali, which they apply to any text considered sacred, such as the Sanskrit Vedas. So Judson, the missionary, described his Burmese Bible as translated from the Hebrew and Greek Pali.— Forchhammer's *Report on the Literary Work for* 1879-80. Rangoon, 1882.

* See Note A at the end of the work.

the statues of Godama. The present Emperor, a most zealous defender of his religion, resolved with one blow to annihilate this sect, and accordingly gave orders for their being searched for in every place, and compelled to adore Godama. Fourteen of them were put to a cruel death ; but many submitted, or feigned to submit, to the orders of the Emperor, till at length he was persuaded that they had all obeyed. From that time they have remained concealed, for which reason I have never been able to meet with one of them, to inquire if any form of worship had been adopted by them. All that I could learn was that the sect was still in existence, and that its members still held communications with each other. They are for the most part merchants by profession. This little which I have gleaned concerning them has rather induced me to believe that they may be Jews, for the doctrines attributed to them agree perfectly with those of this people, who, we well know, have penetrated into almost every corner of the known world, even to the remotest parts of Asia.[1]

---

[1] At page 241 of his *Narrative* Yule gives his opinion that the Zodi sect really consisted of the latitudinarian Buddhists whom Judson, the celebrated missionary, in his journals and letters, calls semi-atheists and semi-deists. ' One held the fundamental doctrine that Divine wisdom, not concentrated in any existing spirit, or embodied in any form, but diffused throughout the universe, and partaken in different degrees by various intelligences, and in a very high degree by the Buddhas, is the true and only god.' The views varied with the individual.

In 1827 the execution, some years before, of certain reformers of the existing Buddhism is mentioned by Crawfurd in his *Journal of an Embassy to Ava*, p. 392. ' The reformers were generally, or I believe always, laymen. They principally decried the luxury of the priesthood, and ridiculed the idea of attaching religious merit to the building of temples.'

17. THE Talapoins in the Pali language are called Rahan, which means holy men, in allusion to the holiness of life which they ought to show forth in their actions. They are the priests of the country: not that they offer sacrifices or oblations, or make public prayers for the people, for each one exercises these acts of religion himself before the Pagodas, but because it is their duty to attend the dead to their grave, and to recite the Tarà, a species of sermon which they make to the assembled people. They may perhaps with greater propriety be called cloistered monks; for they live together, observe celibacy, and are bound to certain rules or constitutions. There is not any village, however small, which has not one or more large wooden houses, which are a species of convent, by the Portuguese in India called Baos. The construction of these Baos is of various nature, for the Talapoins of the kingdom of Ava build them of one shape, and those of Pegù of another. Every Bao has a head, who is the greatest of the Talapoins, and is called Ponghì. This personage has under him a species of deacon, called Pazen, who is his helper. The community is composed of Scien, who are as it were the clergy and disciples of the great Talapoin, youths who put on the habit for two or three years. For it is the custom in the Burmese Empire to clothe with the habit of Talapoins all the young men as soon as they arrive at the age of puberty, not

---

[1] For a more recent and, on the whole, appreciative account of Buddhist monks in Burma, the reader may refer to Bishop Bigandet's Notice of them in his second volume, where everything of importance is fully and judiciously dealt with. The order, he thinks, suffers from the ignorance and idleness of its members, and defects of discipline. The Census Report, 1891, p. 138, speaks in high praise of the attitude of the monks in regard to their education of the people.

only that they may thus acquire merit for their future trans-migrations, but also learn to read and write. All the Tala-poins who live in the different Baos of a province are under the jurisdiction of a superior, who corresponds to the provincial of our religious orders; and those of the whole Empire are subordinate to the Zaradò [Sayadaw], or grand master of the Emperor, who resides in the capital, and may therefore be called their General. The Baos are the buildings in which the Burmese architecture is most gorgeous. Some are completely cased with fine gold both within and without, particularly those which the Emperor and his sons built for their Zaradò.

18. The habit of the Talapoins consists of three pieces of yellow cotton cloth. Those who have rich benefactors even make it of silk, or of European woollen cloth. The first piece is bound to the loins with a leathern girdle and falls down to the feet, the second is a cloak of a rectangular shape which covers the shoulders and breast, and the third is another cloak of the same shape, which, being folded many times, is thrown over the left shoulder, the two ends hanging down before and behind. Every time the Talapoins go out, either to accom-pany the dead, or for any other purpose, they are obliged to carry over their right shoulder the Avana, a sort of fan made of palm leaves,[1] and one of the disciples carries a piece of leather to sit upon. Every morning the Talapoins must go round the houses begging boiled rice and other eatables; and for this purpose they take with them a black vessel in which they put confusedly all that they receive, and this same vessel serves them as a plate to eat from.

19. Those Talapoins who are Pazen or Ponghì are forbidden by their rules to cook with their own hands, to labour, to plant or traffic, and are not even allowed to send others into their Baos to cook for them. They must not make any pro-vision or preserve any sort of food. They cannot take with their own hands anything to eat however small, or anything else for their private use, which has not been first presented to them.

---

[1] The word Talapoin is derived from the Pali name of this palm leaf, and was introduced to Europe by the Portuguese.—*Hobson-Jobson*, by Yule and Burnell. Mr. Taw Sein-Ko thinks it is a Talaing compound, meaning ' Lord-mendicant.'

For this reason they are obliged at almost every moment to go through the ceremony called Akat, which signifies a presentation or oblation. It is as follows. Whenever one of them has occasion for anything, he addresses to his disciples this formula: 'do what is lawful;' upon which, they take up the thing he may want and present it to him with these words: 'this, Sir, is lawful.' The Talapoin then takes it into his own hands, and eats it or lays it by, as may suit his convenience.

In performing this ceremony the Talapoin must stand at the distance of a cubit from his disciple, otherwise he is guilty of a sin; and if what he receives be food, he commits as many sins as he eats mouthfuls. It is, moreover, unlawful for the Talapoins directly to ask for anything: they are only allowed to accept of what is spontaneously offered to them by others. But this law is very little attended to.

The possession of all temporal goods is likewise forbidden to the Talapoins; they cannot even touch gold or silver. They must not have emancipated slaves; but must content themselves with what is barely necessary. But these are rules which they regard very little; for, after covering their hands with a handkerchief, they have no scruple in receiving very large sums in gold and silver: they are insatiable in their lust after riches, and do little else than ask for them. Godama ordered that the habits of the Talapoins should be made of pieces of cloth picked up in the roads or streets, or among the tombs; they still observe one part of the law, they tear the cloth into a great number of pieces, but take care that it shall be of the finest quality. The law of continency, externally at least, is observed with the greatest scrupulosity by these men, and in this respect they might even serve as an example to many of our religious. Not only it is not permitted for them to sleep under the same roof, or to travel in the same carriage or boat with a woman, but even to receive anything directly from their hands; and indeed to such a height are these precautions carried, that they may not touch the clothes of a woman, or caress a female child however young, or even handle a female animal. But their scruples with regard to clothes are at an end, when they are given to them, for they maintain that in this case the clothes are purified as it were by the merit of the almsdeed. For the better preservation of chastity it is further decreed, that the Talapoins do not eat anything after mid-day, and particularly at evening, as many of their greatest men have maintained that to eat at these times too much heats the blood and excites the passions. So indispensable is celibacy esteemed by the Burmese for the sacerdotal state, that not only do they forbid to their own Talapoins the use of marriage, but they can never be brought to look upon any one as a priest who does not observe it. It is for this reason they are inclined very much to esteem our Catholic missionaries, but refuse every kind of honour to the Armenian priests and the Mohammedan Sherifs, merely because they are engaged in the married state. Whenever a Talapoin is detected in the violation of this law, the inhabitants of the place where he lives expel him from his Bao, sometimes even driving him away with stones ; and the Government strips him of his habit, and inflicts upon him a public punishment. The Zaradò, or grand master of the Talapoins under the predecessor of Badonsachen, being convicted of a crime of incontinency, was deprived of all his dignities, and narrowly escaped decapitation, to which punishment he was condemned by the Emperor.

To these rules and constitutions we may here add several others which are contained in the great book called Vinì, the constant perusal of which is much recommended ; indeed there exists an express command that every Talapoin should commit the whole of it to memory. It is written in the sacred language Palì, but is accompanied with a translation in the vernacular Burmese. It is divided into different chapters, each of which treats of something regarding the Talapoins, in their dress, food, habitations, etc. I will here notice some of the principal regulations.

20. The first thing that the Vinì prescribes is, that in each convent, or at least in all those where there is a respectable number of Talapoins, one should be elected to act as superior. To him it belongs to watch over the observance of the rules, and to correct and admonish those who neglect them. If he discover that any one of his subjects has in his possession gold, silver, or anything else which a Talapoin is forbidden to keep

or touch, he must throw it away with his own hands, and think that in doing so he is casting away an unclean thing.

21. A Talapoin is not allowed to buy, sell, or exchange anything whatever. Hence he must never say, 'I want to buy a thing,' but merely ask its price. And if he is obliged to sell or exchange anything, he must not speak of it in direct terms, but say, 'Such and such a thing is useless to me, but I have need of your goods, etc.'

22. In treating of the precept of never touching a woman, it is added in the Vinì that this prohibition extends to one's own mother; and even if it should happen that she fall into a ditch, her son, if a Talapoin, must not pull her out. But in the case that no other aid is near, he may offer her his habit or a stick, and so help her out; but at the same time must imagine that he is only pulling a log of wood.

23. The Talapoins are exhorted to observe in particular four virtues, which consist in the proper use of the four things more immediately necessary to man: food, raiment, habitations, and medicine. Whenever a Talapoin makes use of any of these things, he ought to repeat continually one of these considerations. 'I eat this rice, not to please my appetite, but to satisfy the wants of nature: I put on this habit, not for the sake of vanity, but to cover my nakedness: I live in this Bao, not for vainglory, but to be protected from the inclemencies of the weather: I drink this medicine merely to recover my health, and I desire my recovery only that I may attend with greater diligence to prayer and meditation.'

24. Another counsel of the Vinì is the observance of the four cleannesses, as they are called; which consist in the confession of all failings, in avoiding all occasions of sin, in the practice of great modesty in the streets and public places, and finally in keeping free from the seven sins. The Talapoins must likewise keep in mind that a priest who does not fulfil the duties of his state is a useless incumbrance, and that for such a one to take part in the alms of their benefactors is nothing better than robbery. In the use of the things which are necessary to them they must be moderate and economical, always considering that what they consume is the property of the benefactors. They must sleep in their habits, or, if they

put them off, must be careful to place them at the distance of two cubits from their bed.

25. Digging is an occupation unlawful for Talapoins, for fear of killing some insects; or, if they do employ themselves in this manner, it must be in a sandy soil, where there is no danger of meeting with insects. And such ought to be their care in this regard, that not even with a stick or with their feet should they stir the mould, lest by chance some insect be crushed. For the same reason they are not allowed to cut down several kinds of trees, nor even to gather the leaves or the fruit; and before they can lawfully make use of any fruit, their disciples must open it with their nails or with a knife, to let out the life which they suppose it contains.

26. It is most strictly forbidden to the Talapoins to sleep in the same room with women, children, or even with female animals. And if one of them by neglecting this rule falls into sin, he immediately contracts an irregularity, and is driven away from the society of all other priests. The same punishment is awarded to theft, killing of animals, and vainglory.

27. All who have received the order of Pazen are obliged to shave every part of their body, even the eye-brows; though at present this law is not observed with regard to the last. In the performance of this ceremony the Pazen must consider that the hairs thus shaved off arise from the uncleanness of the head, that they are useless things, serving merely for the purposes of vanity; and at the same time he must be as unconcerned as a great mountain, which is being cleared of the useless herbage that has grown upon it.

28. The full moon and the fifteenth day after in every month are festivals for the Talapoins; so that they have twenty-four in the course of the year. On these days they are to assemble in the Sein, or sacred places, there to read the Padimot, which is a summary of all the sins and faults against their constitutions.

29. They have besides a great fast or Lent, which generally lasts three months. During this time they are expected to be more careful in sweeping the Pagodas and keeping them in order. No one must go out of the Baos without weighty reasons; all secular and worldly thoughts and occupations

must be laid aside ; and the whole attention be given to prayer, meditation, and the study of the Pali. Even during their walks they ought to be employed in meditation ; no useless or idle word must escape their lips, much less a discontented or angry one ; their whole conversation must be of God and his benefits, and of the means of acquiring sanctity, and tend to show that they are only desirous of being delivered from their passions and inordinate desires. They must restrain themselves to the food that is absolutely necessary, and allow little or no time for sleep ; but rather give themselves up to the consideration of death, and of the love we ought to have for all living beings.

30. When any Talapoin has been guilty of a violation of his rule, he ought immediately to go to the great Talapoin, his superior, and, kneeling down before him, confess his crime. And here it must be observed that the sins of the Talapoins are of different sorts. The Padimot gives five or six kinds ; the first is called Parasigà, and comprises four sins, of which each one is warned at his ordination, as will be seen when we come to the description of this ceremony. These are incontinency, theft, murder, and giving oneself out for a holy man. But confession is not sufficient for the remission of these crimes ; since nothing remains for those guilty of them but to lay aside the habit of a Talapoin, to put on white, which is the sign of mourning, and withdraw themselves into some remote place, there to do penance. The second class is called Sengadiseit, and in it thirteen sins are reckoned. 1. Voluntary pollution, for if it happens in sleep this is no crime, unless it be thought of with pleasure upon waking. 2. All immodest touches of women with intention of sin. 3. Amorous or lascivious conversation. 4. The asking for the gift of a female slave under pretence of necessity, but with intent of sin. 5. Acting the part of a procurer. 6. The intention of building a Bao without the aid of any benefactor. 7. Laying the foundations of one in a place where there are many insects, which will undoubtedly be thereby killed. 8. A calumnious charge against another of incontinency in general. 9. The same with the specification of the crime. 10. The sowing of discord among Talapoins, when obstinately persevered in after

three admonitions in the Sein. 11. Abetting and encouraging the sowers of discord. 12. The habit of violating the rules in small things, notwithstanding the admonitions of others. 13. Giving scandal to laymen by small faults, such as telling lies, making presents of flowers, and such like. All these thirteen sins, as well as those of four or five other inferior classes, are subjected to the law of confession. And this confession must be made, not merely before the great Talapoin, but also before all who are assembled in the Sein. A penance is then imposed upon the delinquent, which consists of prayers, to be recited for a certain number of days, according to the time that he has suffered to elapse without confession; and these prayers must be said in the night. A promise must also be given to refrain from such faults in future, and pardon asked of all the Talapoins for the scandal given, and a humble request presented to be again admitted among them.

Besides this there is another species of penance, which is practised when any one doubts of having committed some sin. But all these confessions and penances are null and invalid if a sin is represented as of a lighter species, when in reality it should be classed with the thirteen just mentioned: or when the confession is made to a person guilty of the same crime. Such is the law; but it must be observed that at present it is little attended to. For the Talapoins now content themselves with a kind of indefinite formula of confession, something like our *confiteor*.

31. Another duty of the Talapoins is the recitation of the Tarà, or preaching to the people. Their sermons in general have for their object the recommendation of almsdeeds; not, however, to the poor, but to themselves. In the performance of this duty they ought to have for model the sermons or Godama, in which there is much said of alms, and the merit attached to them : they contain indeed many useful lessons of the other virtues, but these are all passed over by the Talapoins, who confine themselves to alms as far as regards themselves, but take no notice of those to others.

32. What has been hitherto said regards merely those Talapoins who have received the order of Pazen or priest. The Scien or disciples are bound to the observance of ten precepts,

by which they are forbidden—1. to kill animals, 2. to steal, 3. to give themselves up to carnal pleasure, 4. to tell lies, 5. to drink wine, 6. to eat after mid-day, 7. to dance, sing, or play on a musical instrument, 8. to colour their faces with sandal-wood, 9. to stand in elevated places not proper for them, 10. to touch gold or silver. The Scien who is guilty of one of the first five is expelled from the community; but the five last may be expiated by a proper penance.

33. It must be acknowledged that the Burmese owe much to the Talapoins, for the whole youth of the Empire is educated by them. Scarcely are the children arrived at the age of reason when they are consigned to their care; and after a few years most of them put on the dress of a Talapoin, that they may be taught to read and write, and may also acquire merit for themselves and their relations. The ceremonies that accompany the putting on of the habit are very attracting to the young people, as they are really a kind of triumph. The young candidate, dressed in the richest manner, as if he were one of the first Mandarins, is mounted on a superb horse and conducted through the village or city, amid the sound of musical instruments, and surrounded by a great crowd of people. A number of women go before the procession, carrying on their heads the habit, bed and suchlike utensils of a Talapoin, together with fruits and other presents for the great Talapoin of the convent, whose office it is to perform the ceremony.

As soon, therefore, as the procession reaches the appointed place, he proceeds to cut off the hair of the young candidate, and then, stripping him of his secular dress, clothes him with the habit belonging to his new state.[1]

34. The respect with which the Burmese regard their Talapoins, especially the Ponghì, or superiors of the Bao, and the honours they lavish upon them are excessive, so as almost to equal those they pay to their god. Whenever a layman meets a Talapoin in the streets he must respectfully move out of the

---

[1] Thus in Burma and Siam Gaudama's farewell to the life of the world is commemorated at the present day. See two interesting chapters on Buddhist baptism and life in the monastery in Shway Yoe's work.

way to let him pass; and when any one goes to visit a Ponghì, he must prostrate himself before him three times, with his hands raised above his head in token of reverence, or rather of adoration, and remain in this posture during the whole of his audience. The Talapoins have, besides, so much authority, that sometimes they even withdraw condemned criminals from the hand of justice. Indeed, under the predecessors of the present king, a capital punishment was a rare occurrence; for no sooner did the Talapoins hear that a criminal was being led to execution, than they issued from their convents in great numbers, with heavy sticks concealed under their habits, with which they furiously attacked the ministers of justice, put them to flight and, unbinding the culprit, conducted him to their Bao. Here his head was shaved, a new dress was put upon him, and by these ceremonies he was absolved from his crime and rendered inviolable. But during the present reign they do not venture upon such bold measures, unless they are sure of the protection of the Mandarins. In thus saving the lives of criminals, they believe that they are doing an act of piety; for, as their law forbids them to kill any living thing, even though it be hurtful to man, such as serpents, or mad dogs, they think that it must, on the other hand, be meritorious to preserve the lives of others, although by so doing they inflict a grievous injury on society. The person of a Talapoin is inviolable, and it is reckoned a great crime to strike one of them, though ever so slightly.

But it is in the ceremonies that take place after the death of a Ponghì, that the veneration of the Burmese for their Talapoins is particularly displayed. For as their state is regarded as one of peculiar sanctity, it is supposed that their very persons are thereby rendered holy; and hence their dead bodies are honoured as those of saints. As soon as a great Talapoin has expired, his corpse is opened in order to extract the viscera, which are buried in some decent place, and then it is embalmed after the fashion of the country. This done, it is swathed with bands of white linen, wrapped many times round it in every part, and upon these is laid a thick coat of varnish. To this succeeds a covering of gold, which adheres to the varnish, and in this manner the body is gilt from head to foot. It is now put into a large chest, and exposed to the veneration of the people.

It is this chest or coffin on which the greatest care and expense is bestowed. Indeed the great Talapoins are accustomed to have it made several years before their death, whence its beauty is frequently such as to excite the curiosity not only of the natives of the country but also of foreigners. It is usually gilt all over, and adorned besides with flowers made of polished substances, sometimes even of precious stones. In this superb receptacle the body is exposed in public for many days, nay often for entire months, during which time a continual festival is celebrated about it; bands of music are always playing, and the people flock in crowds to offer their presents of money, rice, fruits or other things necessary for the ceremony, by which the expenses of the funeral are defrayed. When at length the day arrives for burning the body, it is placed upon a large car with four wheels, to which are fixed a number of great ropes, so that the people may drag it to the place of sepulture. It is pleasing to see the ardour with which the whole population—men and women—engage in this labour. They believe it to be a work of the greatest merit; and hence, having divided themselves into two bodies, strive with the greatest earnestness who shall have the honour of conveying the body to its destination. The vehicle is pulled first to one side, then to the other for some time, till one party gaining the advantage bears it off in triumph. At the place where the burning is to take place, the people are amused for some time with fireworks, which consist entirely of a species of large rockets. Beams of teak-wood, of the length of six, seven, or even of nine cubits, and from a palm to a cubit in diameter, are bored to receive a mixture of saltpetre and pounded charcoal. To some of them are fixed long strips of bamboo to guide them in their ascent, and thus they are carried up into the air as soon as fire is applied to them. Others are placed upon carriages and made to run round the spot where the body is to be burnt. In the meantime great quantities of wood, gunpowder, and other combustible materials are heaped about the coffin, and the ceremonies are concluded by setting fire to this pile. This is done by means of an immense rocket, which is guided to it by a cord. Immediately that it touches it the pile takes fire and the whole is soon consumed. But these funerals seldom end in this joyful manner; they are almost always signalised by numerous accidents; for the enormous pieces of wood, which are carried into the air by the rockets, and particularly the carriages to which others are attached, and which run up and down without any one to guide them, never fail, besides innumerable bruises and fractures of limbs, to cause the death of several of the spectators. Yet so infatuated are the people with these fireworks, that they do not consider that as a festival which goes by without them ; and hence, in the dedication of a Pagoda or a Bao, or on any other occasion of rejoicing, these always form a principal part of the festivities.

35. It has been remarked that most of the youth of the Burmese Empire put on the habit of a Talapoin for the sake of their education, but it must not be thereby supposed that they all become Talapoins. The greater part, after some years, throw off the habit and retire to their home. But many remain in the Baos with the intention of becoming priests. These are first of all admitted to the rank of Pazen, or assistants of the greater Talapoins, upon whose death they succeed to their places. But not even for the Pazen, or the greater Talapoins is there any obligation to remain always in the state they have embraced ; still the greater part continue to wear the habit for many years, numbers for their whole life.

36. The ceremonies which are observed upon the admission of candidates to the order of Pazen, resemble very much the ordinations of deacons and priests in our Church. They are contained in a book, written in the Pali language, called Chamoazà, which may, therefore, be considered as their Pontifical. It will here be proper to transcribe a description of the ceremonial. It takes place in the Sein, which has something of the form of a church, in the presence of all the Talapoins ; the eldest of whom, called Upizzè, presides. He has another Talapoin for assistant, named Chammuazarà, which may be translated *master of ceremonies*.

The first part of the ceremony consists in giving to the pos-

tulant the Sabeit, or black pot, with which he goes begging
rice. But before he receives it, he must approach the presiding
Talapoin, and repeat three times this question:—'Are you,
sir, my master Upizzè?' This done, he advances towards the
master of ceremonies, by whom he is interrogated as follows:
'Oh candidate, does this Sabeit belong to you?' Answer,
'Yes, sir.' 'Does this cloak belong to you?' Answer,
'Yes, sir.' 'Does this tunic and do these habits belong to
you?' Answer, 'Yes, sir.' Then the master of ceremonies
says to the postulant, 'Draw back from this place, and remain
at the distance of twelve cubits;' then, turning to the assembled Talapoins, he thus goes on: 'Oh, ye priests here
assembled, hear my words. This youth now before you humbly
begs from the Upizzè to be admitted to the sacerdotal state:
and truly this is the time proper and becoming for priests.
Now then will I instruct the candidate; wherefore, O candidate, give ear. But remember that it is not lawful for you
now to lie or to conceal the truth. There are certain defects,
that are perfectly incompatible with the sacerdotal state, and
which hinder a person from worthily receiving it. Therefore
do you, when you shall be interrogated before the congregation
of priests on these defects, reply with sincerity, make known
every quality that you are conscious of possessing, and every defect under which you labour. Be not silent, and have no shame
or fear in your answers. Now, therefore, in the presence of all
this assembly, you must answer the interrogatories of the priests.'
 Some of the priests then examine him on the following
heads:—'Have you, who seek to become a priest, any of the
following complaints? The leprosy, or other such odious
maladies?' Answer, 'No, sir, I have none such maladies.'
'Have you the scrofula, or other similar complaints?' 'No,
sir, I have none such.' 'Do you suffer from asthma, or
coughs?' 'No, sir.' 'Are you afflicted by those complaints
that arise from a corrupted blood; by madness, or the other
ills caused by giants, witches, or evil Nat of the forests and
mountains?' 'No, sir.' 'Are you a man?' 'I am.' 'Are
you a true and legitimate son?' 'Yes, sir.' 'Are you involved in debt, or the underling of some Mandarin?' 'No,
sir, I am not.' 'Have your parents given their consent to

your ordination?' 'Yes, sir, they have given it.' 'Have you reached the age of twenty years?' 'Yes, sir, I have.' 'Are your vestments and Sabeit prepared?' 'They are.'

The examination being finished, the master of ceremonies thus goes on: 'O fathers and priests here present, be pleased to listen to my words. This youth now before you begs from the Upizzè to be admitted to the sacerdotal state, and has been instructed by me.' Upon this the postulant approaches the fathers to ask their consent to his ordination, for which purpose he is to say: 'I beg, O fathers, from this assembly to be admitted to the sacerdotal state. Have pity on me; take me from the state of a layman, a state of sin and imperfection, and advance me to the sacerdotal state, the state of virtue and perfection.' These words must be repeated three times.

Then the master of ceremonies takes up the discourse as follows: 'Oh, all ye fathers here assembled, hear my words. The youth here before you begs from the Upizzè to be admitted to the sacerdotal state; he is free from every defect and imperfection; and he has got ready all the vessels and necessary habits. He has, moreover, in the name of the Upizzè, asked the permission of the assembly of fathers to be admitted to the sacerdotal state. Now, therefore, let the assembly complete his ordination. To whomsoever this seemeth good, let him keep silence; but whoso thinketh otherwise, let him declare that this candidate is unworthy of the sacerdotal state.' And these words he repeats three times.

Afterwards he proceeds. 'Since then none of the fathers object, but all are silent, it is a sign that the assembly has consented. So, therefore, be it done, and let this candidate pass out of the state of sin and imperfection into that of the priesthood; and thus, by the consent of the Upizzè, and of all the fathers, let him be ordained priest.'

After this he further says: 'The fathers must note down under what shade, on what day, at what hour, and in what season, this ordination has been performed.'

Besides this, the newly ordained priest must be admonished of the fourteen things that priests may lawfully make use of, and of the four from which they must abstain. Hence the master of ceremonies thus proceeds with the instruction :—

'In the first place, it is the office of a priest to beg for his food with labour, and with the exertion of the muscles of his feet; wherefore, O newly ordained priest, through the whole course of your life you must gain your bread by the labour of your feet. And if alms and offerings abound, and the benefactors give you rice and other kinds of food, you may make use of the following things :—1. Of such as are offered to all the Talapoins in general, 2. of such as are offered to each one in particular, 3. of such as are usually presented in banquets, 4. of such as are sent by letter, 5. of those that are given at the new and full moons, and on festivals. All these, O new-made priest, you may lawfully use for food.' To this he replies, ' Yes, sir, I understand what you tell me.'

The master of ceremonies resumes his instruction :—

'Secondly, a priest is obliged to make his clothes of the rags thrown about in the streets or among the tombs, however dirty they may be : hence, throughout your whole life, you must put on no clothes but these. If, however, by your talents and learning, you procure for yourself many benefactors, you may receive from them, for your habit, the following articles : —Cotton and silk, or cloth of red wool or yellow wool ; of these you may lawfully make use.' The new priest answers as before, ' I understand.' The instruction goes on :

' The habitation of a priest must be in houses built on the trees of the forest ; in such, therefore, must you live. But if your talents and your learning gain for you many benefactors, then you may inhabit the following kinds of houses :—those surrounded by walls, such as bear a triangular or pyramidal shape, and those that are adorned with bas-reliefs, etc.'

After the usual answer, the master of ceremonies proceeds:—

' Now that you have been admitted to the congregation of priests, it is no longer lawful for you to indulge in carnal pleasures, whether with yourself or with animals. He who is guilty of such things can no longer be a priest, or be numbered in the company of the saints. To what shall we liken such a one ? To a man whose head has been severed from his body. For as the head can never again be united to his body, so as that he shall live, so is it impossible for the priest, who has sinned against chastity, to be restored to the society of

his brethren.   Beware then of committing any such crime.'
The priest answers, 'I have heard, sir, be it so.'
The master of ceremonies resumes :—
'It is unlawful for a priest to usurp or steal what belongs to
another, even though to no greater amount than the quarter of
a Ticale.*   The priest who is guilty of a theft, even though to
no greater amount than this, must be considered as having
thrown off the sacerdotal state, and as belonging no longer to
the society of the saints.   Such a one may be compared to
the dry leaf of a tree ; for as the leaf can never again become green, so the priest, who has stolen from another, can
never again be a member of the sacerdotal body, can never
again belong to the society of the saints.   Wherefore do you,
throughout life, abstain from all such thefts.'   The candidate
answers as before, and the master of ceremonies proceeds :—
'It is moreover unlawful for priests knowingly to kill any
living thing, even though it be but the meanest insect.   He,
therefore, who shall so destroy any creature can no longer be a
priest, can no longer belong to the holy society.   And to what
shall such a one be likened ?   To a stone broken in pieces.   For
as its parts can never again be united, so is it impossible for
this man ever to be joined with his brethren.   Beware then,
and keep yourself for ever from these faults.'   The newly
ordained replies, 'I have heard your admonitions.'
The master of ceremonies proceeds : 'To him who has been
enrolled among the number of the priests, it is most particularly prohibited to be vainglorious, to give himself out as a
holy man, or as distinguished by the possession of any supernatural gift.   Whoever, therefore, either through vainglory or
imprudence shall thus boast of himself, can no longer be a
priest, or a member of the holy society.   And to what shall
we compare the man who transgresses ?   He is like a palm-tree
that has been severed in two.   For as it can live no more, so
is such a one unworthy to be again admitted among the priests.
Take care then for yourself that you give not in to such ex-
cesses.'   The newly ordained replies as before, 'I have heard all
of which you have admonished me.' †

---

* About a shilling English.   † See Note B at the end of the work.

CHAPTER XVI

37. It has been said above that one of the principal duties of the Talapoins is the Tarà or preaching to the people; and that in the performance of this duty, they ought to propose as their model the sermons of Godama. The book which contains them is called *Sottan, or the Rule of Life,* and is one of the principal works which the Burmese possess. Besides a great deal on almsdeeds, to which alone, as has been remarked, the Talapoins attend, it contains some fine morality; and some parts of it deserve to be laid before the reader.

38. The first thing worthy of notice is the method prescribed by Godama to those who, like himself, devote themselves to the instruction of others. In this, two things are requisite: first, order in the matter; secondly, a proper intention, for in preaching, a man ought to propose to himself nothing but the instruction of others, and their well-being; thirdly, a disregard for alms, as no one ought to preach merely with the hope of receiving presents from others; fourthly, modesty, by which all derision or abuse of others and all self-commendation is avoided.

39. Among the sermons of Godama there is one called Mengasalot, that is to say, most excellent sermon, and it is so named as being the one most esteemed by the Burmese for the number and excellence of the precepts it inculcates. It is in such repute with them that all the children who are placed in the Baos for their education are obliged to learn it by heart. Anandà, the first disciple of Godama, is said to have handed it down to posterity. It is as follows:—

'To him who can admit of no unlawful act, even though it be sought to be committed in secret: to him who by the

I

knowledge he has received perfectly comprehends the four inevitable states, through which every living being must pass : to him who is possessed of the six supreme powers, to the most excellent God Godama I offer my solemn adoration.   And so be it.'

This, O most illustrious priest N. N., is the manner in which I, Anandà, the oldest of the divine disciples, have heard the great precepts delivered by the observance of which a man is preserved from evil-doing.   On a certain day, when the Lord God was in the celebrated convent of Sautti [Thawattie or Sravasti in Oudh near Fyzabad], built by that famous rich man N. N.,* late in the evening a certain Nat came to him without making known his name, but the admirable splendour that issued from his body and illumined all the objects in the con-vent, sufficiently showed his illustrious lineage.   He immedi-ately entered the room where the Divine Wisdom then was, and having adored him with the greatest respect, began his re-quest as follows :—'Great and omnipotent God, supreme master of the law, a multitude of just souls, both among the Nat and among men, aspiring after the perfect repose of the Niban, have hitherto been searching after the means by which the hearts of creatures may put off all evil inclinations ; but in vain.   Thee, therefore, do we supplicate, who alone knowest all these things, to reveal them to us.'   To whom the God re-plied :[1] 'O Nat ! know that to keep far from the company of the ignorant, to be always in the society of the learned, and to give respect and honour to whom they are due, are three means of overcoming any inordinate affection.   O Nat ! by the choice of a place of abode proper to one's station, and adapted for satisfying all the common wants of life : by having always in store some merit acquired in a former life, and by ever main-taining in one's own person a prudent carriage : by these three precepts likewise may a man be preserved from evil-doing.   O Nat ! the vastness of learning, the comprehension of all things that are not evil, the perfect knowledge of the duties of one's

---

* It is said that this convent cost 90,000,000,000 crowns.
[1] In this sermon Buddha has condensed almost all the moral virtues.— Bigandet, i. p. 123

state of life, and the observance of piety and modesty in words ; these are four most excellent means whereby we may renounce all wicked actions. O Nat ! by ministering to one's father and mother their proper sustenance, by providing for the wants of one's wife and children, by the purity and honesty of every action, by almsdeeds, by the observance of the divine precepts, by succouring in their necessities those who are united to us by the ties of kindred, finally by everything else in which there is no sin, by all these means may we be preserved from evil deeds. O Nat ! by such a freedom from all faults, that not even the inferior part of the soul manifests any affection for them, by the abstinence from all intoxicating drink, by the never-failing practice of all the works of piety, by showing respect to all, by being humble before all, by sobriety, by gratitude to our bene- factors, and finally by listening from time to time to the preaching of the word of God, by these means also may we overcome our evil inclinations and keep ourselves far from sin. O Nat ! the virtue of patience, docility in receiving the admonitions of good men, frequent visits to priests, spiritual conferences on the divine laws, frugality and modesty in our exterior, the perfect observance, that is, the observance to the letter of the law, having ever before our eyes the four states into which living creatures will pass after death, and finally, the meditation on the happy repose of the Niban, these are all distinguished precepts for preserving man from wickedness. O Nat ! that intrepidity and serenity of mind which good men preserve amid the eight calamities of life, in abundance and want, in censure and praise, in joy and distress, in popularity and abandonment, the absence of all fear or inquietude of heart, the freedom from the dark mists of concupiscence, finally insensibility to suffering, these are four rare gifts that remove man far away from all affection to evil. Wherefore, O Nat ! imprint well upon your heart the thirty-eight precepts I have just delivered, let them be deeply rooted there, and see to put them in execution.'

40. Another time when Godama was standing in the above- mentioned convent, he expounded to the assembled Talapoins the five rules for alms, according as opportunities present themselves for exercising them. These are, hospitality to our

guests and to travellers, ministering to the wants of sick Talapoins, and, in times of scarcity, to those of all persons, and,
finally, the payment of the first-fruits of rice and fruit to the
Talapoins. Speaking of the merit of alms, he declared that
those given to animals stand lowest in the scale, next come
such as are administered to widows, then those to persons who
observe the five commandments, and practise the ten good
deeds. Superior in merit to these are alms to the saints, to
the Talapoins and to God, and particularly the erection of a
convent. But all these are surpassed in merit by the adoration of the three most excellent things, God, the law, and the
Talapoins; and still more meritorious is prayer for the salvation of all living creatures. The most meritorious action of all
is the deep meditation on the miseries of life, and the conviction that we cannot free ourselves from them.

Before passing to the Niban, Godama confirmed all these his
precepts, and added, that the real adoration of God does not
consist in offering him rice, flowers, or sandal-wood, but in the
observance of his laws.

41. In another sermon, Godama speaks of the different
objects of our charity, and of the merits acquired by succouring them. He mentions fourteen of them, 1. animals, 2.
huntsmen and fishermen, 3. merchants, 4. the Talapoins,
then different classes of saints, and lastly God. Alms that are
given to animals carry with them five rewards: long life,
beauty, prosperity both as to soul and body, great strength,
and knowledge; and all these will be enjoyed through a
hundred transmigrations. The same will be the reward of
alms to huntsmen and fishermen, but through the course of a
thousand transmigrations; the third species of almsgivers will
enjoy them through ten thousand, and so on in proportion
through all the classes of Talapoins and saints till we come to
God, when the reward will last for an infinity of transmigrations.

42. In a sermon, which Godama delivered for the instruction
of a young Brahmin, he explains the reason why, in the world,
some are born rich and others poor, some beautiful and others
deformed; which diversity he derives from the good or evil
deeds committed in preceding lives. In another, he prescribes

the manner in which the festivals on the days of the new and full moon, and of the first and last quarter, ought to be observed. Whoever wishes to acquire great merit must not limit himself to the customary adorations and offerings on these days, but must spend them in meditating on the favours of God and the excellence of his law : he must be contented with one simple dish in the morning, and with little or no sleep at night, which should be passed in reading good books ; and he must keep himself separated from his wife. As it is, moreover, forbidden to do any work on these days, every one must be careful to despatch all necessary business the day before, that so he may be free from all cares or distractions. It is likewise the duty of all people to exhort each other to the proper observance of the festival.

43. A young disciple, who had refused to learn anything of almsdeeds or other works of piety, was one day met by Godama, who thus accosted him : 'All who aspire to perfection must be careful to avoid the four works which do hurt to living creatures ; as well as the fourteen base deeds, and the four Gatì : by thus flying away from evil, and ever seeking to acquire merit in this life, as well as in future ones, they will at length attain to the Niban. The four works that do hurt to living creatures are murder, theft, deceit, and adultery. The four Gatì are committed by judges, when, on account of presents, consanguinity or friendship, they decide unjustly : when through hatred to the party who has reason on his side they pronounce against him : when through ignorance they give judgment in favour of him who does not deserve it ; and, finally, when through fear or respect of persons, as of Mandarins, or rich or powerful men, they commit injustice. Those offenders also are here comprised who do not divide property equally as they ought, through love, fear, hatred, or ignorance. Besides this, a man must refrain from the six things that are called ruinous ; which are the love of intoxicating liquors, the custom of wandering about the streets at unseasonable hours, too great a passion for dancing, games, and spectacles, gaming, frequenting vicious company, lastly, slothfulness and negligence in the performance of one's duty. For from these spring six great evils. Drunkenness is the cause of the loss of goods

and reputation, of quarrels, diseases, immodesty of dress, disregard of honour, and incapacity for learning; unseasonable wanderings expose a man to great dangers, and, by keeping him from his family, oblige him to leave the chastity of his wife and daughter unprotected; and moreover his possessions are thus liable to depredations. He may likewise be taken in the company of thieves and be punished with them. A passion for shows draws a man from his occupations, and hinders him from gaining his livelihood. In gaming, success is followed by intrigues and quarrels; loss, by bitterness and sorrow of heart, as well as dilapidation of fortune; the gamester is incapacitated by law to give testimony, nor can he have a wife or mother-in-law, for no one loves the gambler. Finally, frequenting the company of the vicious will lead a man into the houses of women of ill fame, into drunkenness and gluttony, into deceit and robbery, and all kinds of disorders.' Godama then passed on to speak of false friends; whom he described as always making show of friendship without having its reality, professing a love which they do not feel, giving little that they may receive much, and being friends to a man only because he is rich, or because they have need of his favour. Those too are false friends who give a promise in words, but are far from fulfilling it in their actions, and, finally, those who are ever ready to assist a man in evil, but never in doing good. ' But,' the God proceeds, ' there are four species of real friends; first, those who are such both in adversity. and in prosperity: secondly, those who give good advice on proper occasions, even at the peril of their lives: thirdly, those who take care of whatever belongs to him they love: fourthly, those who teach a man what is good, who are delighted in his prosperity, and sorrowful in his misfortunes.'

Godama then goes on to instruct the young man in the mutual duties of fathers and children, masters and slaves. Children are, in particular, obliged to respect their parents, to provide for all their wants, and to reflect often on the benefits they have received from them in their earlier years, and on the care they then took to assist and nourish them; they ought also to cultivate their fields, to listen to their words and advice, and to give some alms for them. Parents, on the other hand, have five duties to discharge with respect to their children. They must keep them far from all wickedness, procure that they always have good companions, they must instruct them, and teach them to give alms and do other pious works, and, when they have arrived at the proper age, be careful to marry them. The duties of scholars towards their masters, and of the latter to their scholars, are nearly the same as those just mentioned. Scholars are to give their instructors honour and respect; they must make way for them whenever they are in their company, must go to meet them, wash their feet, and attend upon them, especially in sickness; finally, they must be diligent in learning what they inculcate on them. Masters, on the other hand, ought to teach their pupils all things that are useful, and be desirous that they should become as learned as themselves.

The duties of the husband to the wife and of the wife to the husband are five. The husband should speak to his wife respectfully, should not ill-treat her or beat her like a slave, should not desert her to live with another woman, and, finally, should commit to her the care of his house. The wife, on her part, should look after the kitchen, and be careful to provide all things necessary for her husband, and the whole family; she should collect the goods of the house, and be attentive to their preservation, and should never be slothful in doing her domestic duties. Finally, speaking of masters and slaves, Godama says, that the former should adapt the labours of his slaves to their strength and capacities, should give them their maintenance, and treat them well, but particularly be attentive to them when sick. Slaves should get up to work in the morning before their masters, and to go to bed after them at night; should look to the interest of their masters in their labours, and in everything else, and, finally, should take nothing but what is allowed them.

44. Godama has left many instructions for the Talapoins, in which he exhorts them, from the consideration of the miseries of human nature, of the perishableness of all earthly things, and especially of corporeal beauty, to put away all carnal desires and aspire to the Niban. In another of his sermons he says, that we should divide our goods and share them with the

poor, in the same way as travellers in a desert country share their provisions with their companions; for the poor are our companions in the journey to a future life. He adds, that an alms done by a poor man is of infinitely greater merit than that of a rich one; that the only faithful companions, who will not desert us in the life to come, are our good deeds, and that the only good that will continue with us unaltered, even to old age, is the observance of the law; for this no thief can take away.

45. In another sermon which Godama addressed to his son after he had become a Talapoin, to teach him how to overcome his inordinate appetites, his anger, and his pride, he suggests to him various considerations on the constitution of his body. That nothing about it is permanent, but all its parts are subject to perpetual changes. And since he must lose it by death, therefore he ought to say within himself, This is not my body. And as the earth is immovable, and all things that are thrown upon it, even if it be gold and silver are but as filth, and as water carries all things away with it, both good and bad, and as fire burns all that comes in its way without distinction, so ought he to be fixed and unalterable, superior to all things and intent only on the Niban. One day, as this his son was asking about his inheritance, Godama answered him, that this was not the time to think of such things, and that he ought to wean himself from all attachment even to the things most necessary to him, such as rice, his bed, etc. When he gave him into the care of one of his disciples to be instructed in letters, he was also careful to exhort him to lay aside every sentiment of pride, to forget that he belonged to the royal stock, and that he was the son of a God. In another place he teaches him not to let his affections be occupied by this world, and not to give himself up to the pleasures of sense, but to aspire to the Niban alone: moreover, that, having what is sufficient to satisfy his hunger to-day, he should not think of to-morrow; and that, having one coat, he should not wish for another. He admonishes him to observe the five sorts of modesty proper to the five bodily senses, not to look upon indecent objects, not to listen to lascivious songs, not to give way to murmuring, to abstain from the immoderate

use of perfumes, not to exceed in the pleasures of the palate, and to restrain the hands from unlawful touches. He recommends to him modesty in his exterior, but to avoid at the same time all vain ornaments in his dress, and, finally, exhorts him to conceive a loathing for the laws of transmigration and to aspire to the Niban.

46. Godama had two sisters who, not having been married, were made Talapoinesses. They were, however, vain of their great beauty. The God, to show them how frail all beauty is, created a most beautiful damsel, and placed her beside him at a time when his sisters were coming to see him. They were struck with envy on seeing her, but he in an instant caused her face to become wrinkled, all her teeth to fall out, and her hair to turn grey. The two sisters were thereby convinced of the vanity of their beauty, and became saints.

47. It once happened that a Talapoin conceived a criminal passion for a woman, who however died before he had accomplished his desire. Godama caused the dead body to be kept till it had become putrid, and worms issued from every part of it. Godama then made the following discourse to the assembled multitude : ' Man, when he is alive, can move himself and pass from one place to another, but when he is dead he is nothing but a motionless trunk. This body, which is composed of 300 bones, of 900 veins, and as many muscles, is full of intestines, phlegm, and mucus; from nine different apertures disgusting matter is discharged ; a stinking perspiration exudes from all its pores, and yet there are people so foolish, as not merely to cherish their own bodies, but also to fall in love with those of other persons. This body, which even when alive is so disgusting, when it is dead becomes a carcase, which its own relations cannot look upon without horror. After two days it begins to swell, on the third it becomes green and black, worms come from it in every part, and, when in the grave, it is gnawed by the most despicable insects. Whoever considers these things will be persuaded, that in the body there is nothing but decay and misery ; and, therefore, he will cast off all affection to it, and turn all his desires to the Niban, where these evils do not exist.'

48. In another sermon, delivered before a number of Nat

and Talapoins, Godama speaks of the various means of obtaining the Niban. Those who pride themselves in their birth or
in their possessions, or indulge in any such criminal complacen-
cies, which are as it were a wall of separation, can never reach
to the Niban. No one ought, therefore, to be ashamed of his
want of them. He gives also the following counsels to the
Talapoins, by which they may escape the law of transmigration. They must observe modesty in their five bodily senses;
they must not run after feasts and such vanities; they must
abstain from highly seasoned meats; they must not make use
of any of the thirty-two species of vain and idle words; they
must not take delight in thinking of any thing unlawful;
when in sickness or pain they must not be impatient, nor give
way to weeping and lamentation; when in the woods they
must not be afraid, nor run away, but must remain unmoved
in their proper places; they must extinguish in themselves all
evil inclinations; they must not too frequently change their
habitation; they must not be scrupulous and irresolute in
acting; they must, above all things, be assiduous in prayer and
meditation; they must not seek after magnificence and super-
fluity; they must not be given to sleep, but, dividing the
night into six parts, they must employ four of them in prayer
and meditation and in repeating the Vinì, one in providing for
their corporal wants, and one only in sleep; they must fly
from sloth, lying, immoderate laughter, vain joy, and play;
they must abhor sorcery, and not give credit to dreams; when
abused or derided they must not give way to anger, and when
praised must not be puffed up; they must not envy others,
their Bao, their dress, etc.; they must not flatter benefactors
to draw alms from them, nor preach sermons in which they
display their desire of them; they must not admit of any
bitterness or acrimony in talking, nor deride, nor despise, nor
injure others; they ought, finally, to accommodate themselves
to the opinions of others, not to give occasion for dissension.

A Talapoin ought never to consent to any bad thoughts,
such, for example, as regard indecencies, or the injury of one's
neighbour; and he who does consent to them, and take
pleasure in them, indeed who does not drive them away from
him, shows that he has no fear of sinning, and is therefore in a

state of sinful cowardice. But he who does not consent to such thoughts, but hastens to drive them from his mind, truly seeks after sanctity, and has a real desire of the Niban.

The Talapoins immediately on waking should hasten with alacrity to prayer and giving thanks to God, saying within themselves, 'How great a favour has God bestowed upon me, in manifesting to me his law, through the observance of which I may escape hell and secure my salvation.' Talapoins who do this increase every day in merit, and extinguish within them all the remains of concupiscence: hence they will soon acquire those dispositions which are the sure preparation for the Niban. There are three degrees of suffering, the first is, when a man takes pleasure in agreeable things: the second, when he is afflicted with disagreeable ones: the third, when he is neither pleased with prosperity nor afflicted by adversity, and the last is the state of sanctity. Talapoins, therefore, ought to force themselves to look upon all things with this disposition, and then they will be free from all hurtful desires and will arrive ultimately at the Niban.

Meditation on the constitution of the body of man is also much recommended in this sermon to the Talapoins; that thus its weakness and misery and vileness may be ever before their eyes. They should often say to themselves, 'This body of mine is the receptacle of a thousand impurities,' etc. They should think in particular of the respiration and perspiration; because by such thoughts the mind is freed from many vain and useless fancies, and disposed towards holiness. To say within one's self, 'I have no power over this my body: it is not subject to my will: I cannot secure it against alteration, or decay, or destruction,' this is an act of the greatest merit, and conducts to perfection. They are once more recommended to shun all vanity and curiousness in their apparel or in their furniture, to be contented with whatever food is offered them, to observe modesty in their looks, particularly when abroad in the streets, not staring about them or suffering their eyes to look more than four cubits before them. They should be grave in their gait and firm as a chariot. They should break off from their friends and relations, considering that death will one day effectually separate them; and that good works are our only hopes, and our only true friends.   In such thoughts as these should the day be spent, and thus the heart will be fixed in doing all that is good.

Finally, Godama menaces them with the pains of hell, if they do contrary to what he has commanded them.   And when they have passed through all its torments, they will be driven into another mountain there to endure new miseries, to be torn by crows and vultures, to be covered with clothes of fire, and to carry always in their hand Sabeits of living fire.

CHAPTER XVII

SUPERSTITIONS OF THE BURMESE

49. THERE perhaps is not an nation in the world so given to superstition as the Burmese.[1] Not only do they practise judicial astrology, and divination, and put faith in dreams, but they have besides an infinity of foolish and superstitious customs. No sooner is an infant born, than they run to some Brahmin to learn what is the constellation that presided at its birth, and this is written upon a palm-leaf, together with the day and hour of the birth, to serve for the divinations of which we shall just now speak. The *Beden*, which, as has been said, is a book of judicial astrology, distributes the stars into a number of asterisms or constellations, distinguished by the names of different men, animals, etc. They believe, or at least feign to believe, as did the ancient Greeks and Romans, that many men and women after their death were transformed into

---

[1] For existing superstitions see the chapter on Manners and Customs in Spearman's *British Burma Gazetteer*. Many are mentioned in the codes called Dhammathats, and though immemorial, are for the most part in Dr. Forchhammer's opinion, not indigenous, but derived from India through Brahmans; tattooing and a few other oddities excepted. 'The *punnas* (Skr. *Punya*, Pali *Punna*) are Brahmans, who at various periods settled in Burma, generally living in separate quarters in or near the capitals of Burmese kings. The royal astrologers and *gurus* were always *punnas*: from the capital they spread all over the country in the capacity of teachers, astrologers and physicians. The Sanskrit and Bengali works found with them belong to the Tantrasastras, Jyotisastras and Kamasastras of Gangetic India: they study chiefly the *Samaveda*.'—Forchhammer's *Jardine Prize Essay*, p. 21. Bishop Bigandet tells us how he learned from one of these Pounhas the mode of finding out by calculation the state of the heavens at any given hour whatever, a mode entirely based on the Hindu system. Bigandet, i. p. 29. The presence of these Brahmans at the Royal Court is often mentioned by our Envoys: they may be seen any day, telling fortunes at the pagodas. The Indian Brahmans employed themselves in the same way many centuries ago. See the quotations from Strabo, Fah Hian and others in Sykes' *Notes on India*, London, 1841, pp. 33, 127.

these constellations, and hence they give to them different
influences, corresponding with the attributes of the person or
thing whose name they bear.   Thus the following history is
told of the origin of the constellation, called in the *Beden*,
Navè.   A giantess who lived to the east of Pegù, having
conceived the desire of taking a husband, transformed herself
into a rich lady, and thus accomplished her desire.   At her
death, the body was placed upon a car, to be conveyed to the
place of sepulture, but both the car and body disappeared in
an instant, and was placed in heaven among the stars, in the
figure Navè.   Hence all who are born under this constellation
are deformed and rude in manners, but rich ; and the males
are in general great merchants.

Of another constellation called the head of the stag it is
related that a king, going out one day to hunt, met a doe big
with young.   It fled away at his approach, but through fright
brought forth in its flight.   The king caused the young one to
be taken care of, and used to go every day to visit it.   This
offended the queen, and she caused the animal to be killed,
upon which it was transformed into a constellation.   The king
afterwards died with grief for the death of his favourite.
Wherefore those who are born when this constellation prevails
generally die of grief.   And of this kind are their stories
concerning all the constellations.

50. The Burmese possess a large volume containing a full
account of all their superstitious observances, and of the
different omens of good or evil fortune, to be drawn from an
immense number of objects; as from the wood with which
their houses are built, from their boats and carriages, from the
aspects of the sun, moon, and planets, from the howling of
dogs, and the singing of birds, etc., and also from the involuntary movements of the members of one's own body.   We will
here translate some portions of this book, as specimens of the
superstitions which paganism conducts to.

51. This book, which is called *Deitton*, in the treatise on
the wood used in building, distinguishes various kinds.   Such
beams as are equally large at the top as at the bottom are
called males: those which are thicker at the bottom than
above are females : the neuters are those in which the middle

is thickest ; and when the greatest thickness is at the top, they are called giants ; finally, when a piece of wood on being cut, and falling to the ground, rebounds from its place, it is called monkey-wood. Whoever lives in a house made of male wood, will be happy in all places, and at all times, and in all circumstances ; but if the wood of any person's house be neuter, continual misery will be his lot, and if it be of the gigantic species he will die. By dividing the two pieces of wood which form the stairs into ten compartments, and observing in which the knots occur, we may also learn a man's fortune. If a knot be found in the first compartment, it is a sign that the master of the house will be honoured by princes ; if in the second, that he will abound in rice and all kinds of provisions ; but if there be one in the fourth division, then a son, or a nephew, or a slave, or an ox of the master will die ; a knot in the sixth division is a sign of riches in oxen and buffalos ; but one in the eighth portends the death of his wife ; and finally one in the tenth is an augury of great possessions in gold and silver and such other valuables.

52. From the wood used in the construction of the houses the *Deitton* passes to the holes in which the poles that support them are fixed : for if these be square, it is a sign of sickness : and divers other prognostics are drawn from the manner in which they are dug, and from the different substances that are met with in making them. Hence various rules are given for choosing a spot of ground for the foundation of houses.

53. The next sources of superstition are the boats and carriages ; for from the knots that are in them good or bad success is assigned to the possessors ; as also from the different objects they meet with on their progresses, on different days of the week.

54. All involuntary movements of the eyes, the head or the forehead are considered as indications of the lot of those in whom they are observed, as their happiness, or of the honours they will receive, or of a litigious disposition, etc.

55. The sun and the planets afford numerous signs from prognostication. When any of them approaches the disk of the moon, and especially if any of them passes over it, great evils are apprehended ; as the destruction of kingdoms, and the ruin

of countries.   If the sun rises with a terrible aspect, great
murders will follow; but if it appear with extraordinary
brightness, then there will be war.   In those four months in
which Venus is not seen, in any month when an eclipse or an
earthquake happens, and in that in which the year commences,
it is unlucky to marry or to build a house or to cut one's hair,
as death by drowning or some such dreadful catastrophe will
be the consequence.

If the planet Mercury approaches the moon, it is a sign that
the embankments of the rice-grounds will be ruined and the
waters dried up.   If Saturn approaches it, there will be war
upon the confines of the kingdom; and if Mars comes near,
all things will be sold at high prices.   If this planet passes to
the left of the Pleiads, it is a sign of a great earthquake; and
so of many other combinations of the planets, from which
auguries are derived.   The appearance of comets is also considered as ominous.

56. In the time of war, or during a lawsuit there is a curious
way of finding out the success to be expected.   Three figures
are made of cooked rice, one representing a lion, another an ox,
and a third a elephant.   These are exposed to the crows, and
the augury is taken according to which is eaten.   If they fall
on the figure of the lion, it is a sign of victory, if they eat that
of the ox, things will be made up by accommodation, but if
they take the elephant, then bad success is to be looked for.

57. When a dog carries any unclean thing to the top of a
house, it is supposed that the master will become rich.   If a
hen lay her egg upon cotton, its master will become poor.   If
a person, who is going to conclude a lawsuit, meet on the road
another carrying brooms or spades, the suit will be long, and
in the end he will be deceived.   If the wind should carry away
any of the leaves of the betel, when, according to custom, it is
being carried to the house of a newly married woman, it is a
sign that the marriage will be unhappy, and that a separation
will ensue.

If in going to war or to prosecute a lawsuit, a person meet
with a fish, there will be no war, and the lawsuit will cease; if
he see another catching a goat, the Mandarins will exact many
presents, the client will be deceived, and the lawsuit a long

one; if he meet any one carrying packages, then everything will succeed to his wishes; if he meet a serpent, the affair will be long; if a dog or a female elephant or a person playing on the instrument called Zaun, a species of cymbal,[1] all things will go well.

58. In divers places this book also speaks of the prognostics to be taken from the cawing of crows, from the baying of dogs, from the different situations and forms in which bees make their combs, from the manner in which fowls lay their eggs, from various birds, such as the vulture and the crow, which light upon the trees or the roofs of houses, and from the shape of the holes made by mice in different substances. It treats also of dreams; and from the hour of their occurrence and the things represented in them shows what auguries are to be drawn. But we should never finish were we to extract all the follies of this book, for they are so numerous, and, at the same time, so inconsistent with common comfort, that, as one of our oldest missionaries has observed, if a man were to be entirely guided by it he would not have a house to live in nor a road to walk on nor clothes to cover him nor even rice for his food; and yet the blind and ignorant Burmese place the greatest faith in it, and endeavour to regulate all their actions according to its directions. And when they find that to a certainty some misfortune is hanging over them, they have recourse to the diviners and to other superstitions, by which the bad omens may be corrected.

59. These superstitions are common to all the Burmese, but there are others that belong to particular persons, and to which they are beyond all measure attached. Of this kind are dreams, and the observance of lucky and unlucky days; for they believe that some days are peculiarly unlucky for beginning a journey either by land or water, and that others, on the contrary, are very lucky. But they have in particular an implicit confidence in their soothsayers, who are most commonly Brahmins. They are consulted on every affair of importance, and on every event, even though it depend entirely on the freewill of man. If a man thinks of undertaking a journey or instituting a lawsuit,

---

[1] The zaun is a stringed instrument.

he runs to the soothsayer to learn what will be its success. If a person falls sick, or loses a slave or some animal, not only will he consult the diviner on the probable end of his malady, but he asks where he is to find a physician, or in what direction he is to go in search of what he has lost. In order to reply to these questions the Brahmin will first draw his horoscope in the manner of the following scheme :—

Rahù	Venus	Sun
North-west	North	North-east
Age 12	Age 21	Age 6
Jupiter		Moon
West		East
Age 19		Age 15
Saturn	Mercury	Mars
South-west	South	South-east
Age 10	Age 17	Age 8

The Burmese, as has been before remarked, admit eight planets, from which the days of the week have their names. But since there are but seven days, Wednesday has two planets, Mercury, which presides from sunrise to mid-day, and Rahù, whose reign is from mid-day till night. To these eight planets, disposed in the order in which they stand in the scheme, different ages are assigned, the sun being the youngest, as it is only six years old. The ages of men are supposed to have some connection with the ages of the planets, and on this ground the calculation of a man's fortune proceeds ; for some of these planets have a malignant and others a benign influence. The four placed in the cardinal points are good planets, the others evil ones, particularly Rahù. The passage of the age of men into that of the planets is always of bad augury ; and the worst passage is that from the age of the moon to the age of Mars. For example, when a man enters upon the seventh year of his age, he passes from the age of the sun to that of the moon ; and when he enters the twenty-second, he is said to pass into the age of Mars. Now if any one desires to know how he will succeed in an affair, as for example if he will meet with dangers in a journey he is going to undertake, the diviner will first ask him the day of his birth, and then his age. He next divides the latter by eight, since there are eight planets, and then counts the number that remains upon the horoscope, beginning with the planet that presided on the day of his birth, and passing round through the houses of the planets. The house where the number finishes will give the fate of the enterprise, according to the aspect of the planet that is in it. Thus, for example, suppose a person born on a Monday, whose age is twenty-three ; divide this by eight, and there will remain, after the division, seven. If now we begin from the house of the moon, as the person was born on a Monday, and count through those of Mars, Mercury, etc., we shall finish in Venus, and the good or bad success of the undertaking must be determined by the nature of this planet. If a person were born on a Wednesday after mid-day, we must begin to count from the house of Rahù, and go on through that of Venus, etc. If after dividing the age by eight there be no remainder, then the augury must be taken from the planet of the birth ; so that for a person born on a Monday, and in his twenty-fourth year, the moon is the fatal planet ; for eight divides twenty-four exactly, without leaving a remainder.

60. The Burmese diviners, in the same manner as gypsies among us, read a person's fortune in the palm of his hand and the lines it exhibits. Thus if the palm be red, it is a sign of a large circle of friends ; but if it be black it is a sign of misfortune. Black lines in the hand denote prudence, and if they reach the upper part of the palm, they promise happiness. A great number of lines is a sign of very great happiness, and of the possession of many friends and a numerous offspring. When there is but a single line in the thumb or little finger, the person so marked will live 110 years ; if there are two lines his life will be of eighty or ninety years ; if three, of seventy ; and if

four, of sixty. Long fingers show that a person has many daughters, short ones that he is lascivious. If the little lines on the top of the forefinger are disposed in circles, happiness is predicted; but if they merely describe the arc of a circle, misery and great afflictions must be looked for. In all these auguries, the right hand of a man, and the left of a woman is to be consulted.

61. Talismans are also much in use among the Burmese; and they are of several kinds. Some they wear round the neck, others round the wrist; and they think to be preserved by them from sickness and all kinds of witchcraft. There is one species much esteemed among the soldiers, consisting of a piece of lead or other metal, which is buried in the flesh. They imagine by these means to make themselves invulnerable. The figures of tigers, dogs, and other animals, which they paint upon their legs and thighs, may also be considered as so many talismans, for they believe that through them they will be safe, not only from these animals, but also from every kind of assault whatsoever.[1]

One of their most potent talismans is a handle of ivory or buffalo's horn, upon which are carved several representations of a certain monstrous ape. The history of this creature is as follows:—A Nat of the name of Mannat, being dead, passed into the womb of a female ape, who shortly after brought forth this famous monster. Its name is Hanuman, the compound of the word Hanu, signifying an ape, and its former appellation.[2] The stature of this monster was enormous, being four leagues and a half; it was possessed of the greatest agility, for at one bound it could leap up to heaven, or pass a sea of the breadth

---

[1] Mr. Eales, the compiler of the Burma Census Report of 1891, at p. 270, vol. i., states that credulity and quackery are still common. In 1881 a Shan 'doctor' was convicted before me as Judicial Commissioner at Rangoon of culpable homicide on the following facts: A Burman, desirous of protection against sudden death, allowed a picture of the paddy-bird of Pegù to be tattooed on his thigh by the Shan, and then, after his feet and hands had been tied together, to be pushed from a boat into the Irawadi river, when the current carried him away helpless, and he was drowned. The Shan had told him that the charm would save him from sinking; and several respectable witnesses for the defence swore that they had seen similar experiments result in the bound man floating unhurt.

[2] Hanuman is the monkey-god of the Hindus, and this history is an altered version of an episode in the Râmayâna.

of 100 leagues; and it had besides the property of transform-
ing itself into an ape of the ordinary size. Its strength was
prodigious, as it could break any mountain in pieces, or transport it from one place to another; finally, it was gifted with
immortality, so that none but the great king Ramamen could
destroy it. It could both understand and speak the language
of men. One day it mistook the sun for a fruit, and having
a great desire to eat it, jumped up to it, and seized it with its
hands to bring it down. But the Nat of the sun cursed it for
its boldness, and as a punishment sentenced it to be reduced to
an ape of the usual dimensions, to lose all its strength, agility,
and immortality, and to remain in this condition till the great
king Ramamen should appear, who by stroking its back three
times, would restore to it, together with its size, all its other
great qualities. And in fact, after this malediction, Hanuman
became a common ape, as powerless and as weak as any other of
its kind; and so it remained till king Ramamen appeared.
He, having been informed of the curse and the prediction, and
being about to wage war with the king of the giants, sent for
Hanuman, and having stroked its back three times, restored it
to its former state, hoping now to derive great assistance from
it in his enterprise. And indeed he afterwards employed it in
the most arduous undertakings; and, through its means,
obtained a complete victory over the giants, and recovered his
wife from their hands. Wherefore the Mandarins and all, the
people believe, that by carving the figure of this monster upon
the ivory or bone handles of their daggers or swords, they communicate to them the virtue of cutting through every obstacle,
and of warding off the blows of any hostile weapon.

62. Besides these, we may also reckon among the superstitions of the Burmese, the use of amatory philtres, and of
numerous recipes for obtaining a return of love; a fear of
witches, admitted in the greatest excess; and the medicines
against incantations, much praised by their physicians. It is
impossible to persuade the Burmese that there is no such thing
in nature as witches, and that they are not extremely malicious
and hurtful. They both believe in them, and have many superstitious practices for discovering them. The following is one
among many. The suspected woman is placed upon a little

bier, supported at each end by a boat, and a vessel full of ordure is emptied upon her. The boats are then slowly drawn from each other, till the woman falls into the water. If she sinks, she is dragged out by a rope of green herbs tied round her middle, and is declared innocent; but if she swims, she is convicted as a witch, and generally sent to some place where the air is unwholesome.[1]

---

[1] This ordeal by water is common to Hindu law and practice, and found among the nations of Europe. The last judicial conviction of a woman for witchcraft in England was in 1712, and in Scotland some years later : the last judicial execution in Europe was in Switzerland in 1782. But the practice of ducking witches survived far into this century. See the *Encyclopædia Britannica*, Articles *Ordeal, Witchcraft*, and the long discussion in Lecky's *Rise of Rationalism in Europe*, ch. i. According to Shway Yoe this superstition is still common in Burma. Mr. Taw Sein-Ko has supplied me with the following note on the book which Sangermano calls Deitton :—' Deitton in Pali would be Ditthum, which is not given by Childers in his Dictionary. I am inclined to derive this word from *dishta*, appointed or settled, and *um*=AUM, the mystic symbol which precedes every incantation. I have not met any Deitton either in Pali or Sanskrit, but have seen several in Burmese. I think this treatise deals with a subject similar to the geomancy of the Chinese, and was originally used in deciding on the position of the king's palace and other public buildings.'

MORAL AND PHYSICAL CONSTITUTION
OF THE BURMESE EMPIRE

CHAPTER XVIII

CHARACTER OF THE BURMESE

1. THE Burmese are, in general, of a moderate stature, their limbs are well proportioned, and their physiognomy open and not unpleasing. There are far fewer lame or deformed persons amongst them than amongst us, which must be ascribed primarily to the absence of the manner of swathing children which we practise, but which is totally unknown to the Burmese. The infant is left to the care of nature till it arrives at the age of eleven or twelve, before which time it is not encumbered with clothes, but is left to be formed to strength and endurance by the action of the elements upon its naked body. And, in fact, by these means all their limbs become fully developed, and they acquire great strength, activity, and insensibility to hardships. They are not only able to endure the greatest heat, but are just as indifferent to rain ; and as in Pegù, more than any other part of India, the rains are remarkable for their violence and frequency, continuing from the beginning of May to the end of October, their patience in this respect is often put to the test. It is by no means rare to see men, especially those who travel on the river, sleeping in the open air while the rain is descending in torrents. The complexion of the people is an olive-brown, but it varies in shade according to the mixture of nations and the exposure to the sun. Hence the women are generally fairer than the men, and the children springing from the marriage of a Burmese with a Siamese woman are of a lighter colour, while

on the contrary, where the man is a Siamese and the woman a Burmese, they are darker than the rest of the people.

2. From the nature of their Government, which, as has been said, is above all measure despotic and tyrannical, it will easily be imagined that the Burmese are distinguished for that servility and timidity which is always the characteristic of slaves. Indeed every Burmese considers himself such, not merely before the Emperor and the Mandarins, but also before any one who is his superior, either in age or possessions. Hence he never speaks of himself to them in the first person, but always makes use of the word Chiundò, that is, your slave. While asking for a favour from the emperor, the Mandarins, or any respectable person, he will go through so many humiliations and adorations, that one would imagine he was in the presence of a God. Even if he is desirous of obtaining something from one who is his equal, he will bow, and go on his knees, and adore him, and raise up his hands, etc.

3. It is a proverb in America that the slave must be governed by the bastinado, and this is certainly the case with the Burmese. Neither the love of fame, nor honour, nor conscience is the spring of their actions, nothing but power can prevail on them to do anything. The fear of punishment alone renders them obedient to the laws and to the imperial edicts, and gives them valour in war.

4. But if they are abject and dastardly towards the Emperor and the Mandarins, they are in the same degree proud and overbearing to those whom they think beneath them either in rank or fortune. There is no contempt, oppression or injustice they will not exercise towards their fellow-men, when they can assure themselves of the protection of the Government. They are thus vile and abject in adversity, but arrogant and presumptuous in prosperity. There is no one amongst them, however poor and mean, who does not aim at the dignity of Mandarin. For it is a frequent occurrence here for a man to be raised in a moment, by the caprice of the monarch, from the lowest state of poverty and degradation to the rank of minister or general, and it is amusing to observe the instantaneous change such an event makes in a man's demeanour. He may have been modest, affable, and courteous before, but

now he affects a tone of superiority and of gravity, and puts on an imposing and severe air, so that one would hardly recognise in him the man of yesterday.

5. Another characteristic of the Burmese is an incorrigible idleness. Although the fertility and extent of their country would seem to invite them with the prospect of great riches, yet they are so indolent that they content themselves with cultivating what is absolutely necessary for their maintenance, and for paying the taxes. Hence, instead of spending their time in improving their possessions, they prefer to give themselves up to an indolent repose, to spend the day in talking, smoking, and chewing betel, or else to become the satellites of some powerful Mandarin. The same hatred of labour leads to an excessive love of gaming, and also to thieving, to which they are much addicted. The severity of the laws against theft is not sufficient to restrain their rapacity, and the whole empire is overrun with robbers.

6. Among the principal precepts inculcated on the Burmese, there is one that forbids lying; but perhaps there is no law less observed than this. It would seem that it is impossible for this people to tell the truth; nay a person who ventures to do it is called a fool, a good kind of man, but not fitted for managing his affairs. Dissimulation is the natural companion of the last-mentioned habit, and the Burmese practise it to perfection. They may have conceived an implacable enmity to another, they may wish him every kind of evil, and be endeavouring by words and actions to ruin him, but not the slightest sign of their dislike will be observed in their exterior deportment towards him; they will wear a face of the greatest complacency in his presence, and they will transact business with him, and talk with him as if he were their dearest friend. On the contrary, have they fixed their affections on anything, and determined to make it theirs, then they will feign an absolute dislike to it.

7. But as every rule will have its exceptions, it must not be supposed that the Burmese have not some good qualities, and that estimable persons may not be found amongst them. Indeed, there are some persons whose affability, courtesy, benevolence, gratitude, and other virtues contrast strongly with

the vices of their countrymen. There are instances on record of shipwrecks on their coast, when the sufferers have been received in the villages, and treated with a generous hospitality which they would probably not have experienced in many Christian countries.

8. It must also be acknowledged that the observance of festivals among the Burmese and their liberality do them honour. In a month called lunar, the days of the new and full moon and of the two other quarters are feasts. On these days every one ceases from all labour, and with the greatest recollection and modesty, goes to the Pagoda, to adore Godama and to offer him their presents of cooked rice and fruit. Even if the weather be tempestuous or rainy, and the Pagoda distant a league from their habitation, they will not fail in this act of religion. When they have finished their offerings and adorations, many return to their homes, but others remain in the vicinity of the Pagodas, and in the public halls and porticos, of which there are always several in these places, spend their time in reading religious books, or in discoursing of God and his law. They content themselves with one meal before mid-day, and even pass the night in these places at a distance from their wives.

9. Though beggars are rare in this country, on account of the cheapness of provisions, the Burmese do not want opportunities of exercising their liberality. For besides giving a daily alms to their Talapoins, they all lay by something to be applied to some work of public benefit, such as a convent of Talapoins, a Pagoda, a hall, a portico, a pond, a bridge or a well. They are very fond of thus signalising their generosity, and will often deprive themselves of comforts, to have the pleasure of being benefactors to the public. It is indeed true that human views of vanity, or ambition, often enter into these actions, but still religious motives always more or less exist. For the Burmese believe that every good work they perform will be rewarded in their future transmigrations, by beauty, or riches or learning, or perhaps by their becoming Nat. But whatever may be the motives for the works, the public generally profits by them. And its sense of the benefit is expressed by the honours paid to the benefactors. They

are saluted by the titles of Pratagà, Chiauntagà, Zaratagà, etc.,
that is, benefactors to the Pagodas, convents, or halls, and
these titles are as honourable with them as those of Duke or
Marquess among us. Their vanity is also flattered by the
festivals that are celebrated on the days when a convent
is given to the Talapoins, and, as it were, dedicated, or a
Pagoda or bridge thrown open to the public. The Saduccò,
or convocation of the people to congratulate the person on the
completion of his undertaking, is a principal part of the
festivities on these occasions. A splendid banquet is given to
those assembled, which is succeeded by music, singing, and
dancing. Boxing-matches, in which the Burmese are very
expert, are also made, and prizes given to the victors, consisting of handkerchiefs, pieces of cloth, and money, and sometimes
a species of comedy is exhibited with puppets.

10. Were it not for this liberality of the Burmese people,
all persons, but especially travellers, would suffer great inconveniences. For the Government takes no care of the roads or
the bridges; and as there are no inns or places of public
entertainment, the traveller would often have to pass the night
in the open air, were it not for the halls and porticos that
every here and there are met with. He would, moreover,
probably die of thirst, but for the wells and ponds, where he
may stay to refresh himself, and cook his rice; for the traveller,
as well as the soldier, as we have said above, is obliged to
carry with him his provision of rice and napì. If the people
cannot afford to construct a well, at least they will place two
vessels of water, and a cocoa-nut shell with a handle for a cup,
that passengers may quench their thirst.

Nor are the Baos less beneficial to the public than the
works just mentioned. They are the schools, and indeed the
only ones in the empire, as the task of education is entirely
committed to the Talapoins. Hence in these convents all the
youth of the kingdom are placed, as soon as they have attained
their sixth or seventh year, and they generally wear the habit
for two or three years.

11. There is yet another point in the character of the
Burmese that merits praise; and this is their respect for age.
In every society the old men are treated with the greatest con-

sideration, the first seats are surrendered to them ; and reverence and veneration are always observed in speaking to them.

12. It may also be put down among the good qualities of this people, that they consider all men as equal in condition. Excepting the Mandarins and Talapoins, who, by reason of their offices and sacred character, are regarded with an excessive reverence, all men are treated as equal. Even the Mandarins, when deposed, and the Talapoins, when they throw off the habit, are regarded with no peculiar marks of distinction. The Pariahs of the caste looked upon as the vilest in India, or from the coast of Coromandel, or the Caffres, and negroes of Guinea, who are regarded and treated by Europeans as little better than beasts, may come into their confines, and the Burmese will receive them with the same respect as the natives of the most favoured country, and will have no scruple of transacting business, or even of eating with them.

The slaves are, for the same reason, treated as children, and as forming part of the family of their masters; indeed it is not a rare thing for them to become the sons-in-law of their master. But it must be remembered that slavery is not for life in these parts. If a man can save sufficient to pay the debt for which he was enslaved, he becomes free. It often happens that a man will sell his children or his wife or even himself, to pay the taxes and imposts ; though these transactions should be looked upon rather as pledges than sales, as the slavery thus entered into is never perpetual. Hence none but the slaves of the Pagodas, and those who are employed to burn and bury the dead are considered as infamous, and with these alone no one will contract marriage.[1]

---

[1] The charitable and religious practices described in this chapter are still common, and excite the admiration of strangers. Monasteries, pagodas, resthouses, bridges and wells are built from religious motives and to commemorate the founder or a father or husband. As in olden time in Europe, when memorial churches, crosses, chantries and wells were common objects, the practice has given much development to art.

CHAPTER XIX

13. THE dress of the Burmese is very simple. That of the men consists of a piece of striped cloth, generally of cotton but sometimes of silk, tied round the middle and hanging down to the feet, being from eighteen to twenty cubits in length. It is at times thrown over the shoulders, and when walking they will often entirely gather it up round the middle. When they pay a visit to a person of quality, and when they go to the Pagodas, they put on a garment like a shirt of white linen, or else of the nankeen of the country, which is open before and reaches to the knees.

14. The dress of the women is also a piece of striped cotton or silk, of a square or nearly square form, which they tie round the middle, and the unmarried girls fold it over the bosom. It is open in front, so that in walking the legs and part of the thigh are exposed. But when they go abroad or to the Pagodas, they put on an outer dress, similar to that of the men, only a little shorter, and over the shoulders they throw a mantle of muslin or silk.

15. Both men and women wear on their feet a sort of sandal, made of wood or leather; and the latter species are for the most part covered with red or green cloth of European manufacture. Both sexes take great care of their hair, keeping it very long, and, to preserve its lustre and colour, anointing it at least once a day with the oil of sesame, called by the Portuguese in India Gingili. The men gather it on the top of the head ; and, to hinder it from falling, tie round it a white or coloured handkerchief. The women simply tie it with a red ribbon, and let it fall down behind. From their earliest childhood all are accustomed to dye their teeth black,[1] to hide, it would seem, the spots which the constant use of betel produces upon them.

---

[1] The custom has since died out in Burma, but is still found in Siam.

This is a creeping plant, the leaves of which are strongly scented, and which is used for mastication here, and in all parts of India. It is prepared for this purpose by rolling up in it a piece of slacked lime, of a red colour, with a little tobacco, catechù, and areca, which is a fruit of the size and shape of a nutmeg. It is said that by these means the phlegm is expelled, to which the Indians are so much subject.

16. The passion for ornaments of gold and silver is universal among the Burmese, so that if there were no laws to restrain them, they would spend their whole substance in dress; but to prevent this, it is ordained that no one shall wear cloth brocaded with gold or silver flowers, except the queens and the wives of the Mandarins. But every person wears on the finger at least one ring set with a diamond, ruby, or some other precious stone; and the girls before their marriage and the boys till the age of sixteen or seventeen wear golden necklaces of various shapes, bracelets of the same metal on their arms and anklets of silver about the legs; all but the royal family are prohibited to have the last of gold, under pain of death.

17. All the Burmese, without exception, have the custom of boring their ears. The day when the operation is performed is kept as a festival; for this custom holds, in their estimation, something of the rank that baptism has in ours; and is, in fact, the distinctive mark of the nation. The hole is at first very small; but it is gradually enlarged by introducing into it a thin plate of gold, about an inch broad and four or five long. This is rolled up; and, as its own elasticity always tends to unroll it, the hole is thus continually made larger.

18. The men of this nation have a singular custom of tattooing their thighs, which is done by wounding the skin, and then filling the wound with the juice of a certain plant which has the property of producing a black stain. Some, besides both their thighs, will also stain their legs of the same colour, and others paint them all over with representations of tigers, cats, and other animals. The origin of this custom, as well as of the immodest dress of the women, is said to have been the policy of a certain queen who, observing that the men were deserting their wives, and giving themselves up to abominable vices,

persuaded her husband to establish these customs by a royal
order; that thus by disfiguring the men and setting off the
beauty of the women, the latter might regain the affections of
their husbands.

19. We must now pass on to speak of the food, beds, and
houses of the Burmese; and in this part of their economy they
are as sordid and parsimonious as they are splendid and extravagant in their dress. They have always in their mouths that
their dress is seen by everybody; but no one comes into their
houses to observe what they eat and how they are lodged.
Hence the food, beds, and houses of these people are simple
and even rude in the highest degree. In every part of the
empire, excepting Rangoon, where, on account of the concourse
of strangers, it is at all times allowed to sell venison, pork,
fowls and fish, the food is of the worst quality and to an
European is absolutely disgusting. It consists of rice simply
boiled in water without salt, one or two kinds of stews or
curries, one acid and the other sweet, but both composed of
herbs and of leaves of trees, seasoned with the napì or half
putrid fish, of which we have spoken above. Every herb and
the leaves of every tree, provided they are not positively
venomous, are used in these dishes; and the very richest kind
is that which contains the flesh of some animal that has died.
Notwithstanding the law of Godama that forbids the killing
of any living thing, yet fishermen are encouraged, for the sake
of the napì, the only seasoning ever used in the Burmese
dishes. Hence the people who live along the river are in a
better condition than others, as they have plenty of fish for
their curry. The hunting of stags and hares is also tolerated;
but a strict Burmese will by no means engage in it, or indeed
kill even a wild animal. The Burmese make two meals in the
day, one about 9 o'clock in the morning, the other at sunset.
A quantity of rice boiled hard, so that the grains do not stick
together, is put on a wooden plate, supported by a leg of the
same material, and round this, two or three people seat themselves upon the bare ground or on simple mats, and they
employ their fingers in eating. Besides the acid and sweet
curry, they have commonly another sauce made of pounded
napì and red pepper.

20. On occasion of festivals, or the death of any member of the family, when they are accustomed to invite everybody to their houses, three or four curries are presented to the guest, with fried fish and meat, and sometimes cakes made of rice-flour and jagra, a species of sugar made from the palm.

21. The usual beverage of the Burmese is pure water. Formerly, indeed up to the commencement of the present Emperor's reign, they were allowed the use of wine, or rather to make themselves intoxicated ; for it is considered no more sin in these countries to drink to the greatest excess than to take a single draught of wine. But when we say wine, we must not be understood to speak of the juice of the grape, which does not grow in these parts, but of a liquor prepared from rice, or from the sugar of the palm, dissolved in water and distilled after a fermentation of two or three days. This is also the method pursued by the Carian in making their wine ; for they are allowed to use it, as their law does not command them to abstain from it. The same privilege is enjoyed by the Christians, provided they are not natives; as they are, in this case, subject to all the restrictions of the kingdom in this respect.

22. The bed consists of a simple mat spread on the ground and a small pillow. But the latter is a luxury not indulged in by travellers, who instead of it generally put a piece of wood under their head. The rich have sometimes a low wooden bedstead on which they place a mattress two or three inches thick. White sheets are not known here, but one or two cotton cloths are used for coverlets : travellers have not even these, but make use of the clothes which they have worn in the day as their covering at night.

23. The houses have but one story ; and their size varies according to the number of persons constituting the families by whom they are built. They are generally of cane or bamboo, woven like basket-work and covered with straw, and are supported on poles. The Mandarins and some rich men have their houses of teak-wood, supported by pillars of the same material. The interior is separated into different apartments by partitions of bamboo, and all the houses, excepting those of the Mandarins, are of the same form. The

roofs are made of thin tiles, nearly square, and turned up
about an inch at one end, for the convenience of fixing them
on the rafters. The form of the roof varies according to the
rank of the master of the house. Mandarins have theirs of a
different figure from those of common people; and according
to the dignity of each one of them the shape of his house is
determined.

24. Houses, such as we have described, are peculiarly adapted
for countries subject to earthquakes; and it would be well if
in some parts of Europe liable to these visitations such buildings were in use. But it is not to guard against the effects of
earthquakes that the Burmese construct their habitations in
this fashion; for though they are sometimes felt, yet they are
far from being frequent. When they do occur they do not
create much fear, merely on account of this form of the houses;
but though the earthquake of itself causes no alarm, the
uproar and noise made by the people are at least calculated to
do it. No sooner do they feel a shock than they begin beating
the walls of their houses with pieces of wood and with their
hands, and shout so as to terrify every one who is not aware
of the cause: and a person who hears it on a sudden cannot
help being alarmed by it. The people make all this uproar
to frighten away an evil genius by whom they believe that the
earthquake is caused. During the whole year after an earthquake has happened no new houses are built, out of a motive
of superstition.

25. The royal palace is distinguished from the houses of the
Mandarins by its size, the number of the apartments, and a
great court, where the Emperor gives public audience, seated
upon a carpet, under the shade of a white parasol. It is here,
too, that he receives the homage of the Mandarins, who daily
come into his presence; where they remain on their knees, as
if he were a God, from time to time raising up their hands,
and holding them joined over their heads, and always receiving
his orders in this posture. It was once the custom that the
Emperor should every day in these audiences make some new
regulation, regarding either the dress or the general government of his kingdoms. The conversation of the courtiers in
the presence of the monarch seldom contains anything but

L

flattery, in which they strive with each other who shall be most extravagant.

Teak-wood is used in the building of the palace, as in other great houses ; but it is much stronger, and indeed may be considered as the only fortress in the empire. All the cannons and other fire-arms are here deposited, as well as the ammunition and stores ; and hence, when the palace is taken by an enemy, the whole kingdom is supposed to be conquered.

26. The etiquette to be observed in the shape and size of the houses is very precise with the Burmese ; as nothing less than death can expiate the crime, either of choosing a shape that does not belong to the dignity of the master, or of painting the house white—which colour is permitted to the members of the royal family alone.[1] There is never more than one story in the houses, as we have before remarked, for it is esteemed an indignity to live under other people, especially under women.

27. The outward appearance of the houses, whether of cane or wood, is pleasing ; but inside they present a scene of confusion and dirtiness that is highly disgusting to a European eye. And this is the case, not merely in the dwellings of private individuals, but likewise in the palaces of the Mandarins, and even in the Baos of the Talapoins, which are esteemed the richest and most magnificent edifices in the country. The foreign merchants at Rangoon are permitted to build after any fashion they please, and may even use bricks, as in Bengal and on the coast of Coromandel, which is unlawful for a Burmese. But they generally prefer the houses of teak-wood ; not from any want of bricks or lime, but because the wooden houses are more adapted to the dampness of the climate. Such few brick buildings as do exist are used more as magazines than as dwelling-houses.

28. In their hours of idleness the Burmese engage in several games of hazard. One of the most esteemed is called cognento. It is played with a species of wild fruit, which is set up in the

---

[1] 'His Majesty has prohibited the use of brick or stone in private buildings, from the apprehension, I was informed, that if people got leave to build brick houses they might erect brick fortifications.' 'Strict observance is paid to the form which is indicative of the rank of the occupant ; nor dare any subject assume a mode of structure to which he is not legally entitled.'—Symes, pp. 185, 243.

earth, and which is to be knocked down by throwing at it. This game is very much like one played with walnuts by the children among us; but in the Burmese empire not merely children but even the old men will consume whole days in this divertisement. They have besides a species of game of goose, and cards of ivory, which have been introduced from Siam.

Among their more athletic games may be mentioned one in which they make use of a ball made of strips of bamboo, which is struck, not with the hands, but with the feet. In this game the young men will sometimes spend several hours together. But there is nothing of which they are more passionately fond than fighting-cocks. Every young man must have one of these animals: he arms its heels with little knives; and its victories are for him a subject of the greatest exultation.

29. The musical instruments of the Burmese are of several kinds. The one most used is the drum, which is generally made of a piece of bamboo or very thick cane, covered with skin. Another instrument is in the shape of a wheel, with a number of bits of brass or copper hung loosely on the inside; there is besides a species of oboe, and these are the instruments generally used at festivals and public functions. But there are others which are only played upon in private houses; such as one called the crocodile, from its resemblance to that animal, being a kind of lute. There is also another, called in the Burmese language Pattalà. It has the shape of a little boat, and is made of pieces of hard bamboo fastened together; these are struck with two little sticks, and the sound produced, echoing in the hollow of the instrument, is not unpleasing. This instrument is known to the negroes of Guinea, and in the European colonies of America.

30. It is difficult to describe the Burmese dance. The performers in it, both men and women, moving slowly round the place of the entertainment, exhibit continual contortions with their bodies, their heads, their hands, and their fingers. The first time I saw these dancers I took them for a troop of mad people. On occasions of the festivals we have described, when speaking of the funerals of the Talapoins, when the great rockets are let off, if these fireworks ascend straight up into the air, without bursting or running obliquely, the makers of

them burst out into the wildest shouts and songs, and dance about with the most extravagant contortions, like real madmen. These rockets, for several days before the festival, are carried in procession about the town, preceded by musical instruments, and by a crowd of those who are at the expense of the entertainment, dancing, and singing the praises of the rockets, and of the powder that is to make them fly up to heaven.

31. The laws of Godama forbid polygamy: but still, when they have the means of maintaining them, the Burmese, besides their lawful wife, have two or three concubines, who, however, are kept separate in different houses, to avoid dissensions. The same laws also command a man to live with his wife till the death of one or the other; and the public opinion agrees with them in esteeming a man as degraded who is separated from his wife. Nevertheless nothing is here more common than divorces, caused principally, perhaps, by the speedy loss of beauty by the women.[1] While young they are winning and gay: but after their first child-bearing, they become so changed and deformed that they can scarcely be recognised for the same. The quality of their food, which is far from giving much nourishment, may be one cause of this, but it must principally be referred to the strange treatment of women in child-bearing which is here practised. No sooner is the infant come to light than an immense fire is lighted in the apartment, so large that a person can hardly approach it without experiencing considerable hurt. Yet the woman is stretched out

[1] Bishop Bigandet confirms these remarks, see p. 173 of his vol. i. Some part of the written law about marriage and divorce is given by our author in ch. xxiv. For a full discussion see my *Notes on Buddhist Law*, which contain much learned commentary by Dr. Forchhammer. The present law may be shortly stated as follows. A Burmese Buddhist marriage may be dissolved, without recourse to a Court, when both husband and wife consent. Otherwise the marriage can only be dissolved for definite reasons, similar to those admitted by the Hindu law as justifying separation, *e.g.* adultery and certain diseases. Polygamy is now rare, and the numbers of married males and females almost exactly balance each other, being 1,306,722 husbands to 1,307,292 wives.— Census Report 1891, p. 115. 'Marriage is, of course, more common in Burma than in England. The tie is so easily undone by divorce, and a wife is so often a means of support instead of being a burden to a husband, that few Burmans reach the age of 23 without being married.'—*Ibid.* p. 113. Nicolo de Conti, the oldest known European traveller to Ava (*circa* 1430), says that the men of this country are satisfied with one wife.

before it, and obliged to support its action on her naked skin, which is often blistered from its effects as badly as if the fire had been actually made for this purpose. This treatment is persevered in for ten or fifteen days without intermission, at the end of which time, as it will easily be supposed, the poor woman is quite scorched and blackened.[1]

32. In concluding a marriage the customs of the Burmese are somewhat different from ours. With us it is the woman who brings the dowry, and she goes to live in the house of the husband ; but in this country the man, on the contrary, goes to the house of his bride's parents, and must take with him a dower according to the resources of his family. When a young man has fixed his affections upon a girl, his first step is to send some old persons to her house to speak with her parents. If they and their daughter consent to the match, the contract is immediately made, and the bridegroom, accompanied by his friends and relations, goes to the house of his father-in-law, where he continues to reside for three years. If at the end of this time he is discontented with his situation, he may then take his wife and go to live somewhere else. Frequently marriages are contracted without the consent of the parents of either party, and even in direct opposition to their wishes. For the Burmese law allows of no restraint in these matters, but leaves young people at liberty to follow their own inclinations, nay, even forbids all opposition to them, and all attempts on the part of the parents to force upon their children an odious marriage.[2]

There is a curious custom observed on the night of the marriage, of which I have never been able to discover the origin. A troop of lads will on these occasions assemble round the house, and throw upon it such quantities of stones and

---

[1] These practices are still common, and as a result the reproductive period among the women terminates before 40 years of age. But trained midwives are now being sent to every district of Burma.—Census Report 1891, pp. 90, 110.

[2] Formerly the young couple were contracted in marriage by the parents, whose act created the matrimonial status, as at Hindu Law still. But as stated in the Census Reports of 1881 and 1891, child-marriage is now unknown, a result imputed to the independence and self-respect of the women. In Burma about one-half of the whole population are returned as unmarried : in India the proportion is only two-fifths.

wood as to break the roof and the utensils in the rooms, and sometimes to do considerable injury to the inmates. This sport continues till morning, and there is no way of escaping from it but by observing the greatest secrecy in celebrating the marriage. It is difficult to conceive any reason for this extraordinary practice.[1]

33. It now only remains for me to speak of the customs of this people with regard to the sick and the dead.[2] The simplicity and lightness of their food on the one hand, and the excessive perspiration to which they are subject on the other, while they render the Burmese enervated and feeble, and devoid of all colour in their countenances, preserve them from many maladies produced in Europe by the quality of the food, by fulness of habit and by the coldness of the climate. On this account inflammations of the lungs, the quinsy, rheumatism, the gout, consumption, and those complaints that are caused by a full habit of body, as apoplexy, are unknown here; though there is something like rheumatism arising from the damps. Even the complaints that they have in common with us, such as putrid fevers, etc., do not appear in so terrible a form, and are not accompanied by symptoms of exhaustion, convulsion and delirium, nor are they so obstinate as in Europe. But then the Burmese are afflicted with all the maladies caused by weakness and relaxation of the organs; and it may be affirmed with safety that the greater part of the deaths are the consequence of disorders in the digestive organs, such as dysentery, tenesmus, and diarrhœa. The most fatal disease of this class is one called datpiech, which means a loss of digestion. It is generally the effect of a dysentery or diarrhœa which has been neglected or imperfectly cured, and consists

---

[1] This matter is discussed by Shway Yoe in his Chapter on Marriage, which is referred to by the Census officer as an authority on marriage customs.

[2] For some recent remarks on Burmese medicine, see the *British Burma Gazetteer*, vol. i. p. 398. The student of folklore will find much interesting information in Shway Yoe's Chapter on Wizards, Doctors, and Wise Men. Medicine is mixed up with magic. Dr. Forchhammer points out the Indian origin of the science. 'Nearly all technical terms in the Burmese idiom, referring to astronomy, astrology, palmistry, medicinal substances, and therapeutics, are words of Sanskrit, and not of Pali origin. Not a single *original* Burmese work treating of the above subjects has as yet been found.—*Jardine Prize Essay*, p. 21.

in a complete loss of the digestive powers, so that the food is voided in the same state as it was taken into the mouth. The sufferers under this complaint are soon reduced to skeletons of mere skin and bone. Europeans, even more than the natives, are subject to the complaints just mentioned, which must be attributed to their excess in eating, and to their use of the spirits made in India as the arrack of Batavia and the rum of Bengal.

34. There is another complaint, found in this country only, to which all people are subject at a certain age. It is called teh, a word signifying to mount, and takes its name from its commencing in the feet and ascending upwards through all the members of the body. It presents the appearance of a stupor or numbness, by which the patient is at last deprived of all feeling, and even of speech. The Burmese attribute it to the wind, but its true cause seems to be the congealing and torpor of the humours, particularly of the nervous fluid, from the want of exercise, as also from the intemperate use of viscous and acid meats. Hence young people and labourers, as well as those who in spite of the law make use of strong liquors, are free from this disease ; but those, on the contrary, who lead a sedentary life, as the Talapoins, are very subject to it. Its only cure seems to be a violent friction of all parts of the body with the hands to excite pain ; and in this two or three persons are employed. Sometimes, where the hands produce no effect they have recourse to their feet, and tread upon the sufferer, with more or less violence as the circumstances require, till animation is restored. The Portuguese in India have given the name of kneading to this remedy, from its resemblance to the kneading of dough for bread ; but still experience shows that it is efficacious, always providing that too many persons are not set to work, and that it is not too violent ; for in this case it may itself be the cause of death. I have myself seen instances of persons surprised by a sudden attack of the teh, which has been followed by death ; but I have always doubted whether it was not the effect of suffocation, considering that eight or ten vigorous men were employed in kneading with all their force the body, neck, breast, etc., of the patients.

35. Another malady of a more malignant nature, and not confined to the Burmese empire, but spread over all India, is that called by the Portuguese, mordazzino, consisting in a violent indigestion, which causes what the physicians call cholera. The continual evacuations both by vomit and stool will reduce a man in a few hours to such a state of exhaustion that he is scarcely to be recognised for the same person. To these evacuations succeed a cold sweat, hiccups, faintings, and death if proper remedies are not immediately administered; but of these the poor Burmese, owing to the gross ignorance of their physicians, have none; for, instead of making use of emollients, they give astringent medicines, which only hasten death. The Christians in India have a remedy for this complaint which has often been found efficacious. They beat the bare arm with two fingers without intermission till the part becomes inflamed and painful. This may be called a revulsive remedy. Sometimes the indigestion has an effect totally different from the one just described, which is to make the stomach incapable of expelling the indigested matter, and in these cases the convulsions of the patient are indescribable. This species of the cholera, to which the name of the dry mordazzino is given, is perhaps more dangerous than the other.

Before the conquest of Arakan the small-pox made great ravages among the poorer sort of the Burmese, not so much perhaps by reason of its own malignity, as from the prejudices that hindered the proper remedies being applied for its cure. For, among other things there was the custom of shutting up all who were attacked by it in places remote from all assistance, sometimes even in the uninhabited parts of the empire, to avoid contagion. But the Arakanese slaves taken in the wars, having seen inoculation practised with success in their own country, have introduced it among their conquerors, and thus done them an essential service.

36. But, generally speaking, in their treatment of maladies the Burmese are far from pursuing that sound and reasonable system of medicine which is founded on the anatomy of the human body and the principles of mechanics. It is true that Godama, whom no subject seems to have escaped, has set down in his sermons, the number of bones, veins, and nerves con-

tained in the human body, but this without ever having dissected a single subject; and there is besides a classical book of medicine in the Burmese tongue, which tells us that the human body is composed of four elements, air, water, earth, and fire ; that ninety-six complaints may arise in it, some caused by fate, some by the passions of the soul, or by the season, or by the food ; that those springing from the passions are seated in the heart, and those caused by the food in the bowels ; finally that the symptoms of complaints are manifested in the five senses of sight, hearing, etc.   Still the whole *materia medica* of the Burmese is confined to a few prescriptions of various roots, barks, and other simples, principally furnished by the Sciam, who find them in great abundance in their woods.   Few, however, of their prescriptions are calculated for the purposes to which they are applied, by reason of the quantity of hot ingredients, such as cayenne, nutmeg, cloves, etc., which they contain.   The virtue of the medicinal roots is supposed to depend particularly on the time when they are dug up, and hence at certain periods, but especially during an eclipse of the sun or moon, the physicians go out into the woods in search of them.   But the greatest fault of the Burmese pharmacy is that any one is allowed to practise it, without having gone through any examination, and without any licence or diploma.   Hence it often happens that rustics, accustomed only to handle the spade and the plough, and scarce able to write, on a sudden take up the profession of medicine and make themselves physicians.   And this is no slight evil, as it is one of the vices of the nation to be passionately fond of exercising their skill in this way.   It is amusing to stand by the side of a sick man and listen to the advice of the persons who come to visit him.   Everybody, even the most ignorant old woman, has something to recommend, as a specimen of his skill whereby the sick man will infallibly be cured.

When a physician is called in, he brings with him a little bag full of small pieces of cane or bamboo, containing powders, pills, etc. ; for here the medicines are prepared by the physician himself.   After putting a few questions to the patient he opens his bag and gives him one of his pills to be taken in warm water, and on departing leaves three or four other doses to be taken in the course of the day or the following night. They are very liberal with these medicines, as they know that the confidence of the sick man in their skill will depend entirely on their quantity. Sometimes, as when the complaint is violent, they will remain several hours by the side of the patient, administering their remedies in the paroxysms of the disorder. No sooner has he swallowed them, and even almost before they can have reached the stomach, they ask if they have done any good; and if the answer be in the affirmative, they will repeat the dose every hour; but if the answer be, No, they try some other pill, or powder; till at length the stomach becomes so overloaded with drugs, and these generally of the hottest quality, that they alone often produce a fatal termination of the disorder. And this happens more frequently perhaps to the rich than the poor; for the former, immediately they fall ill, send for physicians in every direction, each of whom must administer his remedy. I have frequently made the observation, that of two persons, one rich, the other poor, and both attacked by the same complaint, the poor man has recovered, although his symptoms were much more threatening, while the other has died.

37. The Burmese physicians never think of observing the stools of the patient: they take no notice of the tongue, and though they feel the pulse, it is done in so ridiculous a manner, as to preclude all possibility of deriving any knowledge of the disorder from it. They will observe the pulsations in two different parts of the body, as in the arm and the foot, to find if they are equal, for they think that when the blood is affected it does not pulsate equally in all the arteries; but the force of the pulse or its regularity is totally unattended to. But, as the pulsations, so long as they are sensible, are equal all over the body, according to them the blood is never disordered; and hence they persevere in giving their medicines to the last moment, and oftentimes they will force open the mouth of the dying man with a stick, to make him swallow them. Even when the pulse has totally ceased in the extremities, and a man is just on the point of expiring, they will continue to assert the efficacy of their medicines, and as long as any

movement of the blood can be perceived, promise to effect a cure.

38. With regard to diet, they confine themselves to the prohibition of certain meats; but are so far from diminishing the quantity of food, in fevers, and other acute disorders, that they rather increase it, and order the patients to eat more than before, on the strength of the proverb, that a man cannot die as long as he eats. Besides this prejudice they have two others equally absurd, that purges should not be used in fevers, and that hot medicines are proper in these cases; and hence it will readily be imagined how these maladies generally end. In fact, I have frequently seen trifling fevers, by these means, growing into violent ones, and finishing in the death of the patient.

The unwillingness that they manifest for using cathartics in cases of fever proceeds, perhaps, from the want of good opening medicines. The only drug they have for this purpose, is the seed of the ricinus, which is a most powerful purge; and this often produces such serious inconveniences in fever patients, that it is not surprising that they should be afraid of using it. And indeed the effects of this drug must be dangerous for sick people, seeing that robust and healthy men are sometimes so reduced by its action as to lose their sight and hearing. Our missionaries have indeed discovered a root possessing pretty near the same qualities as jalap, and another having those of ipecacuanha; but the Burmese are too prejudiced to adopt new medicines, especially when introduced by foreigners.

39. The treatment of women in childbirth which we have described, by which they are exposed to the action of a fire large enough to roast them, as also the hot medicines which they give them to facilitate the voiding of the secundines and lochia, as will naturally be supposed, seriously affects their health. And indeed there are few who afterwards do not always suffer from hæmorrhage, inflammation of the uterus, diarrhœa, and fever; and thus but few reach an advanced age. Hence it may be considered an advantage here that the women are twice or thrice as numerous as the men.

40. When the physicians find, after several days spent in attempting a cure, that the disorder will not yield to their

remedies, they have recourse to another expedient to save their reputation. They gravely declare that a complaint which is not cured by so many and such excellent medicines must have been caused by the evil Nat, or by the incantations of the witches. And the people are too ignorant not to admit the subterfuge; for they firmly believe that great disorders may be thus caused in the human body. There is one in particular which they ascribe to witches, to which they have given the name of *appen*. It is described as a mass of flesh, bones, and sinews, which is produced by magic, and introduced into the body. They imagine also that the Nat who preside over trees, mountains and fields, and particularly a certain one of the woods, whom, to distinguish him from others, they call Natzò, or evil Nat, are the authors of many diseases. Hence it is easy for a physician to persuade a sick man, already imbued with this notion, that his malady arises from the malice of Nat or witches, especially as he pretends to discover this by feeling the pulse. In these cases he will prescribe some superstitious observance, and administer what he calls the medicine of the witches; or if it be the Natzò that has caused the evil, he will set before him rice and cooked meats, roasted fowls, fruit, etc., which, as he says, are of their own nature good; or else he will make the devil or Natzò dance. For this purpose a middle-aged woman, to whom they give the name of wife of the Natzò, must dance, and go through a number of contortions, to the sound of a drum or some other musical instrument, in a tent erected for the occasion, in which is placed a quantity of fruits and other things as an offering, but which turn to the account of the dancing girl. By degrees she feigns to become infuriated and utters some incoherent words which are regarded as the answer of the Nat, who has been thus consulted with regard to the conclusion of the malady. If all these superstitious remedies are of no avail, the physicians have still another subterfuge, for they declare that the power of the Natzò is too great to be overcome.

41. The Barnabite missionaries, whom the Society of the Propaganda, about a century ago, sent into these parts, and in whose course of studies medicine and surgery are included, that thus, whilst they are gaining souls to Christ and His religion,

they may also administer to the temporal wants of their neighbours, have very much exerted themselves to disabuse the
Burmese of the superstitions and prejudices with which they
are imbued respecting the cure of their complaints. In those
places where they mostly reside they have in part succeeded ; but
it has been impossible entirely to wean them from their ancient
usages, perhaps chiefly from their impatience under suffering,
and their eagerness to be instantly freed from their maladies.
Hence, supposing, as they do, that two or three doses of a good
medicine is sufficient to cure any disorder, if after two or three
days they still continue ill, they immediately conclude that the
physician is unskilful, and have recourse to some one else ; and
if he does not complete their cure within the space of two or
three days, they will discard him also and send for another ;
and thus they go on, till probably the complaint, having spent
itself, requires no further remedies, and the sick man recovers :
and happy is the physician who has been last called in ; he will
have all the credit of the cure, and will be esteemed a clever
practitioner.

42. But in surgical matters the Burmese are more inclined to
have recourse to us. They have themselves no regular surgeons,
and hence, in cases of fracture, dislocation, contusion, etc., they
have recourse to the Barnabite missionaries, who are the only
persons acquainted with the use of the lancet—for the Burmese
method of bleeding is to wound the affected part superficially
with a knife, and then to put upon it a species of cupping
glass—and they alone are able to effect a cure in the cases just
mentioned. It must, however, be confessed, to the praise of the
simplicity and frugality of the food, that wounds and sores are
easily cured in this country. The blood of this people does not
possess that inflammatory tendency which is observed among
us Europeans, and hence a simple application of camphorated
spirits of wine for a few days will cure the most dangerous
wounds without any fear of inflammation ; and an ointment
made of wax, oil, and tobacco or pitch, will in a very short
time drain and cicatrize the most inveterate sores.

43. But though their food is so simple, still the great
quantity of napì that they use renders the Burmese very
subject to cutaneous disorders. Lepers are numerous among

them ; they are obliged to live separate from the uninfected ; but as they are not prohibited to marry, this complaint is continually propagated. The lepers are almost the only beggars in this kingdom. In the cities of Tavai and Martaban the leprosy is so common, that there is scarcely a person who is not in some degree infected with it. This is so remarkable with regard to Martaban, that the complaint has its name from this city. Besides this, there is not a single Burmese whose skin is not in some way diseased either with the itch, which sometimes creeps over the whole body, or by whitish spots.

44. It now only remains for us to speak of the funerals of the Burmese. As soon as a person is dead, the body is washed and wrapped up in a white cloth ; visits of condolence are then made by the connections and friends, who, allowing the immediate relatives to indulge their grief by tears and lamentations, take upon themselves the care of the funeral, causing the wooden coffin to be made, preparing the betel, and lapech, which is to be given to all who assemble on the occasion, calling in the musicians etc. The use of music in funerals is general among the opulent Burmese, and more so among the Peguans. It consists of one or two drums, a species of trumpet and an instrument made in the form of a wheel, with little pieces of copper of different sizes hung loosely on the inner circumference, which, being struck in cadence, produce an agreeable harmony. The manner of playing on these instruments at funerals is not the same as at festivals. There is one custom of the Burmese, which is deserving of imitation in every civilised country, and this is that called Sanenchienzù, that is to say, society of friends. A hundred or more heads of families unite together in a kind of confraternity for the object of affording mutual assistance to each other on all occasions, but particularly at funerals. Hence on the very day of a person's death, all the other members of the society to which he belonged hasten to bring money, rice, or anything else that may be useful to the relatives of the deceased, to whom these presents afford great alleviation in their grief, especially as thus all concern is removed as to the expenses of the funeral, which, on account of the passion of this people to bury their dead with the greatest possible magnificence, are often very considerable.

For besides the coffin, made of large planks of teak-wood, with its pedestal, and the provision of betel and lapech, a great quantity of gifts, consisting of various kinds of fruits, white cotton cloths, and money, must be distributed to the Talapoins and the poor. The Mandarins and officers have the right of being deposited in a gilded coffin, and the rich generally obtain the privilege by force of presents. The corpse is kept a longer or shorter time in the house, according to the age or quality of the deceased, the species of complaint of which he has died, or the day of his death. Old persons and those who are remarkable for having constructed some public edifice are kept two or three days if the heats will permit it. Children, who have no surviving brother or sister, and all such as die suddenly, must be buried immediately, as well as those whose death happens on the last day of the moon; for their funeral must take place on the same day, and it is strictly prohibited to defer it past midnight.

When everything is ready, the funeral pomp commences. First in the procession are carried the alms destined for the Talapoins and the poor, and next large baskets full of betel and lapech, generally borne by a sort of female Talapoins, dressed in white. These are followed by a number of Talapoins from different Baos, two and two. The number of these, as well as the quantity of alms to be distributed, varies according to the means of those who provide the funeral; but in general they do their utmost, and there have been instances of families reduced to beggary from having given too magnificent a funeral, and one exceeding their revenues. After the Talapoins comes the bier or coffin, which, excepting the deceased be a Mandarin, in which case, as we have said, it is gilded, is painted red. It is carried by eight or more persons, who are either friends of the deceased, or belonging to the same confraternity with him. Upon the coffin the richest clothes of the deceased are displayed. When there is music, it ordinarily precedes the bier. Immediately following are the wives, children, and nearest relations of the deceased, all dressed in white, which is here the mourning colour, weeping violently, and calling upon the deceased, and asking him a number of questions. In the funerals of Mandarins, their satellites go before the body, carrying the ensigns of his dignity, his instruments of office, his betel-box, pipe, sword, looking-glass, etc. When a person has died without relations women are hired to act the part of mourners. The bier is followed by a crowd of people, which is greater or less, according to the extent of the kindred, friends and dependants of the deceased. But all funerals are accompanied by a great number of people, even those of the poor, for the Burmese have a natural inclination for this act of piety and respect. Indeed there are some who go about to the houses calling on every one to come and attend the funeral. As soon as the coffin has arrived at the place of sepulture, the senior Talapoin delivers his sermon, which consists of a list of the five secular commandments and the ten good works that each one is obliged to perform. When the sermon is finished, the body is delivered to those whose office it is to burn the dead, and these, placing it on a species of wooden rack, set fire to it, while in the meantime the alms are distributed to the Talapoins and the poor, and quantities of betel and lapech to all who have followed the procession.

But these ceremonies are not practised on all occasions, as there are cases in which the corpse is not burned, but buried. All whose death is sudden, those who die of the small-pox, children and women dying in childbirth are buried, as well as those who are drowned, for they must be interred on the banks of the river or lake where the accident has happened.[1]

On the third day after the funeral, the relations, all dressed in white, accompanied by some friends, return to the place where the body has been burned, to collect the bones that have remained after the fire. These are placed in an urn and buried, and those who can afford it erect a monument of bricks or stone over them. In the meantime, till the eighth or ninth day, a kind of wake is kept up in the house of the deceased during the night, to which there is a great concourse of people. On these occasions tea is handed about, as well as sweetmeats, made either of the sugar of the country, or else

---

[1] A person dying of cholera was buried the same day. The body of a woman dying in labour before the birth of the child was subjected to a horrid rite, to prevent the woman's soul haunting the place as an evil spirit. For details, see Crawfurd, p. 279.

of that extracted from the sugar-cane, and particularly great quantities of lapech, which, as we have before said, is a species of very strong tea, well calculated to keep off sleep. These nights are passed either in conversation or in reading poetry or history, for which purpose some persons of a fine sonorous voice are engaged. All this is done with the view of consoling the relations of the deceased, and diverting their minds from brooding over their loss. On the eighth or ninth day the whole ceremony finishes, and at the conclusion a charitable feast is given to the Talapoins and to all those who have assisted at the funeral.

45. In carrying the body to be burned there are many super-stitions to be observed. One of these is that the procession must not move towards the north or the east; and for this reason the Burmese cemeteries, which are generally large open places, lie to the west of the cities and villages. Hence also all who die within the walls of a city must be carried out through the same gate, which is therefore called the gate of sorrow, and even condemned criminals are led through it to execution. If any one dies in the suburbs the procession must make the circuit of the walls to get to the appointed place, for a dead body is never allowed to be brought into any city.

CHAPTER XX

46. WE do not here enter into a disquisition on the origin of the Burmese language, for this is a question of very difficult solution ; but with regard to its character, we may say in general that it possesses a degree of strength and grace which we do not meet with in our European tongues. By means of certain expletives a tone of gravity, submissiveness, elegance and affability may be given to the discourse, according to the quality of the person to whom it is directed. The singular and plural numbers have always joined to them some particle which at the same time denotes some essential quality belonging to the thing spoken of. For example, for a Mandarin they would say, *Men tabà*, that is, Mandarin one person ; a priest, *Ponghi tabà*, that is, priest one person ; a man in general is called *Tajauch*, an animal *Tachaun*; to express anything round, for example an egg, they say *U talon*, that is, egg one round ; finally, when speaking of anything flat, as a table, they say *Pin tabià*, table one flat. For inanimate objects, which do not possess any remarkable quality like those above mentioned, they make use of the particle *cù* ; thus *tit, nit, son*, one, two, three, with the addition of this particle become *tacù, nitcù, soncù*, one thing, two things, three things, etc.

47. The Burmese language is exceedingly difficult to a European, and that from many causes. For, in the first place, its construction is totally different from ours ; secondly, it has a great quantity of guttural and nasal aspirates in the pronunciation of a number of words ; thirdly, many words have a nearly similar sound, though in signification they are widely

---

[1] For the latest views on the language, and the use of synonyms as well as tones (points which Sangermano here notices), see Appendix I.

separated. One or two examples may make this better understood. *Zà* signifies to be hungry, *Zan*, uncooked rice, and *Zà*,
salt. *Tà* means to hinder, *Tha*, to rise, and *Thaa*, to preserve.
Chiaa means to delay, *Chia*, to fall, and *Chiaà* signifies both
to hear and a tiger. Fourthly, the greatest difficulty in this
language arises from the quality, that every different modification of the same thing will have its own phrase; so that a
word, which expresses any action, cannot be used in expressing
a modification of it. Thus, for example, among us the verb to
wash is applied to linen, to the hands, etc.; but among the
Burmese a different phrase is used for each one of these
operations. So that for to wash the hands they use one word;
but to wash the face requires another; the word for to wash
linen with soap is different from the one signifying to wash it
simply with water; and to wash the body, the dishes, etc., are
all different phrases, each expressing the action to wash by a
different verb.

48. The Burmese alphabet has forty-four radical letters,
many of which are taken from the Palì, which is the language
in which their sacred books are written. Of these letters seven
are vowels, comprehending a mute and an open *e*, and a long
and short *o*. There is no declension of nouns, and hence the
cases are only distinguished by certain articles placed after
them; thus, for example, a house in Burmese is *eim i*,[1] to a
house *eim a*; the accusative is *eim go*, the vocative *o eim*, the
ablative *eim gà*; the plural is formed by adding the particle
do, thus houses *eim do*, of the house *eim do i*, etc. There is no
distinction of genders, except in the case of animals; for then,
to form the feminine, the particle *ma* is added to the generic
name of the animal. Thus a dog is *ce choè*, a bitch *choè ma*,
etc. Neither are the tenses of the verbs distinguished by their
terminations, but the present is formed by the addition of the
particle *si*, the past by that of *bi*, and the future by *mi*. Thus
I go is *suà si*, I went, *suà bi*, I will go, *suà mi*; the imperative
is formed in the same way by *tò*, the interrogative by *là*, and
the gerund by *lien*; thus the imperative go is *suà tò*, is he
gone? *suà bì là*, by going, *suà lien*.

49. There is but little variety in the Burmese versification,

---

[1] The particle *i* is the sign of the genitive case.

and the same must be said of the singing and music; at least so it seems to our ears. They have many books of history and general information written in metre. Their lines always consist of four monosyllables, and only the two last of each chapter are in rhyme. If we consider their cosmography, and the taste for the wonderful and sublime which the Burmese manifest, we shall easily imagine that their poetry will be not altogether foreign to the European taste. They have a great passion for this branch of reading, and will frequently hire persons of sonorous voices to sing their poems to them. There are also many who employ themselves in poetical compositions, and these have no want of subjects, as they find them in great abundance in the books that treat of Godama, and the cosmography.

50. There are few among the Burmese who do not know how to read and write; for the Talapoins, to whose care they are intrusted as soon as they attain the age of reason, always teach them to read,[1] as also to write on the palm-leaf or the prabaich, which is a sort of coarse paper made of bamboo macerated in water, and coloured black with charcoal mixed with the juice of a certain leaf. But still the other sciences have made very little progress among these people. Excepting some few, who embrace the profession of the law, and devote themselves to the study of the Damasat, which is their judicial code, all prefer to abandon themselves to idleness, passing the day in conversation or chewing betel: and if there be any who ever think of literature, even their studies never lead them beyond some book of history.[2]

The Talapoins, however, do apply themselves in some degree to study, since according to their rules they are obliged to learn the *Sadà*, which is the grammar of the Palì language or Magatà, to read the *Vinì*, the *Padimot*, which are the books of their constitutions, and the sermons of Godama, which last mentioned

---

[1] They do so still, and are even willing to teach western science. The State Director of Education says the monks generally lead an honest, cleanly life, and so earn public respect.—*Census Report*, 1891, p. 67.

[2] Among all classes the Dzats or Lives of Gaudama in his 500 previous existences are very popular. Bigandet gives some examples, and says they are of the same Indian origin as the fables which delight the nations of Europe. Many of these Birth stories are the same as these fables.

book is called *Sottan*, or the Rule of Life. Besides this, they have also another collection of the revelations of Godama, called *Abidamà*, and this is one of their principal books. It treats of the ideas, the conceptions and volition of all living beings, in the states both of happiness and misery; and is esteemed the most difficult of all their works to be understood.[1]

The study of the Talapoins is however rather an exercise of the memory than of the understanding. They do not esteem the faculties of reasoning and discoursing, but only that of committing easily to memory; and he is esteemed the most learned man whose memory is most tenacious. There are some Talapoins who can repeat from memory the whole of the *Vinù*, which is a book of no ordinary dimensions.

All these books are written in the Pali tongue, but the text is accompanied by a Burmese translation. They were all brought into the kingdom by a certain Brahmin from the island of Ceylon.[2] Besides these there is another book written in Pali, and this is the *Beden* [one of the Vedas or Vedangas], their great treatise on astronomy or rather astrology; a science peculiar to the Brahmins, who employ it not only to regulate the year, but also in fortune-telling.

51. In Burmese there are also many written works, but they are for the most part productions devoid of genius, and composed in a rugged, cold and incoherent style. But still, in some of them, which certain wise men composed for the instruction of the Emperors, and the direction of young men, we meet with precepts of morality worthy of a Christian, and principles of political science, not only sound and reasonable, but nearly of the same nature as those which are known among us as the Machiavelian.

Among these books, the one called *Aporazabon* deserves to be placed the first; it is a species of romance, in which the principal character is Aporazà, an old minister, to whom the Emperor and several Mandarins put a number of questions on the science of government. To give my readers some idea of this work, I will here translate some extracts.

---

[1] Our author refers to the three 'baskets' of discipline, discourses and metaphysics, called Vinayapitaka, Suttapitaka, and Abhidhammapitaka.

[2] The celebrated Buddhaghosa, in the fifth century of our era.

One day the Emperor asked Aporazà what he must do to render his kingdom flourishing and populous; the old minister replied that, in the first place, he must have the success of all his subjects in their affairs at heart, as much as if they were his own; 2. he should diminish the taxes and ciochì; 3. in putting on imposts he should have regard to the means of his subjects; 4. he must be liberal; 5. he must frequently inquire into the affairs of his kingdom, and make himself fully acquainted with them; 6. he must love and esteem his good and faithful servants; 7. finally, he should show courtesy and affability both in his manners and words to all persons. He ought moreover to take measures that the population of his kingdom is augmented, and that his Government acquire honour and respect among foreign nations: he should not molest the rich, but, on the contrary, should encourage their industry and promote their interests: he should show a proper regard to his generals and ministers, who govern in the name of the Emperor, for it is not seemly that they should be publicly disregarded and ill-treated: he should not despise prudent and careful men; and, finally, he should be just and moderate in exacting tributes, and should always proportion them to the products of agriculture and commerce. As a confirmation of this precept he refers to the fruits of the earth, when eaten before they are ripe. 'You see,' he says, 'that the fruits which are gathered ripe from the tree are well-flavoured and pleasant to the taste, but when they are plucked before they have ripened they are insipid, and sour and bitter. Rice that is taken at its proper season is excellent food, but if it is collected before its time it is devoid of substance and nutriment.' He then advises the Emperor not to shut up the doors of his kingdom, that is to say, that he ought to allow all foreign merchants a free entrance, to encourage their commerce and make it flourish.

A short time after the Emperor had ascended the throne, having received intelligence that a chief of the Sciam was approaching with a large body of his subjects to make incursions upon his territories, and disturb the peace and quiet of his subjects, he sent for Aporazà, to give his advice on the measures he ought to take on this occasion. The old minister advised him as follows:—'Oh Emperor! fire is not the only thing that burns and roars and causes death, for water also, which is by nature cold, and flows placidly and quietly over its bed, is the cause of death to those who are plunged into it. Do you, therefore, in your endeavours to destroy your enemy, lay aside the impetuosity of fire, and imitate the slowness and coolness of water. Remember that the wild and furious elephant is tamed by the female ;* give therefore to this chief some one of your relations in marriage, and you will soon see an end of all these troubles.'

Another time when two petty kings had declared war against each other, they both had recourse to the Burmese monarch for assistance. According to his custom, the Emperor sent for Aporazà, who spoke thus on the occasion :—' It once happened that two cocks of equal strength began fighting in the presence of a countryman ; after continuing their combat for some time, they were so overcome with their exertions that they were unable to do anything more, when the countryman sprung upon them and made himself master of them both. Thus ought you, oh king ! to do at present. Let these two princes fight with each other, till you see that their resources are exhausted, and then, pouncing upon them, seize upon their territories for yourself.'

A man of mean extraction was raised by the efforts of an old Mandarin to the throne. But the Mandarin afterwards became overbearing, and even tried to be in some measure the master of the Emperor. The latter bore all this for some time, but at length, growing weary of this insolence, he determined to rid himself of his importunate minister. Wherefore, one day that he was surrounded by a number of his Mandarins, among whom was the one who had raised him to the throne, he directed his discourse to him, and asked him what they do with the Zen which are erected round the Pagodas, after the gilding and painting are finished for which they were raised ; for the Zen is a scaffolding of bamboo, or thick cane, serving to support the gilders and painters of the Pagodas. ' They are taken down and carried away,' replied the old Mandarin,

---

* This is an allusion to the manner of taking the elephants in the woods, which we shall describe in another chapter.

'that they may not obstruct the view of the Pagoda, or spoil its beauty.' 'Just so,' replied the monarch ; 'I have made use of you to ascend the throne, as the gilders and painters make use of the Zen ; but now that I am firmly seated in it, and am obeyed as Emperor by all, and respected by all, you are become useless to me, or rather your presence only disturbs my peace.' He then drove him from his palace, and sent him in banishment to a village.

One day, while this Mandarin was yet in banishment, a dreadful tempest arose ; in the course of which, looking out into the country, he observed that the great trees, which resisted the force of the wind, were not bent but broken or torn up by its fury ; while the grass and the canes, yielding before the blast, returned to their original position the moment it was gone by. 'Oh !' said the Mandarin within himself, 'if I had followed the example of these canes and this grass I should not now be in so miserable a condition.'

I must pass over many other parts of this book, which deserve to be translated, to lay before my readers some extracts of another work, called *Loghanidì* [Lokaniti], or instruction on the manner of living in the world. They are lessons delivered to youth.

The fruit supon is a species of wild fig, beautiful to look at, and promising, by the richness of its colours, a delicious and savoury viand ; but on being opened it discovers nothing but grubs ; so it is with wicked men. On the contrary, the giacca, a fruit of the size of a gourd,[1] the outside of which is covered with prickles, inside contains a sweet pulp, most delicious to the taste ; good men may be compared to the giacca. The beauty and excellence of a woman is to bestow all her cares upon her husband. The grace and beauty of those whose exterior is ugly and deformed are knowledge and wisdom. The excellence and beauty of hermits is patience. The treasure of a woman is her beauty ; that of a serpent its venom. The riches of a king is an army of good soldiers and brave officers ; the riches of a priest is the observance of his rule.

In the world, he who speaks sweetly and with affability will

---

[1] The jack-fruit.

have many friends; but he whose words are bitter will have few or none. In this we may learn from the sun and moon. The sun, by reason of its strong and dazzling light, drives away every star and planet from the heavens while it is above the horizon, and is thus obliged to run its course through the skies solitary and unattended; but the moon, shedding only a soft and tender light, moves on in the midst of the stars and constellations, escorted by a numerous company.

At present we set a value upon nothing but riches and treasures; it is no matter if a man be of an ignoble stock, that he be ill-favoured of countenance, or without judgment, or ignorant; provided only that he be rich, he will be esteemed by all and exalted by all. On the contrary, a poor man is abandoned even by his friends and relations, who run after those who have great possessions; and hence in this world it is money that makes friends and relations. These and many other such lessons of morality are contained in the book we have mentioned.

52. Let us next consider the arts of the Burmese. On account of the great simplicity of their dress and houses, the Burmese have made but little progress in the arts, as will readily be supposed.[1] We do not find that variety of arts which luxury and vanity have introduced into Europe; for excepting the carpenters, masons, and smiths who are employed in making the instruments used in constructing the houses, boats, convents of Talapoins, Pagodas, etc., there are very few artisans to be met with. Every one is able to build his own house of bamboo; and every woman can make all the clothes necessary for her family. In the great cities the inhabitants are mostly merchants or workers in the trades just mentioned; but in the villages and smaller towns both men and women are occupied in the culture of their fields or their rice-grounds, or in growing cotton and indigo; and when the different harvests

---

[1] 'Destitution is almost unknown, and the wants of life in the temperate climate of Burma are more easily satisfied than in the colder countries of Northern Europe. A young Burmese couple can start housekeeping with a da (or Burmese knife) and a cooking-pot. The universal bamboo supplies materials both for building his house, lighting the fire, carrying the water from the well, and even may help to compose the dinner itself.'—*Census Report*, 1891, p. 115.

are over, while the men are going with their carts or boats to provide what may be necessary for them, the women employ themselves at home in spinning and weaving.

53. In the kingdom of Ava the silk-worm is also fed, for the mulberry tree is very plentiful in this part. The silk thus procured is a principal article of dress; almost all the inhabitants of the great cities make use of it, and even in the towns and villages everybody will have a robe of silk for occasions of festivity. Although the silks and cottons of the Burmese do not equal in lustre and perfection those of China, and are not perhaps so fine as those of Madras, or the muslin of Bengal, they still merit praise for their strength and the brilliancy of their colours.

54. Carving in wood has been brought to a tolerable degree of perfection on account of the custom of profusely ornamenting the public halls, the convents of Talapoins, etc., in this manner; but painting is in a very rude state, and is entirely devoid of those beauties which give it so much value with us. In painting flowers the Burmese artists are tolerable, but they have very imperfect notions of drawing and perspective.

55. The manner in which the Burmese construct their wheel-carriages is worthy of notice; not only for their simplicity and strength, but likewise because no nails are employed in them. The excellent wood with which the forests of the Burmese empire abound affords great facilities to its inhabitants in constructing their boats; for they are thus enabled, with little trouble, to make them of all dimensions, as frequently a single trunk is large enough for a vessel. In their shape they are adapted for navigating the river, where alone they are employed; and hence they are made so as to cut the current, which is very rapid, and this particularly in the rainy season; and they draw but little water, by which their passage up the river is greatly facilitated. In this operation they either make use of their oars, or else two or three men on the bank drag along the boat by means of a rope; and where the stream is particularly strong they employ long poles of bamboo sharpened at the end, which they fix in the bed of the river, and thus force it along. When the south-west wind prevails, which is always the case from May to October, the passage up the river

is accomplished with sails, for the wind then blows in a contrary direction to the current, which flows from north to south.

56. The betel boxes and the drinking cups of the Burmese would be regarded as curiosities in Europe. They are made of a very fine basket-work of bamboo covered with Chinese varnish, which is brought in great quantities by the Chinese into the Burmese empire.

57. Besides these arts, the working in gold has been brought to some excellence in these parts. The bellows used by the jewellers, as also by the workers in the other metals, are very different from those common in Europe. They consist of two cylinders of wood, the diameter of which is proportioned to the force of the apparatus. Each cylinder is fitted with a piston of the same material. These are alternately raised and depressed by one or two men, and the air is thus forced out at an aperture in the lower part of the cylinders, whence it is con-ducted through an iron tube into the fire. By means of this apparatus they give great intensity to the fire, so as to melt the hardest metals. In this way they make drinking-vessels of brass in the form of a hollow hemisphere, and frying-pans of iron for their kitchens. The artisans are also proud of their skill in casting bells. Of these every pagoda has two or three, generally very large, and they are rung by striking them on the outside with a stag's horn. Besides these, every pagoda, how-ever small it may be, has a number of smaller bells hung in the crown which is placed at the summit, and the sound pro-duced by them when moved by the wind is very pleasing. Little bells are also employed to hang round the necks of the oxen.

58. Such are the principal arts of the Burmese; and if they are in a low state, this must be attributed more to the destruc-tive despotism of their Government than to the want of genius or inclination in the people, for they have in reality a great talent in this way.[1] It is the Emperor, with his Mandarins,

---

[1] Yule admires the peculiar and often tasteful art of the Burmese in his account of the shops at Amarapura. See pp. 157-165, and the pictures he gives. Of the adornment of the monasteries he says—'One despairs of being able to exhibit to visitors from such a people, in any of our Anglo-Indian cities at least, works which they are likely to appreciate as indicative of our superior wealth and resource.' At p. 377 is found a note on the architecture by James Fergusson. The styles and uses of religious edifices are well described in Bigandet, i. p. 227.

who is the obstacle in the way of the industry of his subjects ;
for no sooner has any artist distinguished himself for his skill
than he is constrained to work for the Emperor or his ministers,
and this without any profit, further than an uncertain patronage. Of the foreign artisans, who at different times have come
to Pegù, some actually established themselves there ; but they
were soon obliged to retire to Bengal or the coast of Coromandel to avoid the impositions of the Mandarins. In addition to these oppressions, the caprice of the Emperor is also a
serious inconvenience for many artisans, for he will oftentimes,
without any reason, permit or prohibit clothes of a new fashion,
and thus, perhaps, ruin those who have made them.

CHAPTER XXI

59. If we except a few medicinal drugs, sulphur, brass, and some other semi-metals, which are imported from foreign parts, the Burmese receive from their own soil everything necessary for the necessities, the comforts, and the luxuries of life, so that were they but as industrious as the Chinese[2] they might soon rival them in manufactures and riches.

60. Rice, in this country, as in every part of India, holds the same place as bread with us. There are several species of it, differing in taste, colour, and form. Thus, there is one kind of a red colour ; and of the white rice some kinds are of a more excellent quality than others, particularly one of which the grains are very small, and which has a strong but pleasant scent of musk. An intoxicating liquor is also prepared from rice steeped in water, and this is esteemed by the Burmese as the greatest luxury, when the Emperor allows its use ; it is also much drunk by the Carian, a nation we have before described as inhabiting the forests of Pegù. The flour of rice is employed by the Burmese, though perhaps not so commonly

---

[1] The scientific reader will find the topics of this chapter in Spearman's *British Burma Gazetteer:* vol. i. chap. ii. Geology and Economic Mineralogy; chap. iii. Vegetation ; chap. xiii. Arts, Manufactures, etc.; chap. xvi. to xx. Fauna. In chap. xvii. Mr. Oates supplies a list of 771 birds of which about 70 species have not been found outside of Lower Burma. For a complete Natural History of Burma see Theobald's edition of Dr. F. Mason's *Burma : Its People and Productions*, Hertford, 1882. Vol. i. Geology, Mineralogy, and Zoology ; vol. ii. Botany.

[2] The thrifty Chinese from Yunnan, Canton, and other parts of China and the Straits Settlements have long been settled in Burma, and are more and more spreading over the whole country. In many villages the best house belongs to a Chinese immigrant. In 1891 the Chinese numbered above 40,000, of whom half were returned as Buddhists, and the rest as Nat-worshippers.

as by the Siamese and Chinese, in making several kinds of pastry.

61. The wheat of the kingdom of Ava is most excellent, and it gives good returns in the grounds that lie along the river, and are subject to its floods, by which they are generally covered during three months every year. It is usually sown immediately the waters have retired, and is harvested in February. Its produce is usually forty-fold. Besides wheat, this empire is very fertile in maize, *panicum*, and a species of grain called *piaun*, which is similar to the Indian millet, being round and of the size of our chickpease. In some parts it is cooked like rice, which it excels in substance, but not in flavour. All kinds of beans and pulse grow with great luxuriance here, and there are even some species unknown in Europe.

62. The citron, the pomegranate, and the orange are the only fruits that the Burmese have in common with us. But it must not thereby be supposed that there is any scarcity of good fruits, for besides all those that are found in the other parts of India, the Burmese have some peculiar to their own country. A Frenchman once endeavoured to introduce the vine, and did in fact succeed in bringing some tolerably good grapes to maturity; so as to show that the climate would admit its cultivation if the natives took the pains to attend to it. The olive is here quite unknown ;[1] but its place is supplied by the sesame or gingili, the grains of which, though not larger than those of mustard, furnish an excellent oil, useful; not only for burning, but also in cookery, though it is said to be rather heating. Under the city of Pagan there is a large well of petroleum, very thick in consistence, and of a strong and disgusting smell. It is carried into all parts of the kingdom for lamps ; but great precautions must be taken in using it, as it very easily takes fire. It is also used for varnishing the houses made of teak-wood, to which it gives a lustre ; and if regularly renewed every year, has the effect of preserving them from decay. But the greatest consumption of this article is at Rangoon, where, united with pitch, it is employed for smearing the vessels. Its colour is somewhat black, and hence it seems

---

[1] Grapes are still grown at Mandalay, and I have seen a fine olive tree at Kyouk-hpyoo covered with fruit.

to be of the same nature as what is called by naturalists Scotch fossil-oil. From Rangoon it is carried to all places along the coasts of Coromandel and Bengal.

63. In Europe there are no fresh fruits during six months of the year, but here every month produces some one; and the celebrated banana-tree furnishes the inhabitants of the torrid zone with its fruits all the year round. The cocoa-tree and the palm are two inexhaustible sources, unknown in Europe, which furnish to the Burmese an immense number both of the luxuries and necessaries of life. The fruit of the former, even whilst yet tender, is filled with a nectareous juice, and a substance of the consistence of butter, both extremely delightful to the taste; when the nut is grown harder this paste acquires the taste of the almond, and, being pressed, yields an oil which is an excellent seasoning in cookery. The coarse exterior rind, which is very stringy, furnishes an excellent material, after it has been washed and pulled to pieces, for making ropes and ship-cables; and it is also used in calking. The inner rind, which is as hard as horn, serves for drinking-cups, ladles, etc. By making incisions in the trunk a juice of a pleasant flavour is extracted, which, after fermentation, becomes a generous wine, and by further fermentation a strong vinegar. The palm-tree is scarcely less useful than the cocoa; for, besides its fruit, it also produces a sweet liquor, which is drawn from its trunk, and which, like that of the cocoa, may be successively changed into cocoa, wine, and vinegar. It has also this further property, that by means of fire it is condensed, and forms a kind of sugar called jagra, quite hard and compact; and this, dissolved in water, and left twelve or fifteen days to ferment, gives a spirit equal in strength to our alcohol. The leaves of the palm are used not only to thatch the houses, but also for every-day letters; and the bark of the branches furnishes good ties for connecting the canes of which the houses are built. Even the trunks of these trees, which, on account of the quantity of pith they contain, are useless for planks or beams, are not thrown away, as they make very good water-conduits. Hence we may see that what some travellers have asserted is an exaggeration, that the cocoa-tree furnishes materials for spinning, as well as wood for all kinds of carpentry.

64. The sugar of the palm just mentioned is not the only one the Burmese possess; for the sugar-cane is cultivated to the north of Ava, in the country of the Sciam, and a very coarse article extracted from it, and made into flat-cakes. The Chinese established in Amarapura have also begun to refine it, and they have been imitated by the natives; so that at present a sugar is made here as white and as refined as that of Bengal.

65. Besides these two kinds of sugar, the Burmese have also many drugs which are useful for conserves; and some which are medicinal; of these we may mention pepper, and the cardamomum, which is found very plentifully in the district of Martaban. Great use is made of cayenne pepper in seasonings; and the common pepper is frequently an ingredient in medicine. A species of nutmeg is also common, of an oval shape, and larger, but less aromatic than those of the Moluccas; as well as a large species of cinnamon, called by the druggists *cassia*. The woods of Tavai and Merghi are full of the sassafras-tree, which is remarkable not only for the sudorific virtues it possesses in all its parts, but also because its leaves, when dried, are useful both in medicine and cookery. In Pegù there is abundance of wax and honey, which is deposited by the bees in the highest trees. Some of the little islands near Negraglia, and off the coast of Tenasserim, are famous for being the resort of the birds, whose nests, formed of a curious gum, are so much esteemed throughout India, and still more in China, for their pectoral, anodyne and cordial qualities. For use, they are boiled in water or in chicken-broth. As to their formation, the most probable opinion seems to be that a marine bird, collecting in its beak the sea-foam, and uniting with it a glutinous substance which it draws from its own stomach, builds these nests with the material so prepared. They are always fixed upon high rocks, and they are gathered by means of ladders, by men trained to the occupation, not without considerable danger. Finally, salt, which seems so necessary a commodity all over the world, far from being rare, as in Bengal, Azen and Junan [Assam and Yunnan], is here most plentiful. In Pegù the very best species is extracted from the sea water; but more is drawn from the brine pits in the plains of Mozzobò, and in other places.

66. Tamarinds, aloes, lac, catechu,[1] indigo, cotton, and tobacco, must also be mentioned among the productions of the Burmese Empire. Catechu is a juice obtained by boiling a certain wood, and hence it is quite wrong to call it Japan-earth or catechu-earth ; the Burmese use it principally in pre-paring their betel ; but is also exported to other places, where it is refined. The labours of the insects that make the lac are worthy. of the study of a naturalist. The indigo would pro-bably be better than that of Bengal, if industry were brought in to assist nature ; but as less attention is here paid to it than in other places, its lustre and fineness are rather inferior. There are two species of cotton, that of a reddish colour, which is rare and most esteemed, and the white or common cotton ; and of this more is collected than the natives can make use of. The tree called *leppan* also produces a kind of down or cotton, which, though it cannot be spun, is good for mattresses and pillows. The tobacco of the kingdom of Ava is not inferior to that of America. The cane, called by the Portuguese bamboo, grows everywhere, and particularly in Pegù, where it increases to a height and thickness truly aston-ishing. Some will measure a foot and a half in diameter, and are large enough to form the principal pillars of a house. Great use is made of the tender roots of the bamboo, which, after having been steeped in water for some time, are used in making curry ; they are also preserved in vinegar.

67. The flowering shrubs and plants of this country are not less numerous or various than the fruit trees, and it would require a volume to describe them all. We must therefore content ourselves with speaking of some of the most remark-able. There is one shrub which grows to a great height, and has a flower like a large spike of maize, the scent of which is very pungent, and is not lost even when the flower is dried. Many species of the jessamine are common, one in particular, the flowers of which are as large as small roses. Lilies are also common ; and indeed there are so many kinds of flowers that it would take too much room to enumerate them. The young people of both sexes gather them to make garlands for their heads, and are very proud of this ornament.

---

[1] The Cutch of commerce.

68. But besides the trees producing fruit, the Burmese have many which are extremely useful to them, for their leaves are the chief ingredient of their curries. In the villages, where there are no markets, the inhabitants are furnished with their kitchen herbs entirely from these trees. But they do not restrict themselves to the trees which have no fruit in preparing the curry, for the leaf of the tamarind and of the mango-trees are very much sought after for this purpose. The former are rather acid, and the latter have an aromatic flavour, and when dressed as a salad, after the European fashion, are really excellent.

69. The shade which the great trees afford may also be reckoned among the benefits that the Burmese derive from them. In particular there is one tree, called *gondon*, which is very serviceable for this purpose. Its roots are so strong that they will penetrate the thickest walls of Pagodas, and often throw them down. Its appearance is most majestic, as its trunk is of an extraordinary height and thickness, and its branches spread on every side over a great space of ground. It is esteemed sacred, because under its shade Godama received the privileges of divinity.[1]

70. The pine-apple is here very common, as also the *santor*, the *guava*, the *jambos*, the *jaceas*, the mango, the *durcione*,[2] and all the other fruits that are found in India and the adjacent islands. There are also some peculiar to the Burmese, as the *marione*. Before ripening this fruit very much resembles our olive, but it afterwards attains the size and appearance of the plum. Whilst in its first state it is excellent for preserves, on account of its acidity, and it is likewise pickled in salt and vinegar; but when ripe it is eaten both in its natural state and preserved in salt. The tree that bears it is exclusively a

---

[1] This tree, called Bodi or Baudhi, under which Gaudama obtained the supreme intelligence, was a banyan tree, the *ficus religiosa*, of which Milton gives a beautiful description in the *Paradise Lost*, Bk. IX. See Bigandet, i. p. 39.

[2] Our author probably means the durian (*durio zibethinus*—Helfer), of Tenasserim, thus described by the old traveller Linschoten :—'They affirme that in taste and goodness it excelleth all kinds of fruits, and yet when it is first opened it smelleth like rotten onions, but in the taste the sweetnesse and daintinesse thereof is tryed.'—Purchas' *Pilgrims*, Bk. x. p. 1779.

native of Pegù, so that it will not even grow in the kingdom of Ava.

71. Before entering upon the natural history of the Burmese Empire, it may be well to mention that the Rev. Father Giuseppe di Amato, of the same order as myself, a man remarkable, as well for his apostolic zeal as for his deep acquaintance with natural history and his skill in drawing, has been now employed more than twenty-seven years in writing on all the branches of natural history, in taking drawings of all animals, serpents, and curious insects, which are natives of the Burmese kingdom, as also in making a collection of butterflies and rare insects, all of which he keeps in glasses hermetically sealed, and arranged in the most perfect order. He has promised either to send this collection, with his writings, to Europe, or to bring them over himself, and give them to the public, and then the curious reader may fully satisfy himself on these subjects. In the meantime I will here briefly describe a few of the most remarkable animals to be met with.

72. The species of animals in this country are certainly more numerous than in Europe. Of all the kinds of poultry known among us the only one not common here is the turkey-fowl, and its loss is completely supplied by the peacocks, which live in great numbers in the woods of Pegù, and are of as fine a flavour as the turkey. Pigeons abound everywhere; it is enough to make a dove-cot and in a short time it will be full. There are also wild pigeons, whose plumage is perfectly green, and large doves. The sparrows completely cover the fields, and often commit great ravages on the sown lands. Of rooks and crows there is an infinity; for they find plenty to live on in the rice that is offered in the Pagodas or thrown to the Nat. In all the towns these rapacious birds may be seen in flocks; and they are so bold that they will even enter the houses and steal any food they can find there; they will open the jars and snatch meat or fish from the hands or heads of people who are carrying them. The turtle-dove is found everywhere. But the falcons, eagles, vultures, and some other species in this part of India, are different from ours. The plumage of the land-birds is generally very brilliant and lively in its colours; and the feathers are an article of commerce for

the Chinese of Junan [Yunnan], who come to buy them, and carry them to China; it is said that they have the secret of extracting the colours by means of aquafortis.

73. This country is also far superior to Europe in the number and variety of its aquatic birds. The banks of the lakes and rivers are covered with them. Among these the duck and the goose are very common; and there is one species of the latter, called ensà,[1] that is, delicious for eating, which is sought after by Europeans as a great delicacy. There is another bird, often met with on the banks of the river, worth mentioning; it is as large as an ostrich, its beak is about a foot and a half long, and it has a kind of bag under its neck, where it deposits the fish it catches. The flights of parrots are astonishingly large; and they are the terror of the Burmese, on account of the damage they do to the fruit trees. Flock after flock will settle upon them and ruin all the fruit, which, not being yet ripe, falls to the ground. To frighten them away, they make use of wooden bells such as they hang on the necks of animals. They employ the same means for frightening away the sparrows from the corn fields. Long cords are tied from tree to tree, and upon these are hung the wooden bells, with large pieces of cloth, which are blown about by the wind. One or two people are employed to shake these ropes, at the same time shouting, or rather screaming, so that the sparrows take to flight.

74. The ass, the mule, and the wolf are the only European quadrupeds not found in the Burmese Empire, and it may even be said that they have the last mentioned, as what they call the dog of the woods is probably a species of wolf.[2] It is about the size of a common house-dog; and generally accompanies the tiger in its nocturnal expeditions, to share the prey. There are numberless varieties of the ape, differing in size, shape, and colour. It is highly amusing for the passengers along the canals, into which the great river Ava [Irawadi] is divided, in that part of Pegù which lies between Rangoon and Bassino, to watch the motions of the apes that crowd the trees on the

---

[1] The *hintha* or *hamsa* of Buddhist books.

[2] The *Canis rutilans*, or jungle-dog of the *Gazetteer*, not now common in Burma.

banks. They leap from tree to tree with such agility as to seem birds rather than quadrupeds; they fight with each other, and mock the lookers on, and chase the fish and crabs that have been thrown on dry ground, in the most ludicrous manner.

The different species of the tiger, the elephant, the rhino-ceros, and the porcupine are numerous, and on the mountains of Martaban the bear is likewise found; but it is not so ferocious as with us. I have also heard from some of the natives, that, in the great forests that lie between the city of Bagò in Pegù, and Taunù, the celebrated ape, called the Orang-Outang, may be met with. Although at the four corners of the Pagodas, and on the staircases in the convents of the Talapoins we see representations of the lion, yet this animal is not a native of the Burmese territories.

75. Horses are by no means uncommon here; they are somewhat smaller than with us, but more active. It is not customary to shoe them, nor are they ever employed in carry-ing burdens or in drawing, for in this oxen are used. The Emperor is the only person who possesses a carriage; and he only because the English East India Company have made him a present of one or two, which are drawn by horses.[1] But he seldom appears in them, as he prefers to show himself in public seated upon a great elephant.

Even the greater Mandarins are permitted to ride on these animals; but all the rest of the people, if they do not possess a horse, must be content to travel in carts drawn by oxen; the tedium, however, of this mode of travelling is diminished by the quick paces they oblige the animals to take. When the Emperor goes out, accompanied by his great body of Man-darins and guards, the streets through which he is to pass must all be swept, and, in the dry season, watered to lay the dust; the doors of all the houses which lie in his route must be kept shut, or else a mat be hung before them, that no one presume to look at his majesty. It is not necessary to close the windows, for these, receiving their light from a great

---

[1] Or more often by men, the kings disliking to see a coachman occupying a seat higher than their own.—Yule, p. 163.

aperture in the outer wall, do not afford the means of looking upon the street, and if there be any little window besides the principal ones it never is on this side of the house.

76. The buffalo is another of the Burmese animals. It is larger than ours, and its horns are longer and more elevated. It is used both in ploughing and in carts. But there is also a wild species, very formidable, not only to man, but even to the tigers, whom they will often surround and kill.

77. Dogs, and these of the most disgusting and dirty description, have multiplied almost beyond endurance ; and this because there is here an absurd custom of never killing them. Every family has a great number of them, so that in some places they are really more numerous than the men.

78. Hares are not common ; and the same must be said of the goat : some few sheep are sometimes seen, but they are not indigenous to the country, having been brought from Bengal. The wild boar is common in the woods, where also stags and deer feed in immense herds : there is one species nearly as large as an ox, which is known by the name of *zat*.

The Burmese Government permits the hunting of these animals in Pegù, and hence venison is always to be bought in Rangoon. They are generally hunted with large dogs; but there is another method of taking them, which it may be as well to describe. In the dark nights, ten or twelve persons get into a cart drawn by buffaloes ; in front of the vehicle two or three lighted torches are carried, and at the sides two persons continually beat two great wooden bells. The deer, which go in herds, dazzled by the light, and astounded by the noise, remain immovable, and the huntsmen with their spears, swords and great knives, kill all they can ; and are often so successful that the cart is not large enough to carry home the booty.

79. In the Burmese villages swine are not very common ; but in the capital, and in Rangoon there is an abundance of them ; for the foreigners residing here feed numbers of them for the sake of the pork, which here, as in China, is always eaten fresh. The Burmese are very fond of it, and esteem it as the most exquisite food ; but their laws forbid them to eat it ;

and the present Emperor has prohibited his subjects either to feed pigs or to kill them. In the markets of Amarapura and Rangoon pork is sometimes exposed for sale, but for the reasons just mentioned, and from the fear that it is the flesh of an animal that has died of some complaint, there are but few purchasers.

80. Among the many kinds of lizards common in this country, the chameleon deserves to be first mentioned. It was formerly believed that this animal fed on nothing but the air;[1] but I myself have had ocular demonstration that this is not the case. I once observed a chameleon upon a tree stedfastly gazing upon a particular spot, whence all of a sudden a large insect came running straight into the mouth of the chameleon, by whom it was instantly devoured. It is a remarkable property of this animal that it frequently changes its colour, which is naturally that of earth, into a brilliant green. There is also another remarkable lizard found in this country, called *tautthè*;[2] it is about the same length as the chameleon, but thicker; and the skin of the back is a beautiful shagreen. It hides itself among the beams of the houses, where it lies in wait for the mice and such other little animals, and night and day keeps up a continual cry of *tau tau*, whence it has its name. The *padat* is a very large lizard, remarkable for being good eating; its flesh is not inferior to that of fowls. The *talagojà* is also a lizard that grows to a great size; some people say that they become crocodiles. Its flesh, and also its eggs are very delicate. Crocodiles are not very numerous in the great river Ava; but in the numerous channels into which it divides itself before reaching the sea, where the water is brackish, and in some perfectly salt, they may be said to swarm. In these channels they are seen every here and there, of all sizes, stretched upon the muddy banks, where, as it is said, they go in order to sleep, which they cannot do in the water. When in this situation they display no ferocity, but at the slightest noise run to the river; but when in the water

---

[1] This is one of the vulgar errors most learnedly refuted by Sir Thomas Browne.

[2] The *Gecko guttatus* of the *Gazetteer*.

they are formidable and troublesome both to men and animals. These channels also abound in a monstrous fish called by us the shark; and by the Portuguese *tuberao*. Out at sea, during a calm, these fish may be observed swimming round the ships and waiting to swallow anything thrown out to them; and it sometimes happens that sailors, who have gone into the water, either to bathe or for any other motive, are seized by them and devoured. It is a difficult matter to take a crocodile: nevertheless the Siamese are very expert at it; they make use of large iron hooks and strong ropes in this occupation.

81. Both the land and water tortoise is plentiful here, and is very valuable to the Burmese for its flesh and eggs.[1] In one part of the river Ava there is a large sandbank, where these animals deposit their eggs in such numbers as to be sufficient for the supply of a great portion of the kingdom; and near an island, contiguous to the great Negraglia, which, from the quantity of tortoises that resort to it, is called the island of the tortoises, the animal itself is taken, and thence carried to Pegù and Bengal. Some of them weigh as much as 500 pounds. The eggs here found are sent by boat-loads to Bassino and Rangoon, and thence distributed all over Pegù. A great part of them are salted, to be used as they are wanted.

82. The quantity and variety of the serpents, natives of the Burmese Empire, and particularly of the woods, is really prodigious. One of these called *nan*, which is an inhabitant of the forests of Pegù, is very formidable; for it moves along with its head erect, in which position it is taller than a man; and whenever it meets any person, without allowing time for flight, it darts upon him, fixes its fangs in his head, and soon kills him. There is a curious story told of one of these serpents that had stationed itself in the neighbourhood of a village, to the great terror of the inhabitants. A reward was offered to any one who would kill it, but no one dared to undertake it,

---

[1] Sometimes more valuable to shipwrecked mariners. Cæsar Fredericke, on his voyage from Malacca steered for Tenasserim, and being unable to find the port, went with twenty-seven others into the ship's boat to get victuals. They found no land, and rowed nine days along the coast, with a small quantity of rice, but at length stumbled on a nest of 144 tortoise eggs.—Purchas, Bk. x. p. 1712.

till an old woman presented herself for the purpose. She placed upon her head a vessel full of melted pitch, and advanced towards the serpent. It made its usual strike at the head, but stuck fast in the pitch, and was soon suffocated.[1] The greatest enemy of this, and indeed of all the serpents of these parts is a spider, known among the Burmese by the name of *pangu*. Although very insignificant as to its size, it inspires terror by its horrible bristly appearance. Its length is about four fingers-breadth, and its thickness in proportion. The belly is covered with hairs of a red colour; it has ten legs, each armed with crooked claws, with which it fixes itself on its prey; and its mouth is provided with two black fangs curved like the claws of a cat; its back, finally, is covered with a hard and scaly case, similar to that of the tortoise. Its bite is poisonous and generally mortal, as is proved from the fact that the serpents it fixes upon almost invariably die. It is continually hunting after them, and attacks them by fixing its claws into their body, and nimbly climbing up to the head, where it strikes in its fangs, and thus kills them; after which it sucks out the brain. A Christian, who once was witness to a struggle between this animal and a serpent of the *nan* species, which we have just described, gave me this account.[2] The *mocauch*, called by the Portuguese the cobra capello, is another terrible serpent. When it meets a man, it immediately swells out its throat, springs upon him, and covers his body with a caustic foam, which causes an insufferable pain wherever it touches the flesh, and is capable of producing blindness if it reaches the eyes. Though the bite is not absolutely mortal when a remedy is immediately applied, still if any principal part of the body has been wounded and the animal was very furious in its bite, a speedy and painful death generally ensues. But the most dangerous serpent here known is one called by

---

[1] The hamadryad *Naja Elaps* is the serpent meant here, as in the somewhat similar story related by Yule, p. 180. Mr. Theobald tells of two adventures in which he seized with his own hands these very large and deadly snakes. Theobald's edition of Dr. Mason's *Burma*, 1882, vol. i. p. 310.

[2] Dr. Mason describes a large, very poisonous spider, but disbelieves the story of the Karens about it killing the cobra and eating its brains.—*Ibid.* vol. i. p. 35.

the natives *moè boè*,[1] and by the Portuguese cobra ceras. It
might with great propriety be named the deaf serpent, for no
noise can ever rouse it. It will even place itself in the middle
of a street, and not all the tumult of men, horses and carriages
passing to and fro can wake it from its lethargy ; but if any
one touches it, though ever so slightly, it instantly raises its
head, hissing most furiously, throws out its tongue and darting
on the aggressor, communicates a venom which no medicine can
counteract. This animal is properly of the viper species, for it
is viviparous ; but its form is different from that of our viper.
I have been assured that the young of this species issue from
their mother's womb by means of holes which they themselves
have made, and thus kill their parent. The venom appears to
be a most powerful acid, and the symptoms, in those who die
of its bite, manifest an universal coagulation of the blood. The
madurà that celebrated specific prepared in the college of the
Father Missioners at Pondicherry, and of which they only
know the ingredients, though it is a singular antidote against
all kinds of bites, whether of mad dogs, or of the other serpents
of Pegù, is of no avail where the *moè boè* has wounded a person : nothing but instant amputation of the limb can save
from immediate death. It is remarkable that death in these
cases is not accompanied by convulsions, swoons, cold sweats
and other violent symptoms, the usual effects of venom.
Another serpent, remarkable for its size, is that called by the
Portugese cobra madeira ; some of these are as long as fifteen
feet and even longer, and their thickness is proportionate to
the length. They are not venomous, but by twining themselves round any animal, and breaking its bones, they kill and
devour it. A man, who was once attacked by one of these
animals, delivered himself from it by stabbing it in several
places with a dagger that he happened to have with him. The
Burmese believe this serpent to be a Nat, and therefore are
careful not to kill it ; and hence, having found one of them
near our church, we were obliged to be secret in destroying it,

---

[1] This serpent is the Daboia or Russell's viper, the Cobramonil or necklace
snake of the early English and Portuguese writers. ' If the animal is so confined
that it cannot fasten on its captor, it will in its rage bury its long fangs deep in
its own body.'—*Gazetteer*, vol. i. p. 635.

for fear of the idolaters. It is said to possess the property of fascinating animals and drawing them into its jaws; and a great boar, which had been fighting with the tigers, was thus devoured by one of most enormous dimensions. Some may perhaps ridicule the idea that it possesses this property, and I myself at first did not give credit to it; but after seeing a large insect, as I have mentioned above, place itself in the mouth of a chameleon, and having been assured by persons whose veracity I could not doubt that they had seen frogs after some contortions, and faintly crying out as it were complaining, jump into the jaws of the macauch or cobra capello, I could no longer refuse to believe it. I have been told by persons deserving of credit that there exists in the Burmese Empire a serpent with two heads,[1] the venom of which is most deadly. Throughout the whole of this country, but particularly in the kingdom of Ava, nearly every species of serpent is used for food after the head has been cut off.

83. The swarms of butterflies, ants, and other insects in this country are prodigious; and the gnats and horse-flies generated in the forests of Pegù, especially during the rainy season, are equally numerous. The horse-flies are seen in clouds along the course of the river, and they are a perfect scourge to the passengers in the boats, whom they will not allow to sleep at night; for to defend themselves they are obliged either to be continually flapping a great fan, or else to be burning tobacco, by the fumes of which the flies are driven away. There are some villages on the banks of the river where the inhabitants are obliged to be both day and night behind large mosquito-nets, where they spin, weave, and pursue all their occupations, for this is the only way of defending themselves against these troublesome insects.

84. Another great nuisance in Pegù are the leeches which, during the rains, abound in the grass and in the waters, so that a person is exposed to their bite at every step. They are actually ravenous after blood, and cannot be made to loose their hold on the flesh but by the application of salt or lime.

---

[1] For the Amphisbæna or serpent with two heads, one at each extreme, see Sir Thomas Browne's *Vulgar Errors*. Like him, 'we must crave leave to doubt of this double-headed serpent until we have the advantage to behold.'

Some of those that live in the water are so large that they may easily be mistaken for small eels, and these are great annoyances to the buffaloes, which are fond of washing themselves in the rivers, for they leave fearful wounds in their flesh.

85. Scorpions also are very common in this kingdom. They are of two species, the whitish and the black. The former are the most dangerous, though smaller in size ; some of the latter species are as large as lobsters, but they are comparatively harmless, for their sting does not cause any irritation or pain. Even the white species is not so venomous as to cause death by their sting.

86. Still more annoying than these are the centipedes, which get among the clothes and into the beds, and cause by their bite an inflammation and torture almost insupportable, which will last for several hours. Some people affirm that, in the great forests of Pegù, there is a species of this animal that grows to the length of an ox, and is thick in proportion, and in moving produces a noise which may be heard at a considerable distance.

87. The Burmese esteem several kinds of insects as articles of food, particularly a species of red ant, which they eat fried [1] or with the napì. Its flavour is rather acid and pungent, and to some European palates would not be disagreeable. But the great delicacy of this country is a worm, not very dissimilar from the silkworm, which is found in the heart of a shrub, called by the Portuguese jental. These worms are so much esteemed that every month a quantity of them is sent to Amarapura for the table of the Emperor. It is eaten either fried or roasted. Some few Europeans are disgusted with it on account of its appearance, but the greater part who have tasted it agree that it is exquisite.[2]

88. But I must not omit to speak of another famous insect of the East Indies, called by the Burmese chià. It is not a worm, as some travellers have painted it, but very much

---

[1] Nicoló de Conti says they eat a red ant, the size of a small crab, as also a frightful serpent without feet as thick as a man, and six cubits long. Dr. Mason states that the Karens esteem the python as food, as also a red ant, the *formica smaragdina*. In an inventory of a Karen's assets I once found some jars of pickled crocodile.

[2] The European opinions still differ on this matter of taste.

resembles a large ant, and hence, as it is white, it has been named the white ant. It lives in communities, and is a most destructive animal, for when a colony of them has found its way into a magazine, a cupboard, a chest, or a library, it will spoil and gnaw to pieces in a single night the most beautiful stuffs and the richest furniture. The only means to keep them away is to anoint the boards of a magazine or chest, etc., with *nustà* or petroleum. But even this is not a sufficient safeguard against one species of the chià found in some parts of Pegù, which is of rather a dark colour, and has a rather disagreeable smell. Another means practised by some for preserving their goods from the depredations of the chià is to place under their houses great Dutch bottles. They seem to have a great horror of the light, or at least to be solicitous to hide their operations from human eyes, for they always make their advances to a place under a covered way made of earth united with a glutinous substance which they draw from their own bodies. When they meet with nothing better they will fall foul of the wood that comes in their way, especially such as is not very hard. After some time these insects change their shape, acquire wings and disperse in the air.

89. To the productions of the Burmese empire mentioned in this chapter, we may here add several kinds of salts, iron, lead and some precious stones, particularly rubies. Throughout the whole of the kingdom of Pegù great quantities of nitre are collected, so that at times it is so cheap, that 300 French pounds may be had for two dollars and a half; but it is forbidden to carry it out of the empire. In a large lake, situated in the vicinity of the Pagoda at Rangoon, there is found a salt which seems to be a compound of nitre, vitriol and alum: it would be very useful in medicine. The kingdom of Ava produces an alkaline earth called *xappià*, which is used in washing. Iron, that metal so necessary to man, is found in great quantities, and of an excellent quality. That drawn from the mines near Miedu is nearly as fine as steel ; and in the vicinity of Pron and Tavai there are also some good mines. Plenty of lead is furnished by the mines in the country of the Sciam ; and tin, of which there is abundance in Tavai, supplies the place of copper. With regard to precious stones, a few inferior sapphires

and topazes are sometimes found; but it is the rubies of the Burmese Empire which are its greatest boast, as both in brilliancy and clearness they are the best in the world. The mines that contain them are situated between the countries of Palaon and the Koè. The Emperor employs inspectors and guards to watch these mines, and appropriates to himself all the stones above a certain weight and size; the penalty of death is denounced against any one who shall conceal, or sell or buy any of these reserved jewels. There are also some mines of amber, which is used by the Burmese for toys and bassi-relievi. Finally, alabaster and the oil of wood must be placed among the useful productions of the Burmese Empire. The former is found in great abundance in the hills opposite the city of Ava, but it is only employed in making the statues of Godama. The latter is procured from a tree called *chien*, by incisions made in the bark. It is an excellent varnish, for besides giving a beautiful lustre to wood, it also preserves it from decay; it may likewise be used in painting, for after it has been boiled a little, if it be mixed with the colours, it very much adds to their vividness.

90. Before concluding this chapter something must be said of the Burmese elephants and the manner of catching them. They have multiplied prodigiously in this empire, by reason of the immense forests with which it is covered. Generally speaking they are also of an enormous size. There are three species known here. Those of the first species have very large tusks, the second smaller ones, and the third none at all, and these are the most wicked and ferocious. It will be understood that these marks apply to the male elephants alone, for the females are universally without tusks. Some have asserted that this animal at certain periods sheds its tusks, but this is not true; and this is also the case with another idea, that when it falls on the ground it cannot raise itself, for in fact the elephant always lies down for its master to mount upon its back. In the Burmese empire it is trained more for the purposes of luxury than any real use, for it is never made to carry any burden further than the provisions of its guide and grass and branches of trees for its own provender. Only in time of war it is sometimes loaded with pieces of artillery, or perhaps

a little baggage. It is the exclusive privilege of the king to ride upon an elephant, but he allows the royal family and the greater Mandarins to use them.

The hunting of the wild elephant is the principal amusement of the Emperor; and indeed this spectacle is the delight of all the inhabitants of the metropolis. As soon as it is known that in some forest there is a herd of elephants, or that there are some, which, on account of their colour or form, deserve to be the property of the Emperor, a number of female elephants are sent out. The wild elephant, upon seeing the females approach, will immediately single out one, and attach himself to her, nor will he afterwards leave her.[1] The hunters then recall all the females, and the amorous elephant will faithfully follow the companion he has chosen, nor will he be deterred even by torrents or rivers. At length he is thus enticed into an enclosure made of strong stakes, and no sooner has he entered than two great beams, which had been suspended over the doorway, are let down, and thus the animal is entrapped. Sometimes he will be very suspicious in going into the enclosure, or may even retire, in which case the hunters, mounted on female elephants, surround him, and by going through a number of evolutions, and shouting and screaming, oblige him to return into the snare. If, as is sometimes the case, he continues restive, or grows angry, and begins to make pushes at the neighbouring houses, there is no remedy but to kill him with musket-shots, a task not always easy, considering the thickness and hardness of his skin. Sometimes the elephant is secured by means of nooses which are disposed so as to catch his feet; but it often happens that people, rashly venturing too near the infuriated beast, to lay the nooses, or through curiosity, are killed by him. The tame elephants are afterwards set to fight the wild one in the enclosure, where they bind him to a great post; and then a few days are sufficient for taming him. Many however die either with grief or from the ill-treatment they have received.

---

[1] The old travellers, Nicoló de Conti, Cæsar Fredericke and Ralph Fitch all speak of the capture of elephants; and Symes, p. 346, has an engraving of the scene. The mode shows the constancy of the Burmans to old customs.—Yule, p. 105.

CHAPTER XXII

91. The Brahmins who come from the coast of Coromandel and the island of Ceylon, and are distinguished from the rest of the Burmese by a vest entirely of white cotton, are the astronomers and astrologers of the Burmese Empire. As they are versed in judicial astrology, in which all the Burmese without exception place implicit faith, and can frequently point out with accuracy the time of an eclipse and regulate the calendar, they are held in great estimation, particularly at court, where a number of them always reside, to be in readiness to answer any questions put to them, to find out the favourable or unfavourable moments for any transaction, in a word, to regulate everything that is to be done ; for, as has been said in a former chapter of the work, the Emperor takes no step without having first consulted the Brahmins.[1]

92. If we look at the manner in which they regulate the calendar,[2] and the exactness with which they often predict eclipses, we must allow to these Brahmins some knowledge of the principles of astronomy ; among other things they certainly are acquainted with that observation made by the ancient astronomers anterior to the celebrated Hipparchus, that after a period of 223 lunar months or eighteen years and

---

[1] See notes, pp. 141 and 134. The white-robed Brahmans are often mentioned by our Envoys. The officials whom Symes met also kept them in their houses, and were guided in all things by their advice.—Symes, p. 221. The Brahmans of Burma in Sangermano's time were descendants of the captives from Arakan, Assam, and Manipur, and of those who were in the country from the time of the Pagan dynasty.

[2] See notes on the computation of time in Chap. I.

ten days the eclipses of the sun and moon return in the same
order and magnitude. Among the Brahmins of the palace one
is chosen to take care of the water-clock which is placed there.
It consists of a large vessel full of water, upon which a little
cup perforated at the bottom is made to float. By degrees the
cup fills with water, and at length sinks, when another cup of
the same size is put on the water, and when this sinks, a third,
and so throughout the day. The period marked by the sinking of the cup may be called the Burmese hour, and as each
cup in succession goes down, a certain number of strokes are
given with a hammer upon a great plate of brass according to
the hour. The number of the hours is seventy, which are
equally divided between the day and night. But as the length
of the days and nights varies in different parts of the year,
therefore the cups are made of different sizes, so that those
which are used in the nigh at the winter solstice mark the
hours of the day in the summer. Both day and night are
divided into four equal parts, and at the end of each quarter
whether of the day or night, a man, by order of the Brahmin,
ascends the belfry that stands in the great court of the palace,
and strikes alternately the bell and a great drum to indicate
the quarters and the number of the hour.[1]

93. The Burmese week, like ours, has seven days, and they
have the same names as with us ; that is, they are called after
the planets, the first day being the day of the sun, the second
the day of the moon, and so on. The months are lunar, consisting alternately of twenty-nine and thirty days ; but as
twelve of these months do not make a solar year, an inter-
calary month is added every third year. The first day of the
year is our twelfth of April; but the year is not supposed to
begin with the morning of this day, but either then, or at
mid-day, or six hours after mid-day, according to the moment
when the sun finishes its course through the ecliptic, for the
Brahmins well know that its annual revolution is accomplished
in 365 days and about a quarter.

The beginning of the new year is always announced by firing

---

[1] There are sixty, not seventy divisions, in the Burmese day. A bell and
drum, of the kind described, taken from the King's Palace, are preserved in the
Phayre Museum at Rangoon.

a cannon, and the Burmese assert that at this moment a great Nat descends amongst them, for they believe that every year has its tutelary Nat. During the three days before the commencement of the new year, or, as they say, before the descent of the Nat, all except the Talapoins, both men and women, divert themselves by throwing water at each other till everybody is wet from head to foot. Even strangers are not spared on these occasions, and the only way to avoid being wet through is to stay at home during the whole time.

94. With respect to the seasons, temperature and air of the Burmese Empire, we must distinguish between the kingdoms of Ava and Pegù. In the latter, which extends from Tavai to the city of Pron [Prome], the south-west and north-east winds divide the year between them so as to cause but two seasons, the rainy and the dry season. From the end of April or the beginning of May to July after the vernal equinox, the dense vapours drawn by the sun from the sea, descend by the force of attraction to the earth ; and meeting with the immense forests that are spread over every part of Pegù, and with the chain of mountains, which, running from east to west, separate Pegù from Ava in the vicinity of Pron, they become condensed and discharge themselves in the most violent rains, which fall without intermission during the whole of this time. At the beginning and end of the wet season the rains are accompanied with tremendous thunder and lightning and violent winds, and great damage is sometimes done, and even lives are lost by the thunderbolts falling upon elevated buildings. On the contrary, after the autumnal equinox, when the sun retires from the southern hemisphere, it draws after it the vapours of the sea, and thus from the end of October or the beginning of November to April, during which time the north-east wind prevails, the season is perfectly dry. Some years there is a little rain in February, but it is very gentle and never lasts long.

95. But in the kingdom of Ava, that is, from the city of Pron, to 26° or 27° north latitude, there may be reckoned three seasons, the cold, the hot, and the rainy season. The four months of November, December, January, and February form the winter ; from the beginning of March to the end of June the heats prevail, and the other four months are the season of

rain. The cold is felt in these parts merely at night and in the mornings, and is more sensible in Ava, which lies to the north, than in Pegù. Heavy mists fall in November and December, but snow is altogether unknown. The only thing that can give the Burmese any idea of the ice and snow of our northern climates are the hail-storms that occur sometimes about the end of April or the beginning of May. In these countries the winter is the most delightful portion of the year, for this is the season for gathering in the rice and all other kinds of grain and pulse. During these months more than at any other time, all sorts of herbs and plants flourish, not merely such as are natural to the climate, but also those that have been imported from abroad, as lettuces, cabbages, turnips, radishes, love-apples, etc.

96. Summer is not, as in Europe, ushered in by the beautiful spring, but the transition from cold to heat is very sudden. In March and April, at which time the cold with us is still very sensible, the greatest heat is experienced in the Burmese Empire, and the thermometer will sometimes stand at what we call the most extraordinary degrees of heat. The trees, which in some parts of Europe only begin to show their leaves in May, in this country shed them during the same month, but it is only instantly to be clothed with new ones ; for here, as in all other parts of the torrid zone, the trees are always green, and though they change their foliage every year, it is done with such rapidity that the new leaves may be said to bud forth before the old ones have fallen off. The kingdom of Ava, although situated more to the north than Pegù, is nevertheless subject to the greatest and longest heats. In the last mentioned of these kingdoms, at the end of April or the beginning of May the rains begin, and thus the atmosphere is purged of the suffocating vapours, and the earth is moistened so as to render the heat more supportable. But in Ava, after a little rain that falls in May, and there are some years when even this does not come, the south-west wind, by reason of the chains of mountains, which stretching in a northerly direction divide the Siamese from the Burmese, and Aracan from Pegù and the kingdom of Ava, taking a course from south to north, carries away all the clouds, and thus deprives the earth of the moisture necessary to cool it till about the middle of August. But at

the same time these same clouds cause the most violent rains in the forests of the Sciam, and in the mountains of Azen [Assam] and Thibet, whence the waters descending produce those inundations of the river Ava which, during June, July, and August cover the lands in its vicinity; and like the floods of the Nile to Egypt, are the source of their fertility. During these months the water sometimes rises to the height of thirty-two feet above its level in February, when it is lowest, and the river is so much extended on each side of its usual bed that in some places it is not possible from one bank to see the other. The waters are generally drained off towards the end of October, when the soil thus fattened by the deposit they have made is wonderfully fertile, and pulse and plants of every kind thrive to perfection in it.

97. The waters of the river Ava have the property of petrifying wood, bones of animals, etc., but this not in every part, but only in some particular spots at a great distance from Rangoon.

98. Although the Burmese do not make use of bread, nevertheless they sow wheat in the places that have been inundated by the river. The greater part of it is carried to Rangoon, where it is either made into bread for the foreigners who reside there, or else into ship-biscuits. Even in the capital great quantities of biscuit are used; for the Mandarins and military officers carry it with them in their expeditions, both on account of the facility of transporting it, and because they have found by experience that it has more substance than rice.

99. After a little rain which falls in May and the beginning of June, and which is called the first rain, two months and a half pass over without any more in the kingdom of Ava. But from the middle of August to the beginning of October, what are called the second rains fall, but not always in the same abundance, and immediately the sowing of rice, cotton, sesame, indigo, etc., begins. It sometimes happens that these second do not come at all, or are not sufficiently plentiful, and then a great scarcity is always the consequence. But still it is never so serious as sometimes in Europe, for Pegù, where the rain always falls in such abundance, is thereby rendered so fertile as to be able to furnish rice to supply the wants of Ava. Nor are

the inhabitants of the latter kingdom entirely devoid of resources when the rice-crop fails, for they make a species of
polenta with wheat cleaned from the outer skin, milk and
palm-sugar, which has a good flavour and is very nourishing.
They will also mix with what rice they have several other sorts
of grain, the seeds of vegetables when they are ripe, and even
wild fruits, and the roots of different trees steeped and afterwards boiled in water. They have besides begun for some
years past to cultivate the *maniocco*, which does not require
much humidity, and will grow in any soil, whence it is well
adapted for supplying their wants.

100. From Rangoon to Amarapura, the air along the course
of the river is generally salubrious, though sometimes new
comers are attacked with fevers; but they may easily be cured
by using bark, and it is only in certain places that there is any
danger of taking them. But in Aracan, the island of Negraglia
[Negrais], to the north of Amarapura, and particularly in the
forests and mountains of the Sciam, the air is generally bad,
and all who venture to stay in these places soon contract
malignant fevers, which quickly prove fatal.

101. Those who live on the banks of the river are provided
by it with water for drinking; but in the interior there are
wells, which mostly furnish good water. To raise the water
from the wells they make use of a lever, to one end of which
the bucket is fixed by means of a long cane, and to the other a
heavy weight. A man, standing on the brink of the well,
plunges the bucket into it, and this when full is raised without
any labour by the action of the weight at the other end of the
lever. The buckets made use of in this machine are of wood,
or else they are large jars; but the most common ones are
made of thin strips of bamboo woven together, covered with
that species of varnish of which we have spoken before.

102. In this country also, as well as in all other places of the
torrid zone, no inconvenience is experienced from living in the
neighbourhood of lakes. For the action of the sun, by rarifying
the atmosphere, weakens or altogether destroys the pernicious
properties of the exhalations which in Europe are the cause of
malaria.

103. The Burmese have no coined money, but in their commercial transactions they make use of gold and silver bullion.[1] Hence they are obliged to employ scales in all payments. The principal weight that they have, and to which all others are referred, is the ticale : it is equal to about half an ounce. The gold and silver used is sometimes quite pure, but ordinarily it is mixed with some alloy ; and of course its value depends on its degree of purity. But the inferior money of Amarapura and Rangoon is lead : its value is not by any means fixed, but varies according to its abundance or scarcity. Sometimes a ticale of silver, with a portion of alloy, is equal to 200 ticali of lead, sometimes to a thousand, and even to more. In Tavai and Merghi [Mergui] pieces of tin with the impression of a cock, which is the Burmese arms, are used for money.

104. And this will be the place for speaking of the manner in which gold and silver are here procured. There are many torrents, the sands of which yield gold. At a place near Rangoon, between the river Cittaun [Sittang] and that of Pegù or Bagò, and at another above the city of Pron [Prome], gold-sands are also found, as well as to the east and the north of the city of Ava. Hence we may reasonably infer, that in the hills and mountains from which these torrents descend there must be veins of this metal, and these very rich. In other places the marks are still more evident, but no one ventures to

---

[1] There was a coinage in Arakan and Tenasserim. In Captain Cox's time the King of Burma made an attempt to establish one. In the sixteenth century, a mixture of copper and lead, called *gansa*, apparently stamped, was used in Pegù. On these subjects, see Yule, p. 258, and for statements of the old travellers about the foreign trade, see his Chap. VIII. Fredericke, Fitch, and Balbi all deal with these matters. The present tikal is equal to about 3½ pounds.

open a mine, as he would have to suffer so many vexations from the Court, that he would soon be obliged to abandon the enterprise to his cost. But the little gold that is thus collected is far from being sufficient for the Burmese, who use great quantities of this metal, not only in their bracelets, ear-rings, and other ornaments, which persons of both sexes are accustomed to wear, but much more for gilding the convents of the Talapoins, the public porticos, and particularly the pagodas, which, being exposed to the rain and the action of the air, soon lose their gilding, and are therefore continually requiring fresh gold to repair them. To supply this demand, gold is imported from the Malay coast, from China, and other places.[1]

105. The silver is drawn from the mines which exist to the east of Canton [Kaungton near Bhamo], towards the Chinese province of Junan [Yunnan], the country of the Sciam. Although these mines are in the Burmese territories they are worked by the Chinese. They produce an abundance of silver, which would be more than enough for the wants of the inhabitants, did not the Chinese on the one hand, and on the other the foreign merchants who frequent the ports of Pegù, notwithstanding the severe laws forbidding its exportation, carry great quantities out of the Empire. Near these mines crystals of different colours are found, with which the Chinese make little idols and other toys. There is one species of a green colour, thought to be the emerald.[2]

106. The Burmese are all given to the follies of alchemy, and there is not one of them who does not believe in the existence of the philosopher's stone, and in the possibility of converting the baser metals into gold and silver by means of certain preparations.[3] The following instance may give an idea of their

---

[1] All this is true of the present day.

[2] Or perhaps jade, for which there is a great demand in China.

[3] These experiments are still common. In his chapter on Making Gold, Shway Yoe states that the last great fire in Rangoon was caused by a searcher after secrets capsizing his crucible, while suddenly pouring in mercury, at three in the morning, which the horoscope had given as a favourable hour. In my judicial work at Bombay I have seen cases where many people were induced by vagabond rogues to part with silver to be transmuted into gold. Alchemy was introduced into Europe from Arabia, and similar impostures were common. Like the Burman Emperor, our Edward III. was persuaded by Raymond Lully

folly in this respect. Among other things which can effect this transmigration, they give the first place to the *ajechè*, which signifies congealed or petrified wine ; and of the efficacy of this they are so persuaded, that the Emperor and his children have often begged foreigners to procure it for them. The Emperor, the Mandarins and numbers of other rich men spend their time in making chemical preparations, and performing experiments for procuring the wished for transmutation ; and it is not a rare occurrence for people so totally to ruin themselves, as they have done sometimes in Europe, as to want the very necessaries of life, by spending all their property in these chimerical pursuits. There have not been wanting impostors to turn these prejudices of their countrymen to their own advantage, by pretending to transform lead into silver, and copper into gold, deceiving the spectators by mere sleight of hand. Among others, there was one who succeeded in deceiving the Emperor, the royal family, and the principal Mandarins ; but this trick was in the end discovered. It consisted in conducting away the lead at the moment of fusion, by means of secret tubes connecting with the vessel, and at the same moment introducing silver through other tubes, so that a real change seemed to have taken place. But at last, not being able to restore the silver he had borrowed from various people, his imposture was discovered, and he paid the forfeit of his cheat by the loss of his head. Still it was publicly reported that he was put to death, not on account of his deceit, but because the Emperor wished to be the sole possessor of the secret, which he had drawn from him by threats and presents.

107. The Burmese have both an internal and external commerce. In the kingdom of Ava, and indeed throughout the whole Empire, except in the great cities, the commerce for the necessaries of life, as food and clothing, is rather a barter than buying or selling. The inhabitants of the places abounding in rice or cotton go to exchange their commodities with those, the produce of whose fields is gingilì, tobacco, indigo, etc. In

---

to treat the art as a source of wealth ; but the frauds that ensued led to the Statute of 5 Henry IV. c. 4, which made it felony 'to multiply gold or silver, or to use the art of multiplication.' The 'Chanounes Yemannes Tale' in Chaucer is a satire on the science of alchemy, and full of details of the art.

all the villages of Ava rice is the ordinary commodity bartered for fish, vegetables, and other things necessary for food. But the Sciam [Shan] are those who carry on the most extended internal commerce, as it is they who sell throughout all the provinces of the Empire that coarse tea of which we have spoken, under the name of lapech, as being used at funerals, in lawsuits, and in making contracts.

108. The external commerce of the Burmese is with various nations. The Chinese of Junan [Yunnan], coming down by Canton [Kaungton] and along the great river Ava, bring to the Burmese capital, in great boats, several of the commodities of their country, as wrought silks, paper, tea, various kinds of fruit, and other trifles, and they return laden with cotton, raw silk, salt, birds' feathers, and that black varnish which, as we have said, is distilled from a tree ; this, prepared and purified, is the celebrated commodity known by the name of Chinese varnish.

The excellence of the ports of Pegù, and the richness of the productions of this Empire, attract merchants with their vessels, not only from all parts of India, but also from China and Arabia. The river of Rangoon, the mouth of which is the same as that of the river Siriam, affords a station for ships, at once easy of access and defended from the wind. The river of Bassino forms a harbour which is still more secure, and from which ships may sail at all seasons, which is not the case at Rangoon, by reason of the south-west wind which often prevails. The dangerous shallows and formidable calms of Martaban hinder any but small barks from entering its port. Tavai has a commodious port, and vessels may ride at anchor in the mouth of its river, under the shelter of two or three small islands. The sea in the vicinity of Merghi [Mergui] is full of little islands, among which, as in secure roads, vessels may winter, sheltered from every wind, or be repaired in the greatest security.

But of all the ports of Pegù that of Rangoon [1] is the prin-

---

[1] Rangoon was founded by Alompra in 1755.—Phayre, p. 157. Symes estimated the population at 30,000, and says it had long been the asylum of insolvent debtors from India, and was crowded with foreigners of desperate fortunes, who supported themselves by petty trade. In 1814 Mrs. Judson writes, ' There are no English families in Rangoon;' and again, ' With the exception of two or three sea-captains, who now and then call on us, we never see a European face.'

cipal, in fact it is the only one of importance; for this is one of the most populous cities of the kingdom, the residence of a governor and viceroy, and it has an easy and continual communication with the capital and other principal places of the Empire, by means of the river, along which all their various productions are brought to it, to be again disposed of to the merchants, both native and foreign, with whom the city is crowded. Until the year 1790, Bassino enjoyed the same privileges, but when it was given as an appanage to one of the children of the Emperor, the Mandarins who were sent to govern it committed so many and such cruel injustices and vexations, that no merchant dared to approach the place. It may therefore be said that the commerce is entirely concentrated in Rangoon, where it is exercised by the inhabitants, as well as by a number of Mohammedan Moors, some Armenians, and a few English, French, and Portuguese, who have taken up their residence there. The ships that come from China and the Malay coast, which latter are for the most English, bring in cargoes of areca and other merchandise, as silks, nankeen, porcelain, tea, etc. The commodities, however, which have the best sale at Rangoon, and return the highest profit, are the sugar and muslins of Bengal, the linen of Madras, and particularly the white and coloured handkerchiefs, which are here universally used for covering the head. Sometimes also vessels arrive from the Isle of France, laden with merchandise that yields an exorbitant profit, such as pottery, muskets, lookingglasses, and articles of iron and brass, with woollen cloths of various colours, which are eagerly sought after in this country, particularly when they are of two colours. For although they are not used for clothing, still they are in great request as coverlets at night, as also for wearing on the shoulders in the daytime like a mantle. The English ships also bring in quantities of these stuffs. Such are the principal commodities brought by sea, though there are some others of minor importance, consisting chiefly of various drugs and spices, raisins, almonds, coffee, and other natural productions of Persia and Arabia, which are brought by the ships of the Burmese themselves.

109. No ship is allowed to enter Rangoon without being provided with a pilot acquainted with the navigation of the

river; for the city is fifteen leagues from the mouth. After
having cast anchor, the captain of the ship, or some one of its
officers, must present himself at the Rondai, which, as we have
said, is a large hall where the Mandarins assemble to administer
justice, to declare the nation to which the ship belongs, the
place it has come from, and the merchandise it carries. If
afterwards anything is found not mentioned in this declaration,
it is considered as contraband. The ship is then disarmed;
all the cannons, muskets, and ammunition, and indeed even
the rudder is carried to land. All merchandise upon entering
pays a duty of twelve and a half per cent.; of which ten per
cent. goes to the Emperor; the rest is divided among all the
Mandarins in Rangoon.

110. The commodities which the Burmese export in return
for those just mentioned are lac, catechù [cutch], and isinglass,
when the ships are destined to China or the Malay coast. The
lac and catechù are used by the Chinese in their colours, the
isinglass for glue. But if the vessels are bound for the west,
that is, for Bengal, the coast of Coromandel, the Isle of France,
etc., the cargo generally consists of vegetable oil, petroleum,
and, above all, teak-wood, either as masts for ships, or cut into
planks of different sizes. Indeed it is for this wood, more than
anything else, that vessels of every nation come to Pegù from
all parts of India. It is found also in Bombay, but in small
quantities, and is excessively dear; whereas in Pegù and Ava
there are such immense forests of it, that it can be sold to as
many ships as arrive at a moderate price.

This wood, while it does not quickly decay, is very easily
wrought, and very light. Cases have occurred of ships made
of it and laden with it, which have been filled with water, but
yet did not sink. Hence all the ships that come to Pegù
return with cargoes of this wood, which is employed in common
houses, but particularly in ship-building.

111. Most of the ships that arrive in these ports are here
careened and refitted; and there are besides two or three
English and French shipbuilders established at Rangoon.
One reason of this is the prohibition that exists of carrying
the specie out of the Empire. For, as merchants after selling
their cargo and taking in another of teak-wood, generally

have some money remaining in their hands, they are obliged to employ it in building a new ship. Though perhaps this is not the only motive for building vessels in Rangoon; but the quantity of teak and other kinds of wood with which the neighbouring forests abound may also have a great influence in this way.

112. If the port of Rangoon entices strangers to build ships there, it also obliges them to sail as soon as possible. For there is a species of worm, bred in the waters of the river, which penetrates into the interior of the wood, and eats it away in such a manner that the vessel is exposed to the greatest danger, since the holes formed by these worms being hidden, cannot easily be stopped up. They attack every species of wood except ebony and tamarind, which are so hard that they are used to make mallets with which carpenters drive their chisels.[1]

---

[1] The reader will find some account of the earlier commerce in the Introduction. A separate treatise would alone do justice to the modern expansions of import and export trade, following the British conquests, the making of roads and railways, and the establishment of steam navigation along the coasts and rivers.

BURMESE CODE

CHAPTER XXIV

ABSTRACT OF THE BURMESE CODE ENTITLED DAMASAT ;
OR THE GOLDEN RULE [1]

THIS Code is divided into ten volumes, which treat of everything relating to donations, heirships, and all other matters
under the jurisdiction of the courts.

Vol. I.

The first volume contains the origin of the Damasat, and
certain rules to be observed by judges in the performance of
their duties.

It relates that in the days of the Emperor Mahasamatà, there

---

[1] Sangermano has the honour of being the first to translate any of the numerous codes of law found in Burma, written on palm-leaves. Symes noticed the
resemblances with the famous Code of Manu. ' I was so fortunate,' he writes,
' as to procure a translation of the most remarkable passages, which were rendered
into Latin by Padre Vincentius Sangermano, and, to my great surprise, I found
it to correspond closely with a Persian version of the Arracan Code which is
now in my possession,' p. 303. Cox carried away some copies. Crawfurd, at
p. 413, notices the divergence from the Hindu Code : and it would seem that
the Dhammathat was not used as a guide to the law in the part of Burma then
under our Government. In 1847 Dr. Richardson printed and translated the
very voluminous Menu Kyay Dhammathat, which has ever since been used in the
Courts. It was composed in 1756 by the Minister of Military Works, by order
of Alompra. In 1877 the Burmese and Pali texts of several other Codes were
printed. Between 1882 and 1884 several translations appeared in my *Notes on
Buddhist Law*. Dr. Forchhammer also printed and translated the Code of
King Wagaru of Martaban, whose reign began A.D. 1280, from a palm-leaf
manuscript, being itself a translation by the Talaing jurist Buddhaghosa into Burmese from the Talaing language. This publication has been adopted by the
University of Oxford as a text-book in the Burmese language. In 1884 the
same learned scholar's *Jardine Prize Essay* on the sources of Burmese Law
was published. The subject is referred to in his two Notes on Early History
and his report on Literature. All these works were printed at the Rangoon

lived a famous hermit, who, having taken up his abode in one of the caverns of the great mountain Emauntà [Himavantâ], which lies to the north of the southern island Zabudibà, occupied himself in the contemplation of those things that prepare man for the Niban. Whilst in this retirement, the solitary was tempted by the daughter of a Nat, who, placing herself before the door of the cavern, begged with prayers and tears to be admitted. Moved by pity the hermit at length consented to allow her to remain for one only night; but the beauty and arts of the young Nat made such an impression upon him, that, relaxing something of his attention to his sublime meditations, he married her, and had by her two sons; one of whom he named Menù, the other Menò, and both of whom afterwards became famous for their sanctity and learning. They, despising the kingdom that their father promised to them, retired to the mountain Emauntà, where, by the practice of meditation, they became Zian; by which just men acquire the property of transporting themselves flying through the air to any

Government Press, and they make up the literature of an obscure branch of learning. In the *Notes on Buddhist Law* and the *Prize Essay*, the many more or less equivalent Hindu texts found in Yajnyavalkya, Manu, Vishnu, etc., are cited; and the reasons given for the proposition that these Dharmashasters are based on the law of India are now, I believe, accepted by all scholars. They contain, however, additions from several sources, viz., 1. The older customs of the Burmese when they were in the same stage of civilisation as the Chins are now. 2. Decisions of Burmese and Talaing kings and judges. 3. Quotations from the sacred books of the Buddhists. Buddhists had some natural difficulty in understanding who the traditional Manu was; and historical memory being weak, the Burmans have forgotten the difference between the lawyer who got the title of Manu in the seventeenth century A.D., and wrote the Manu râjâ Dhammathat, and the more ancient and mythical Manu of India. In the same way the Buddhaghosa who translated King Wagaru's Code in the fifteenth century A.D. is forgotten, and confounded with the renowned divine of the same name, who, about 450 A.D., is said to have returned from Ceylon. The jurist only translated the Talaing Manu into Burmese: but it has gained much in sanctity and importance by having become connected with the greatest theologian of the Buddhist Church.—*Prize Essay*, pp. 65, 75, 77, 107. A third period begins with Alompra, 1750 A.D. The latest Dhammathats reject the Rishi Manu altogether: the rulings of the Wagaru are retained, but it is now Buddha who pronounced them at the beginning of all things. Our statutes call this system Buddhist Law; and the people have a general belief that these Codes are part of their religion, so that they are willingly accepted as authority. Dr. Forchhammer believed that they were introduced prior to the tenth cen-

place they may wish. They then transported themselves into various parts of the world; till at length arriving at the great chain of the mountains Zacchiavalà, they found the code of laws here set down, carved in capital letters upon the rock. They made a faithful copy of them, which, upon their return, they presented as an inestimable treasure to the great Emperor Mahasamatà; who being informed of the wonderful way in which they had been discovered, commanded them to be observed by all his subjects. The successors of Mahasamatà having added some few laws to this code, they were afterwards reduced to a more perfect form, and enriched with various ordinances of one of the princes of the Nat. Finally, this code, which was at first written in the Palì tongue, and kept in the island of Ceylon, was at length brought into the Burmese Empire by a certain Budelagosa [Buddhaghosa], and translated into the vulgar language. And such is the origin of the Damasat.

After this there follow some admonitions and counsels to

---

tury A.D., from Southern India into Indian colonies on the coast of Burma, and being adopted by the Talaings, became the law of the united Burmese and Talaing dominions from the eleventh to the sixteenth century. The possibility need not be excluded of Hindu Codes having been compiled in the Sanskrit language at the Courts of ancient kings of Prome, and perhaps also at Pagan, although no trace of such works has yet been discovered. In Alompra's reign there was a great literary and religious revival : the untractable Talaings and Arakanese had been subdued, and codified laws became more important in so great an empire.

Dr. Forchhammer inclined to the opinion (controverted by Dr. Jolly in an Appendix to his *Tagore Law Lectures*, 1883) that these Burman Manava-Shasters are based on originals older than those found in India. In discussing his views with me, he used to urge that it was the policy of Buddhism to publish its rules to the people, of which the memorials of Asoka are examples, which contrast with Brahminical procedure : that in the Buddhist, Brahminical, and Jain Jurisprudences, the rule of law is the constant, unvarying quantity, the theology the varying, and therefore, presumably, the modern ; and that the great Buddhist States of India must have required a civil law in accordance with their religion. He placed a high value on the many facts and learned arguments adduced by Colonel Sykes in his *Notes on the State of India*, as proving the antiquity of Buddhism, and its becoming the established cult of many kingdoms of old time in India.

Mahasamata is the designation of a just man, an embryo Buddha, selected according to the Milinda Panha, by the original inhabitants of the world, to settle their disputes. For his connection with Manu, see Forchhammer's Preface to iv. *Notes on Buddhist Law.*

the Mandarins and judges for the regulation of their conduct; such as not to yield to the movements of anger and hatred; not to be blinded by the presents of clients, nor to propose in a judgment the hurt or ruin of any one, but only the fulfilling all the dispositions of the law; to make themselves masters of the statutes and laws contained in this code, before attempting to sit in judgment. To judges who act in this manner the esteem and praises of men are held out as a reward, as well as happiness in future lives; but if they do otherwise they will be hated by all, and after death will be condemned to the abodes of the wicked.

When judges and Mandarins are going to enter into the tribunal called Jon [Yon, *i.e.* Court], they must raise up their eyes and hands to heaven. And when they are in the tribunal, they should not be ashamed to ask the opinion and advice of subordinate ministers, as to the best and speediest means of satisfying the parties in a lawsuit. They must neither in their countenance nor speech show any regard to the wealth or dignity of either party, but must listen impartially to both; nor must they be offended if sometimes harsh words are used by the litigants towards them; and with the greatest prudence and sagacity they must hear all that is said either by the persons themselves concerned in the cause, or their lawyers. This is all that is worth extracting from the first volume of the Damasat.

Vol. II.

I.

Of donations.

There are three sorts of donations. 1. Many things are given as a mark of affection. 2. Others are given through fear; and, 3, Others are given from a religious motive, as, for example, alms to the Talapoins. Donations of the first class may be demanded back again, if it should happen that the giver becomes extremely poor; in which case the receiver is obliged to restore the gifts, if they are still in existence; but if they no longer exist, he is not bound to restore anything. But this last regulation does not hold with regard to the second kind of donations, such as are those exacted by robbers, as these may always be demanded, and the receivers are obliged to make restitution, even though what they received is no longer in existence. But all things that are given from a religious motive are alienated for ever from the donor, even though he should fall into extreme poverty; for these are not considered as presents of pure liberality, but as acts of reciprocal donation; since, according to the laws of Godama, all that during this life is given to the Talapoins and the poor, purchases in future lives many advantages and great felicity.

II.

Of promises.

Promises are of two kinds; for sometimes they are made by a person under the influence of fear or anger; at other times calmly and considerately. Those of the first description are not binding, since the anger and perturbation of him who made the promise, hindered him from properly reflecting on what he was saying. But things promised in the other way become the lawful property of the person who received the promise. But it must be here observed, that promises rank among the seven things which cannot be reclaimed after the death of the emperor under whom they were given or promised. And these are deposits, pledges, money paid unjustly by litigants in a lawsuit, things taken by force, or seized upon without a just title, promises, things secretly stolen, and such as having been abandoned by one possessor have been occupied by another. All these by the prescription of the laws remain to the actual possessor, even though he have procured them unjustly.

III.

Of the division of a man's property among his surviving wives.

Wives may be of four different conditions; as they are the daughters of Mandarins, Brahmins, merchants, or agriculturists. A wife who is not of one of these classes cannot have any share in the inheritance. If a man have four wives of these different states, his goods after his death must be divided into ten parts;

P

and of these four go to the daughter of the Mandarin, three to the daughter of the Brahmin, two to the daughter of the merchant, and one to the daughter of the agriculturist. If there are more than four wives, the division must be made in the above proportions. The wife who does not belong to any of these four classes has no pretensions to any part of the inheritance, and can only retain what she has received from her husband during his lifetime.

IV.

Of the seven kinds of slaves.

There are seven species of slaves who are bound to render personal services to their masters. 1. Those who are bought with money. 2. The children of a female slave living in a family. 3. Slaves by birth, that is, those whose parents are slaves. 4. Slaves given as presents. 5. Those who make themselves slaves to deliver themselves from some trouble. 6. Those who in times of scarcity are dependent on others for support. 7. Those who hire themselves out for daily or monthly labour. There are also seven sorts of persons from whom no menial service can be demanded; and these are the freedmen of Talapoins and Brahmins; those who having been slaves, have, with the consent of their masters, put on the habit of a Talapoin, these, even if they afterwards lay aside the habit, cannot again be reduced to slavery; the Brahmins and observers of the law; those who are loaded with debt; and finally, those who belong to others under the title either of habitation or possession.

V.

Of the children who participate in the paternal inheritance.

There are six descriptions of children among whom the paternal inheritance is to be divided. 1. The first-born, that is, the son of the first wife. 2. The children of legitimate children, or grand-children. 3. The children of inferior wives or concubines. 4. The children had by any female slave. 5. Adopted children. 6. Those boys or girls, who, having been received into a house, have been brought up there as children of the family. There are also six descriptions of children who are excluded from the inheritance. 1. Those who, having been consigned to others to be educated, grow up under their care. 2. Boys or girls bought with money, for these, even though they have been looked upon by the father as his children, cannot pretend to a share in the inheritance. 3. Step-sons. 4. Disobedient children. 5. Children had by a prostitute, or woman of ill fame. 6. Children had by a woman who, constrained by necessity, has prostituted herself. These can retain nothing but what the father has given in his lifetime.

Children have no dominion over the substance of the family before the death of the father.

Upon the death of slaves, all their rights over their children, or anything else that they have possessed, descend to their respective masters.

VI.

Of the division of the inheritance among children.

The son of the first wife has four parts; the children of the inferior wives or concubines one part; the children had by slaves have only half a share, and this does not come to them till the death of the mother, as they have no title but that of maternal inheritance. And according to this proportion the property is divided if there be more children.

If a man has had no children, his substance is divided among his relations, and those who have been brought up in his house as children. But in case there are no relations, it goes to the royal treasury.

VII.

Of the division of the family substance in case of divorce.

If a man and wife separate by mutual consent, the family substance must be divided equally between them. And if they afterwards agree to reunion they ought to go to live either in the house of the wife's father, or in another taken in lease.

If a girl, who has been married to a man with the consent and will of her parents, afterwards desires to be separated from him, the husband may take possession of her dower, and even sell her for a slave.

If a woman after the solemnisation of her marriage, but before its consummation, has connection with another man, she loses her dower, which goes to the husband. But if after the consummation of the marriage she commits adultery, she must pay to her husband twice the value of her dower; but may then, if she please, go to live with the man with whom she has committed adultery. But if the dower was very small, the husband may sell her for a slave and retain the price.

If a man after his marriage goes to live in another place, and for the space of three years does not send a letter, or money, or anything else to his wife, she is considered as free, and may enter into another marriage.

VIII.

When parents give their daughter in marriage to a man, who has represented himself as of a noble and illustrious lineage, and it afterwards appears that this was false, they may take back their daughter; and in this case the parents must have exacted the dower brought by the husband before the consummation of the marriage, for if they have neglected this they cannot afterwards exact it as a debt. When a man marries a girl, with the condition of going to live in the house of his father-in-law, to assist him in his labours, he must remain with him three years, but after this time may go and live elsewhere.

If parents, through fear, give their daughter to a Mandarin, they may demand her back if their fear should cease, nor can he refuse to surrender her. But if they have given her, not through fear, but of their own will, they cannot demand her restoration. Parents may give their daughter to a man who has business with them. If a girl falls dangerously ill, and her parents agree to give her to a physician if he cures her, they are obliged to keep their promise; or if they will not give him their daughter, they must pay him the price of her body. Finally, if a girl secretly, and without the knowledge of her parents, contracts marriage, the parents are obliged, in order to save her from infamy, to have the marriage performed before legal witnesses.

IX.

When a girl promised in marriage to a man dies before the solemnisation of the nuptials, the parents ought to use their endeavours to unite their second daughter with their proposed son-in-law, and even to employ menaces to induce her compliance. But if she absolutely refuses her consent, and they have no other daughter, the half of the dower, which was to have been given with the deceased, must be paid to the man.

X.

When a man and wife separate by mutual consent, the household goods are equally divided, and both retain their respective dowers. The sons belong to the father and the daughters to the mother; but still they may follow which of them they please. If it should happen that the wife had maintained the husband, the property is divided into three parts, of which two belong to the wife and one to the husband; but if the husband has maintained the wife, he takes the two parts, and the wife the remaining one. If at the separation the daughter follows the father, he may sell her for a slave, but then he must give half the price to the mother; and the right of the mother is the same over a son who has followed her. If the wife dies after she and her husband have left the house of her father, the husband is heir to all she possessed; but if she dies whilst they are yet living with her parents, the husband inherits nothing of her property.

XI.

Parents may disinherit disobedient children and expel them from their houses; and if these secretly carry away anything, they may be punished as thieves.

All the property which has been gained by a son during the lifetime of his father, must upon the death of the latter be put into the common stock to be divided according to the laws among the heirs.

If a man has become rich and powerful through the favour of others, he ought out of gratitude not only to show respect and honour to his benefactor, but also to supply all his wants in case that he falls into poverty, and if he neglects these duties the judge may give to the benefactor one half of his goods.

Such children as do not perform the above mentioned duties to their parents, or refuse to support them when in want, may be deprived of all their possessions and exiled into distant countries.

If a man do an injury to his father or mother-in-law he may be expelled by them from their house, into which he is not again to be admitted till he has humbly asked pardon for his offence. And if he lift his hand against them he may be despoiled of all he possesses and driven out of the house. Finally, those who do not honour the aged shall be condemned to pay to those whom they have offended the sum of fifty ounces of silver.

XII.

If the husband brings with him to the house of his wife a female slave, whom he afterwards makes his concubine, she must be made free at his death, and if she have had a daughter by him she belongs to the mother.

But if it be a slave of the wife whom the husband has taken for his concubine, she will always be the property of the wife, even after the death of the husband, and though she may have had children by him. The slave of the wife or of the husband and wife conjointly must be liberated upon the death of the latter. And if the woman have had a son by the husband he must also be liberated with his mother, but if she has only had a daughter, then the daughter is made free, but the mother belongs to the husband.

Vol. III.

I.

Of heirships, and the seven ways of dividing them among the heirs.

The following are the cases provided for in this section. How property is to be divided : 1, after the death of the father, among the mother, the sons, and daughters; 2, among the mother and daughters; 3, after the death of the mother, between the father and son; 4, between the father and daughter; 5, after the death of both parents, among the sons and daughters; 6, what proportion of the sons of a former husband; or 7, the sons of a former wife must receive.

In the first case one of the sons is selected, generally the first-born, and he is to succeed the father in his military posts and all his other honours; the sword, horse, bed, and other utensils of his father belong to him, and he may choose one of the paternal fields for his share. All the other property is divided into four parts, of which three belong to the mother, and one to the children. The jewels, rings, and other ornaments given by the father to his children in his lifetime, do not enter into the property to be divided. The slaves are divided according to the above proportion, except that all the women belong to the mother.

II.

In the second case, when the property is to be divided between the mother and daughter, the latter retains all the jewels given her by her father, and besides receives a set of slaves, a yoke of oxen, and a certain portion of rice. All the rest goes to the mother. The reason of this provision is that the daughter remains in the power of the mother who may even sell her for a slave.

III.

In the third case, that is, after the death of the mother, when the division is to be made between the father, and a son residing with his wife in a separate house, the father has a right to the whole inheritance; but still he must give up to his son one field and a yoke of oxen, which, however, he may demand back again if he falls into poverty, provided they be in existence.

But when the father and daughter or daughters have to share the property, the latter, besides the jewels and ornaments they have already received, may claim ten cows, twenty goats, and all the female slaves employed in the domestic service of the house. All the rest belongs to the father.

IV.

After the death of both parents, when the inheritance has to be divided among the sons and daughters, the eldest takes two parts, the second one and a half, and the youngest only one part. And besides, the eldest son or daughter has an ox and a goat.

V.

If, after the death of his wife, a man marries again, the property is to be divided after his death among the children of the first marriage, only the second wife receives one share. But if there be no children, the surviving wife has all the inheritance ; and if she dies before her husband, all her property belongs to him.

But in case there be children from both these marriages, the following rules must be observed. If the property has very much increased since the second marriage, while before this was not the case, it must all be divided into eight parts, of which five are given to the second wife, two to her children, and the remaining one to the children of the former marriage. But if, on the contrary, the great increase took place before the second marriage, and ceased with it, after having set aside the five parts belonging to the first wife, two are given to her children, and one to those of the second wife.

VI.

As after the death of the parents, the eldest son or daughter naturally succeeds to their place, in order that they may always keep in mind the obligation they are under of taking care of their younger brothers and sisters, the laws decree that to them in particular a cow and a goat shall be given.

VII.

When the wife, after the death of her husband, contracts a second marriage, her goods, upon her death, provided the second husband has brought nothing to her house, and the whole property has belonged to her, are divided into four parts. Three are given to the children of her former marriage, and one goes to her second husband. But if there has been a notable increase in the property since her last marriage, the goods are divided into eight parts, and distributed as directed in § v.

In case of the death of both the husband and wife, the general rule is, that the property acquired during the first marriage goes to the children of that marriage, and that acquired afterwards to the children of the second.

These rules are also to be observed in dividing an inheritance among the children of the chief wife and those of the inferior ones. That is, the property received with the first wife descends to her children, and that acquired with the inferior wives to their respective children.

VIII.

The first-born son, after having received his portion of the inheritance, ought to take a paternal care of his younger brothers; and they, on their part, ought to honour and respect him as their father. If he usurps, or attempts to usurp, any thing belonging to his brothers, he forfeits his inheritance, and may moreover be punished by the judge. If the younger brothers wish to leave the paternal house, and to employ their property in alms-deeds, they are not to be hindered.

IX.

If the father, or both the father and mother, are reduced by sickness or old age to such a state as not to be able to do the duties required from them by the Emperor, nor to procure for themselves their necessary food and clothing, all their property is to be divided into two parts, of which one is assigned to the eldest son, if he be capable of succeeding to the duties of his father, who is thence to take care of his parents; he ought also to receive something valuable. The remaining part is subdivided into nine shares, of which one belongs to the eldest son; the remainder is again divided into nine parts, and one given to the younger son; the other eight parts are now again divided as before, one part is given to the eldest son, and the remaining parts to the younger. But if there be more than one younger brother, the division must be made as prudence may require.

X.

If it should happen that a woman, after giving birth to seven daughters, should have a son, the inheritance must be divided in the following manner. The son, although the last-born, must have the same as his eldest sister, the second and third daughters have two shares each more than the fourth and fifth, who have a share and a half more than the sixth and seventh; and the latter are to receive one share each.

In general, the heirs who are on the spot must claim their share in an inheritance between the seventh and thirtieth day after the death of their relation, and those who are at a distance, within the space of three months; after this period has expired they can have no further claim.

XI.

When a father has given one of his sons a sum of money for commerce, this is not mingled with the common stock at the death of the father, but continues to be the property of the son.*

XII.

When a girl contracts marriage contrary to, or without the consent of her parents, her property does not go to her husband at her death, but to her parents. And if a woman has married twice, once with and once without the consent of her parents, her dower then belongs to the children of the first marriage, to the exclusion of those of the second.

XIII.

If a man has had several wives, but only one son, his goods

---

* At present this is not the case. For now the gain alone belongs to the son, but the capital must be returned to the common inheritance.

at his death go to this only son, and the surviving wife has nothing. When there is no surviving child the inheritance is divided among the wives, in the manner before set down.

A hermaphrodite child cannot claim an equal share with the other brothers.

XIV.

Of the divisions of inheritances among Talapoins.

When a Talapoin dies, his relations can have no pretensions to his goods. Upon the death of a great Talapoin, all his furniture and utensils go to the next in dignity, or to his successor; the rest of his goods are divided into four parts, two of which are given to the second Talapoin, and the other two again divided into four parts, of which one is given to the Pazen, the remaining three to the other persons constituting the family.

XV.

Elder brothers have no right to anything that the younger gain by their industry or labour. When a husband dies without children, the wife has the whole inheritance. Before dividing a man's property among his heirs, his wife must take out sufficient to pay his debts, and for alms.

If a son who has married dies before his father has made a division of his property, his children can claim no part of the goods of their grandfather; though he may, with the advice of some prudent and aged persons, give to them a small share.

Vol. IV.

I.

There are four cases of fornication between a man and an unmarried woman. 1. When the girl consents to the violation. 2. When she refuses her consent. 3. When, although she consents, she is not of the same caste or condition as the man. 4. When she consents, and is of the same class. In the last case,

the parties ought to marry each other; in the third they must
be separated, and the man must pay the price of the body of
the woman. If the violation has been forcible, the man must
be punished in proportion to his crime ; and if death be the
consequence of his violence, he must pay to the parents of the
girl, ten times the price of her body.* But if the girl has given
her consent, there is no punishment for the man, even though
the girl should die in consequence.

All who co-operate in seducing girls are to be punished.

II.

A man may punish his wife in the following cases. 1. If she
is accustomed to drink wine. 2. If she is careless of her
domestic duties. 3. If she encourage any gallant. 4. If she is
fond of running about to other people's houses. 5. If she is
very often standing at the door or window of the house. 6.
If she is petulant, and quarrelsome with her husband. In like
manner it is lawful for husbands to punish those wives who are
very extravagant in dress or in eating, those who show a disregard of modesty, or a too great curiosity in looking about
them, and those who, by reason of their beauty, or of the property they have brought for their dower, are proud and overbearing. In these cases the husband must at first bear with his
wife patiently, and admonish her in the presence of others ; but
if she does not amend, he may then punish her and even beat
her. If after this she still continue in her evil courses, he may
put her away, making with her a division of the property.

III.

Of buying and selling.

There are two ways of selling anything. The first is by a
private agreement between the buyer and the seller; the second
is for some third person, having a competent knowledge of the
thing to be sold, to determine a price. The following articles,
however, cannot be lawfully offered for sale. Things that are

---

* At present, death is the punishment in this case.

a great way off; things which are indeed on the spot but are hidden; things of no value; and finally, stolen goods. When a person, after having made a purchase, discovers that he has paid an exorbitant price, he may return the article and reclaim the money, provided five days have not passed since the transaction; but after the fifth day, the sale stands good. Supposing that a person buys, for example, an ox or a horse, and after he has paid only a part of the price the animal dies, he is not obliged to pay the remainder.

IV.

Of those who cannot be admitted as witnesses.

In judging causes, the testimony of persons, respectable by their state in life and their wisdom, disinterested, and who believe in the merit of good works, ought to be received. But there are several persons whose testimony cannot be admitted. These are, those who do not believe in the merit of good works, such as trade with other people's goods, the parties interested in the cause, as well as their relations, friends and enemies, great talkers, sick persons, old men, children, overbearing men, public singers, dancing girls, women who roam about or are of ill fame, goldsmiths, painters, blacksmiths, cobblers, those who are inclined to harbour hatred, asthmatic persons, persons of vile condition, gluttons, gamesters, choleric persons, thieves, physicians, those whose kindred and habitation are unknown, pregnant women and hermaphrodites. All these are incapacitated from giving testimony; though they may be allowed to do it with the consent of the parties. The judge also cannot appear as a witness. A witness too, otherwise unexceptionable, if, before appearing in court, he goes into the house of either of the parties, is thereby incapacitated; but this precaution does not affect persons of weight, as the Talapoins. If a person refuses the testimony of a witness who has all the qualities required by the law, he loses his cause; and the same is the case when a man will not produce his witnesses nor take the customary oath.

When one of the parties brings forward a witness, he is not

obliged to swear ; and when he takes the oath, he is not obliged to produce a witness. If a man before judgment has been pronounced goes to the house of the witness he loses his cause.

V.

Of the crimes a man may be guilty of towards married women, and their penalties.

If a man touch another's wife with his hands, or if he go to visit her when her husband is not at home, or walk with her in lonely places, or talk much with her, or place himself in the door-way, or on the stairs, or go into her bedchamber, he may be made to pay the half of the fine attached to the actual commission of adultery. But still it must be observed, that there must have been something in the character of the man to excite suspicion.

VI.

If a husband surprise a man in adultery with his wife, he may lawfully kill him. But if he have time to fly, and has got as far as the stairs, the husband cannot lawfully kill him ; and if he does, he is guilty of murder.

If a man find that a person, whose character warrants suspicion, is accustomed to give betel and make other presents to his wife, or passes jokes with her, he may bring him before a judge, and force him to pay half the fine for adultery.

VII.

The husband may command his wife not to visit at certain houses, not to frequent lonely places, etc., and if she will not obey, he may accuse her as guilty of a crime.

When a man is guilty of adultery with another's wife, and it is proved to be the first time, he must pay the ordinary fine for adultery ; but for the second offence he is only to pay half the fine ; and if he is guilty a third time, he is free from all penalty.

VIII.

When a woman accuses a man of having violated her person, and he denies it, he must be made to take the oath. If within seven days after no one of the misfortunes described in the oath befalls him, he is acquitted, and the woman must pay a certain sum in punishment for the calumny. But if both take the oath, neither of them must be reputed guilty, only they are bound to pay the expenses of the trial.

It must here be observed that the trial by water, described in the chapter on government, is not proper to be forced upon women in these cases, as men are generally more expert at it than women.

IX.

If a man carries away a married woman, and after the death of her husband sells her, he must give her the price he has received, and, moreover, pay the fine of adultery. If he drives her out of his house, he must pay only the half; and as he has deceived her he has no right whatever over her.

It is not reckoned a crime for a married woman to revile or even to beat a man who by promises or blandishments attempts to draw her to sin; and if the man retorts he may be condemned to pay the woman the usual fine.

X.

If a rich man violates the wife of a poor man, he must pay the ordinary fine; but if a poor man violates the wife of a rich man, the penalty will be the forfeit of his liberty.

If a man, after committing adultery with the wife of a respectable person, flies, his wife must give ten slaves to the injured person or their equivalent in money.

If a drunken man sleep upon the bed of another man's wife, but without being guilty of any indecency towards her, he cannot be punished in any way; but if he takes any liberties with her, he may be condemned in the ordinary way.

XI.

If a slave forms a connection with another slave he must be

punished as a slave; but if the woman be the slave of a brother or near relation to the master of the man, there is no penalty; because the slaves of brothers and near relations are supposed to be members of the same family.

It is no crime for a slave to have a connection with a free woman if she consents to it; but if a free man forms a connection with the female slave of another, he must pay the value of the woman to her master.

XII.

If a woman by deceit induces a boy of thirteen or fourteen to sin with her, she alone is reckoned guilty. When a slave violates a female slave of his master, and she dies in child-birth, the violator must pay the customary fine.

When the adulterer is not able to pay the fine, he must become a slave to the man he has injured; but at the death of the wife he regains his liberty. If a son should be the fruit of this connection, he is free.

XIII.

The fine for the violation of a female slave is the value of a slave; for the violation of a poor woman it is the value of two slaves; for the violation of a woman of the class of husband-men, the value of three slaves; for the violation of the wife of a merchant, the value of four slaves; for the violation of the wife of a physician, the value of five slaves; for the violation of the wife of a wise or rich man, the value of eight, or if he be a person of consequence, of twelve slaves; for the violation of the wife of a lesser Mandarin, the value of fifteen slaves, but if he be a Mandarin of the higher class, of twenty or thirty slaves. When the women thus violated were not wives but only concubines, the fine is diminished one-half.

XIV.

If a man has insulted, or struck, or wounded others, or dishonoured another's bed, he alone, but not his wife or children must be punished. But in case of debt, upon the flight or death of the husband, the wife and children must satisfy the creditors.

XV.

If any man seize another by the hair, he must pay a fine of thirty rupees; if a man strike another on the head, he must pay a fine of fifteen rupees; whoever gives another a blow so as to draw blood from the nose or mouth must pay twenty rupees; whoever beats another with a stick must pay fifteen rupees, or forty, if any bone be broken, or eighty if the flesh is much bruised or blackened. If the man dies from the effects of the beating, the aggressor must be fined in the sum of 300 rupees.

Whoever strikes a Mandarin must pay the sum of 400 rupees, or 500 if the Mandarin be of high rank.

XVI.

But if a person does not actually strike a Mandarin, but merely touches him disrespectfully, he must be condemned to a fine of 150 rupees, or of 100, or 70 if it be one of the lesser Mandarins. And if any one disrespectfully touch a rich man of great consequence he must pay fifty rupees, and forty if he is not of the first class; for thus offending against a wise man the fine is forty rupees; against a soldier thirty-five, and so on in proportion to the rank of the injured person.

XVII.

If any one shall strike a Talapoin, he must offer to him 100 baskets of cooked rice, 100 jars of curry, and 100 hearth-cakes, and must, moreover, humbly beg his pardon. If the injured person be a Brahmin, he must offer him cloth, and clothes, and other utensils, and beg his pardon. Whoever lays hands upon one of the chief Mandarins must pay the value of seventy slaves; if the Mandarin be not of the highest order, the fine is the value of sixty slaves.

The code then goes on to speak of the fines which those

must pay who insult, or strike, or wound persons in conditions superior to their own.

If any one in the public streets lays hands upon another of equal condition with himself, he must pay the value of two slaves. Then the different parts of the body are enumerated which may be wounded in quarrels, and according to the danger or size of the wound the fine is regulated.

XVIII.

If a man, free-born and of a respectable state in life, kills a poor man, he must pay the price of ten slaves; and the fine is the same in case a poor man kills a slave; but if he kills a person superior to himself he must pay the value of seventy slaves; for killing the slave of a Mandarin the fine is the value of fifteen slaves. The murderer of a Talapoin or a Brahmin must pay a fine of fifty ounces of gold.*

XIX.

If two persons quarrel and fight, and one of them is killed, there is no penalty; but if a third person interfere, and he kills one of those engaged in the quarrel, he must pay the ordinary fine for murder; but if he himself is killed, the other two are subject to no penalty.

If any one accepts a commission to murder another, even though the crime is not committed, both he and the person giving the order must pay the full fine of murder.

When two persons mutually insult or strike each other, if they are both of equal condition, each must pay the usual fine, but if one is superior to the other, the fine is increased or diminished one-fourth, according to their respective states in life.

XX.

It is no crime for children not more than ten years old to strike or insult any one. When Talapoins, or Brahmins, or

---

* At present murder is punished with death.

Mandarins, or old men, or children, or mad or sick people beat any one, they are guilty of no crime, even though death should be the consequence of the blows, since it is supposed they did not do it with the intention of murder, but only of correction.

XXI.

If a man insult another, calling him a thief, a wizard, a vile fellow, and such like, he must pay in penalty the price of a man. And if a man in a passion shall tell another that he is a murderer, a killer of other men's oxen, pigs, etc., if this be a calumny, he must pay the price of ten men.

If any one insult his own parents, he must be stripped of all his goods and expelled from his father's house.

XXII.

If any one plays tricks upon a person of higher condition than himself, or throws water or filth upon him, he must be punished with the bastinado. When any one grievously insults another, he must pay the ordinary fine; and if he be a poor man, his face must be blackened with charcoal, and he is to be conducted in this state through all the streets of the city.

Vol. V.

I.

This volume speaks of those who may act as judges. All persons, whether Mandarins or Brahmins, or prudent or pious men, may act in this capacity, provided they have those qualities which constitute a good judge, which are specially these : to be considerate, prudent, wise, eloquent, and well versed in the laws and statutes contained in this book. It then goes on to point out those who more commonly exercise the office of judge, and these are the governors of cities, and the chiefs of the villages or their lieutenants, those who have made a study of the Damasat, and arbitrators.

After the chiefs of the villages, or the governors of towns, have given their judgment in any cause, if the parties are dissatisfied with the decision, they may have recourse to another judge ; and, if this judge has been chosen by consent of both parties, they must abide by his award.

II.

There are four causes for arrest and imprisonment ; debt, quarrels, enmity, and theft. A creditor may arrest his debtor and keep him confined till he has paid him. If a creditor tortures his debtor in such a manner as to cause his death, he may be punished as a murderer. If a debtor wishes to prosecute his creditor for the vexations he has suffered from him, he must first pay the debt before he can begin the prosecution.

If the people of a village seize upon a robber, and in securing him or conducting him to prison he is killed, they are not subject to any penalty.

III.

A debtor must be released when he promises that he will submit the cause to a judge, and abide by his decision.

If a person is bail for another, who afterwards flies, or refuses to satisfy the claims upon him, the surety is bound to make all payments good.

IV.

A man may suffer an injury in three ways : in his body, in his possessions, or in both body and possessions at the same time.

And where an injury has been inflicted, reparation must be made either by restitution or an equivalent.

If a person is made to pay a fine unjustly, which ought to have been paid by another person, he may exact a double fine from the real offender.

V.

Of interest on money.

When a person puts out his money to interest, if he be a poor man, he may receive monthly one per cent.; two per cent.

if he be of the class of Mandarins ; four per cent. if he be a rich man ; and five per cent. if he be a merchant.*

When a person pays back the capital without any interest, he is no longer bound to pay any interest. And so also when a person restores half of the capital and half the interest, he is not bound to pay any interest for the half thus restored. If a person who has lent out money calls in the capital and the interest before the stipulated time, he can only demand the capital, in punishment for having broken his agreement. If the owner of the money lent employs his debtor in doing him various services, he cannot make him pay any interest, but simply restore the capital ; and if he is very vexatious towards the debtor, he loses half of the capital. If a person having gratuitously lent a sum of money, afterwards pretends that he did it with the obligation of interest, the judge may sentence him to lose the whole debt.

VI.

If a woman takes a loan of stolen money, her husband is obliged to restore twice the sum to the real owner, whenever he shall appear to claim it. But if it was not the chief wife, but only one of the inferior ones who accepted the loan, the husband is then bound to pay merely the capital with the usual interest. And if a slave borrows stolen money, the master is only to restore three quarters of the sum.

VII.

When a husband, after having borrowed a sum of money, sets off for a distant country without the knowledge of his wife, and dies on the way, the wife is not bound to pay the debt ; and in like manner if a woman borrows money in the absence of her husband, and dies before his return, the creditor cannot force the husband to pay the debt. Finally, if a person lends money to another's wife in his absence, and under suspicious circumstances, he cannot claim payment from the husband.

---

* At present the interest is five per cent. for all persons.

VIII.

If the near relations of a debtor, as his brothers or sons, should go to the house of the creditor, to entreat him to release their kinsman who was in prison, promising to arrange things so that the debt shall be paid, and the debtor, upon his release, flies or conceals himself, these relations shall be answerable for the debt. But this does not hold if the intercessors were only friends or distant connections.

IX.

When several persons stand surety for a debt, they are all bound *in solidum* to payment, in case the debtor withdraws himself from the country, so that if the creditor meets with one of the sureties, he may exact from him alone the full payment, provided he is not a poor person or slave.

The sureties however are only bound for the capital, but not for the interest. If the creditor, without advertising the surety, arrests his debtor, and he afterwards escapes from him, then the surety is no longer bound to anything, and the same is the case when the debtor makes his escape after he has been consigned by the surety to the custody of his creditor.

X.

When the interest in the space of two or three years comes to be equal to, or greater than the capital, the debtor is no longer bound to restitution.*

When a debtor runs away, all his property must be divided among his creditors in proportion to their respective credits.

XI.

In case of the denial of a debt, the judge may administer the oath to the party most illustrious for his family, or remarkable for his integrity. But if the litigants are equal in

---

* To elude this law creditors have now the practice of making their debtors give them new bonds every year.

these respects, he must require both to take the oath, and the one who refuses loses his cause.

XII.

If a person lends money to a slave, not knowing him to be such, the master is bound to the payment; but if the lender was acquainted with the condition of the borrower, the master is bound to nothing.

XIII.

If a person gives money with the condition of receiving at a stated period a quantity of rice, for example, and the article is not delivered as agreed, he may exact interest for his money. A person who lends another a quantity of rice may at any time demand its repayment, even in a year of scarcity ; and he may also require compensation for any damage he may have suffered through the loan.

XIV.

When two persons are joint creditors of another, and one of them consigns the debtor to the custody of the other, if this one, after receiving his share of the debt, releases the debtor, he is bound to satisfy the claims of the other creditor. If at the time that a creditor holds his debtor in confinement, another creditor appears, and tells him to keep him safe, and if the prior creditor afterwards releases the debtor, upon receiving the payment of his own demands, he is obliged to give to the other creditor one-half of the sum he has received : but if the other creditors do not come forth before his debt has been paid, he is not bound to pay them anything. But if the creditor, having been thus paid, persuades the debtor to run away, he is then obliged to satisfy all the claims of any other creditors who may appear.

XV.

If a person lends money to another, not knowing that he was a slave, or if the borrower afterwards becomes a slave, and he arrests him and tortures him in such a manner as to cause his death, he must pay to the master of the slave half his value. But if the slave only flies, and does not return to his master's house, the creditor is under no obligation of restitution of any kind.

But if he knew that the borrower was a slave, and he die in consequence of the ill-treatment of the creditor, the latter must pay the full price of the slave to his master, or the third part if he merely runs away.

XVI.

If a person accompanies another when he is going to satisfy his creditor, and the debtor runs away without paying, the creditor may require the whole debt from his companion, or if the latter be the slave of the debtor, he becomes the slave of the creditor. These laws take place when a debtor has no children or near relations to succeed to his property.

XVII.

A creditor may arrest his debtor when he refuses to pay; and if he perseveres in his refusal, after three years he may be sold for a slave by the creditor, who may thus pay himself out of the price he receives for him. But if he keeps the debtor in prison ten years and then sells him, he may appropriate the whole price, even though it exceed the original debt.

XVIII.

If a man contracts a debt during the lifetime of his first wife, and after death runs away from his creditor, the latter can have no claim upon the second wife.

But though creditors are allowed thus to arrest and imprison their debtors, they are nevertheless forbidden to punish or torture them in the same way as criminals.

XIX.

Of deposits.

A depositary ought to be a person of a respectable station in life.

The depositary must not restore the deposit to any one but its master; if he does, he must make compensation for all losses.

If the depositary asserts, that the things committed to his care have been stolen, or burnt, or otherwise destroyed, he must produce good testimonies for the fact. If he appropriates the deposit to his own use, and afterwards denies it, he must take the oath; and if within the eight following days, none of the denunciations contained in it happen to him, he is acquitted and absolved from making any compensation.

XX.

When two persons enter into partnership, and buy a boat, a house, or a field for trading, both must employ themselves in the common concern, if they are to participate in the gains. If they quarrel and dispute, he loses the cause who began the litigation, unless the other has exceeded him in injuries and insults. But if the dispute runs so high that they come to blows, that one wins the cause who sustains the greatest injury.

XXI.

No one has a right to anything he has agreed to purchase, unless he has paid down the earnest-money, which is forfeited if he afterwards fails in his promise.

When two persons entering into partnership buy anything in common, and one of them dies, his share of the purchase goes to his heirs.

XXII.

If a person give a lease of a piece of land for one year, and in the meantime sells the land, he must pay to the tenant double the annual rent, unless the field, by reason of the drought, have been totally unproductive.

When a person mortgages his land to obtain money, and within three years pays back the mortgage, his land must be restored to him. But if he does not pay it off in less than five years, he is only bound to one half of the original sum. And if he does not pay it within ten years, the debt is liquidated, and he is not obliged to anything.*

Vol. VI.

I.

Of theft.

Whoever steals a horse must restore two ; whoever steals an ox, must restore fifteen ; whoever steals a buffalo, must restore thirty ; whoever steals a pig or a goat must restore fifty ; whoever steals a young goose or a fowl, must restore 100 ; whoever steals a man must restore ten, or four if he only conceals him.

As for inanimate things, whoever steals anything, must restore, if it be the property of the Emperor, the Brahmins, or the Talapoins, ten-fold ; if of a Mandarin, five-fold ; if of a rich man, three-fold ; and if of a poor man, two-fold what he has taken.

II.

Whoever secretly enters into another man's house in the night, even though when he is caught he has taken nothing, must pay the value of two men ; but if any stolen goods are found upon him, he is fined in the value of four or five men. If a man steals in a street or public place, and is caught by the owner of the stolen property in the town where the robbery was committed, he may be obliged to restore double what he has taken. But if he is pursued, and taken in another town, the stolen goods must be sold in the place, and half the sum arising from the sale be given to the chief of the town.†

---

* In consequence of this law, money-lenders among the Burmese are very solicitous to have their money back before three years are expired ; and if the debtor is unable to repay it, they will make him give them a new bond, that thus they may continue to receive the interest of the money they have lent.

† At present thieves, especially if they are old offenders, are mostly condemned o death.

III.

If, when two persons are living together, one of them takes away or hides anything from the other, he is only obliged to a simple restitution. Those who are watching in the house of a deceased person may lawfully make use of the food they find there ; as also the inhabitants of one village, being invited by those of another to a festival, may make use of anything belonging to the latter.

IV.

If a man lends a sword to one, who afterwards uses it to kill or wound some one, if he was ignorant of this evil intention at the time he lent the sword, he is not guilty of any crime ; but if he knew it, or ought to have known it, he must pay a third of the ordinary fine. When a thief has been pursued and taken, he must not be immediately put to death, but consigned into the hands of the judge to be punished according to the law. But the master of an orchard or of a field may kill a thief, whom he finds stealing there in the night. If, however, a thief is caught stealing fruit in the daytime, he must pay a fine of the value of a man.

V.

If a person should buy an old and worn-out boat from a thief, and after having mended it, should discover its owner, he is only bound to make known the thief, from whom the owner must exact the fine ; as it is presumed that he could not have suspected it to be stolen property.

If two people together buy a stolen garden, and one of them dies before the owner has reclaimed his property, the other is obliged to endeavour to discover the thief, but if he is unable, to restore the whole garden to the true owner.

VI.

If a man, having stolen a boat, gives it to a carpenter to mend, when the owner appears, five times the value of the boat must be paid as a fine ; of which the carpenter must pay one-third, and the thief the other two.   If a slave turns robber and is taken, he must be condemned to death, or else to pay the usual fine for theft ; which must be paid to the judge by him who has received the thief into his house ; half the fine must be given to the master of the slave.

VII.

If a thief being discovered in the night, and closely pursued, leaves behind him the stolen goods, they are to be divided into three parts ; one of which is to be given to the person who discovered the thief, one to the judge, and one to the feudatory of the town.   If anything is missed in a place near which a number of people have been playing, they are bound to pay its value to the owner.   In like manner, when anything is lost in a village, the inhabitants must make it good.*

VIII.

Whoever appropriates to himself things found in the woods or mountains is to be considered as a thief, and treated as such. On the contrary those who restore them untouched to their owners merit great praise ; and moreover they are also to receive a third part of the value of what they have restored, if it is not gold or silver, as then only a sixth part is due to them.   The same law holds when any one finds a lost child or slave, and those must be punished, who, instead of restoring them to those to whom they belong, retain them in their own employ.

IX.

According to the rules of justice and honesty, a person who has found anything should keep it in his possession for three years, and then consign it to the chief of the town or city, who must restore it to the owner when he appears ; and if any one declares the thing to be his, and it is discovered upon examina-

---

* The inhabitants of a town are also responsible for any crime, as, for example, murder, which has been committed in the neighbourhood.

tion that this is not true, he must be condemned to pay twice the value of the thing that was lost.

X.

Natural or adopted fathers, sponsors, and masters may make use of the property of their children or scholars ; the husband has also a right to the property of his wife, and a master to that of his slave.

XI.

Of lying and deceit.

Whoever takes money from another, promising at some stated time to give him some merchandise, but afterwards breaks his word, is bound to pay double the sum he has received.

A calumniator must receive the same punishment that would be inflicted for the crime of which he had accused his adversary.

XII.

When a compromise had been made between the two parties in a lawsuit, and confirmed by a written instrument, if either of them attempts to renew the question, he shall be condemned to lose the cause.

He also loses his cause who will not appear before the judge.

The lawyer who undertakes to conduct a lawsuit is obliged to answer the opposite party in everything, if his client flies away.

XIII.

If one man takes another into places, unwholesome by reason of the malaria, or dangerous, or full of robbers, he must pay the customary fine for any evil that may happen, provided he was not ignorant of the nature of the place. If both were ignorant of it, the one who induced the other to go must pay half the usual fine.

XIV.

If two persons challenge each other to swim, to ride on horseback, or to any similar trial of skill, and any accident happens to one of them, the other is not bound to any penalty. In like manner, if a person, seeing another's horse or carriage approach, warns him to keep at a distance, but he notwithstanding will approach, and in consequence suffers some injury, the latter cannot institute a lawsuit on this ground.

xv.

If a person curses another and some evil happens to him who was cursed, the other must pay twice the value of the evil which has been suffered ; thus if the man dies, he must pay twice the value of a man.

It must here be observed that at the death of the Emperor, a general pardon and remission of all crimes and fines is given, excepting in cases of debt.

xvi.

If, while a stranger is living in a house, a thief comes there to steal, and the stranger pursues him and makes himself master of his clothes, they must be divided into two parts, of which the master of the house takes one and the stranger the other.

xvii.

When a stranger dies, all his goods belong to the master of the house where he was residing. In like manner if a man, who has been wounded by robbers, dies in another man's house, his goods, together with the fine to be paid by the thieves, go to the owner of the house. If a woman is brought to bed in another person's house, she must offer to the master one dress for a man and another for a woman, as also a sum of gold if she be able. When a sick man remains in another's house till his death, and receives all his food and medicine from his host, the latter must be repaid double what the sick man has consumed, and four times as much if, during the sickness, he has waited upon him.

XVIII.

If a sick man, in offering rice or any other species of food to the Nat of the woods or mountains, throws it near the steps of another man's house, he is not guilty of any fault; but if he throws it under his house, and any misfortune afterwards happens to its owner, as, for example, if he dies, the one who has put the rice there must pay the price of the body of the deceased, as well as for all the medicines that have been taken.

XIX.

If a sick man, in warming himself, sets fire to another person's house, he must pay to its owner the third part of the value of his body. And a person who in any other way, as in lighting a lamp, sets fire to a house, must pay the owner two-thirds of the value of his body. If the fire was caused by him whilst he was drunk or in a passion, he must pay the full value of his body. If an inhabitant of a village, whilst carrying fire in his hands, quarrels with the inhabitant of another village, and is the cause of its taking fire, the inhabitants of the last-mentioned place may for vengeance set fire to the village of the incendiary, without being liable to any prosecution.

If a person sets fire to a wood that does not belong to any one, and the fire is thence communicated to a neighbouring garden, the owner may demand reparation for all damages.

Vol. VII.

I.

If a young man, to induce a girl to marry him, gives her a ring or any other pledge, but afterwards marries another woman, he cannot demand back what he had given.

When a person deputes another to go into another town and contract for him a marriage with a woman, giving her at the same time a pledge for the fulfilment of the contract, if when he goes himself to receive his bride he finds some defect in her, as that she is infected with the leprosy, or has known some other man, he may break off the contract and require the pledge to be given back. But this law does not hold when the woman is of the same village as the man, or he has personally been acquainted with her.

If parents have promised a young man to give him their younger daughter in marriage, but deceive him and give him her eldest sister, and if he has consummated his marriage with her, he may retain the elder without losing any of his rights over the younger.

II.

If a young man, after having given the usual dower required for marrying a girl, has a connection with her sister, the former may, if she pleases, break the contract, and the man cannot demand the dower he brought with him.

A father-in-law may drive out of his house a son-in-law who shows great inaptitude for labour, and give his daughter to another man. But he must give to his son-in-law the clothes of his wife, if he is going to marry another woman, or half the value of her body, if he is going to remain single.

III.

If, during the celebration of a marriage, the bride runs away, her parents must give their younger daughter in her place, if they have one, or else restore the dower. But if the bride only hides herself in the house, and refuses to receive her husband, double the sum given as a dower must be paid to him.

IV.

If a man forcibly violates another's daughter, he must, if he be a low person, forfeit all his goods in favour of the girl, and moreover be punished by the judge. But if he be of a more noble condition, he must give her a dower corresponding to her state in life. If his condition be the same as the girl's, he must first be punished, and then must marry the girl, or else give her a dower, which must be equal to the value of her body. When a person, denying a former marriage, is united with a woman, and it is afterwards discovered that a former wife is living, he must be forced to separate himself from his first wife, or else must forfeit all his property to her whom he has deceived. To make a marriage good the consent of the father is always necessary, so that if a mother gives her daughter in marriage in the absence of the father, he, upon his return, may annul the marriage.

v.

If a son-in-law, whilst living in the house of his wife's father, traffics with the money borrowed from another and makes any gain, he must give a third part of all such gains to his father-in-law ; and if the money belonged to the latter, he must yield to him the whole. If a person who has freed a young man from slavery gives him his daughter in marriage, even after the death of his wife, the young man continues to be free. But whatever property he may have possessed, as also that of his wife, and all the daughters he has had by her, belong to the father-in-law ; to whom, moreover, he must give the third part of his gains as long as he remains in his house.

And if the young man, during the lifetime of his wife, goes to live elsewhere, he must pay the price of her body.

The property of a slave who marries a free woman belongs, after his death, to his master.

VI.

If a stranger, after giving the usual dower to a girl, goes to his own country, but with the promise of returning at a certain period and celebrating the marriage, the parents of the girl cannot give her to another, nor take possession of the dower, before the time fixed has elapsed.

VII.

If a man after his marriage returns to his father's house, and for the space of three years does not provide for the clothing of his wife, she is, at the end of that period, free to marry another man. She is also free if she hears nothing of her husband for six years, when he has gone out on a military expedition. But if he is travelling for objects of commerce she must wait seven years, and if from religious motives, ten.

VIII.

A young man should look upon his father-in-law as his natural father, and the father-in-law on his part should consider the former as his own child. If a son-in-law should dare to lift his hand against his father-in-law, upon being corrected by him, he must humbly beg pardon, and according to the greatness of the offence pay in forfeit the price of a slave or an ox. But the father-in-law must use discretion in correcting his son-in-law.

IX.

If a married couple, from their continual disagreements, consent to separate, each one takes his dower, and then whatever has been acquired since their marriage is divided into three parts ; of which the wife takes one and the husband two. But if the husband brought no dower with him, the common gains are equally divided between them.

But if the separation takes place, not by common consent, but at the pleasure of one party alone ; then, if it be the husband who seeks the divorce, he must leave the property to the wife and go out of the house, with only one suit of clothes ; but if it be the woman that wants to separate, the husband, besides taking all the property, may also sell her for a slave.

X.

If a man buys a female slave to make her his wife, and afterwards repudiates her, he does not thereby lose the right of exacting the price of her body. But this does not hold in the converse case, when a woman has bought a man to make him her husband, for in case she afterwards separates herself from him, she loses all right over him.

Here there is an exhortation to judges to punish husbands who ill-treat good wives ; as well as wives who revile and ill-treat good husbands.

XI.

When a husband sets out for distant countries, leaving in his house everything necessary for the maintenance of his wife, the latter may not leave the house and go to her parents. And if the husband is out on the service of the Emperor, or from religious motives, she is not allowed to abandon the house, even if there be a want of necessaries. And if the husband upon his return finds his wife living out of his house, he may have satisfaction by sentence of a judge, who may decree a separation for three years, or, if the husband demands it, a perpetual divorce.

XII.

Even if the husband goes to live with another woman, the wife is not immediately to proceed to a divorce ; but she must wait three years, after which time she is free to do as she pleases. There are, however, causes for which a woman may separate herself from her husband ; as, for example, if he is lazy, or unable to procure what is necessary for the family, if he commits adultery, and some others ; but then the husband has still the right of retaining her dower. But sickness, old age, deformity or any other bodily defect, are not considered sufficient causes for a divorce. Those wives who, notwithstanding the sickness or other defects of their husbands, attend to them, and take care of them, and have patience with them, as a sister does to a brother, or a scholar to his master, deserve to be praised by all the Mandarins and judges.

XIII.

If a husband has taken one of his own female slaves, or one belonging to his wife, for a concubine, and have a son by her, he may give him as a slave to his wife, but not to his eldest daughter ; as in that case he would lose his right to half the value of the body of his son.

If a father sells his son into slavery, the price paid for him must be taken from the inheritance at the father's death, and given to this son; who, moreover, may claim two shares more than any of his brothers or sisters in the paternal inheritance. Moreover, if a brother sells his younger brother for a slave, and dies without children, all his property goes to the one who had been sold.

XIV.

The children of a first marriage cannot complain if their mother, having married a second time, employs all the property in keeping her husband. If he, after the death of his wife, marries one of her female slaves, the children do not lose their right over her after his death; as she always belongs to them, except she has had a male child.

XV.

Parents, on their death-bed, cannot dispose of their property in favour of their friends or connections; and even if they had made them any presents, which, however, have not yet been consigned into their hands, the heirs may retain them after the death of the parents.

XVI.

If a father, in consequence of age or sickness, gives up the care of his property to his wife and son-in-law; upon the death of the wife the administration does not pass to the head of the family, as he cannot dispose of anything without the consent of the son-in-law.

XVII.

When a married daughter, who has been living with her husband, returns to her father's house in her sickness and dies there, half of her goods belong to her parents.

If a father-in-law has given money to his son-in-law for trade, he has a claim not only to the restitution of the original capital, but also to half of the profits, should the man have to return to his own house from the death of his wife. In like manner when parents have given to their daughter money or anything else, by means of which the property of the young people has been increased, upon the death of their daughter they may claim a share with the husband in the inheritance. The same laws hold in case the husband has received anything from his own parents.

XVIII.

That daughter must be disinherited who refuses to live with the man to whom, with the consent of her parents, she was given in marriage.

If a married man leave at his death a son and a younger brother, the latter may claim the clothes and a female slave of the deceased, but all the rest goes to the son.

XIX.

In this last paragraph it is decreed, that not only the fathers of families, but also their sons and grandsons, must contribute to the taxes which are paid to the Emperor or feudatories.

Vol. VIII.

I.

Of the sale of slaves.

There are two kinds of slavery, one temporary, the other perpetual. A man may be sold in both these kinds of slavery. Still there may be cases in which the buyer has no right to any services from the slave ; as when the person sold was previously the slave of another, or when he has contracted debts ; for in these cases the former master or buyer must have all his demands satisfied before the new master can have any right over his slave.

If a slave, within seven days after he has been sold, runs away from his new master, the latter may demand back from the seller the price he has paid. And if within ten days the slave falls sick of any foul malady, the buyer may send him back to the house of his old master, who is bound to provide him with food and medicine, and, if he is cured, to restore him to the buyer.

II.

When any one to obtain money gives in pledge his son, or an ox, or anything else, promising to redeem the pledge within three months, if he fails in his promise, he loses his pledge.

If any one in want of money sells his slave who is involved in debt or other embarrassments, he, and not the buyer, is responsible for the debts of his slave.

III.

When any one sells a slave who afterwards returns to his house, and is sold to another at a higher price, the surplus over the first sale belongs to the man who then bought him.

A person who has sold a slave has the right before any one else of repurchasing him.

IV.

When two slaves of the same master agree to run away together, and one afterwards sells the other, and they divide the price, and then the one who has been sold returns to his old master, if the new master comes to claim him, the old master must give him two slaves, unless he can swear or bring testimony that the whole transaction was without his advice, and then he is only bound to give one.

V.

When a slave, having run away from his lawful master, sells himself to another, but as soon as he has received the price runs away again, and sells himself to a third, if the first and second masters then discover the runaway, they may sue the last possessor for the restitution of the slave, and the reparation of all damages, unless he can prove that he acted through an involuntary ignorance, that he had examined the slave, and used all the necessary precautions, in which case he may demand reparation for what he has paid.

VI.

If a person hires a slave, and takes him with him to another village, where he is obliged to sell him, and the slave then runs away, the purchaser is not bound to pay anything to his original master, as he had bought him from one who had a right over him, since he had hired him.

VII.

If a slave who has been sent to war, or to conduct some business for his master, is taken by the enemy, but afterwards escapes, and returns to his own country, his master loses all right over him.

VIII.

A master may slightly punish a slave ; but if he strikes or beats him violently, he loses a third part of the price of his body ; and if the slave dies from the beating, he must pay twice the value of his body to the slave's parents, or, if they are not living, to the judge. And if a slave runs away to avoid the cruelty of his master, there is no penalty for any one who receives him into his house.

IX.

The master of a runaway slave may exact from him, or from the person who has received him, the gains he would have derived from his services.

If a son or a slave, given in pledge, dies in the house of the creditor, the parents are not thereby freed from the debt, unless during the sickness they ask permission to take him into their own house, and were refused.

X.

If any one hires a slave by the day or month, and he dies in his service, the value of the slave must be paid to his master. If a person, having taken a slave as a pledge, becomes discontented with him, and returns him to his master, and shortly after he runs away, the person who has had him in pledge must seek after him and restore him.

XI.

If a father sells himself for a slave, and at the same time gives his son in pledge to the same or any other master, if the son runs away, his master may demand restitution from the father; and if the father runs away, his master may demand restitution from the son.

XII.

If a free man marries a female slave without the knowledge of her master, the children all belong to the master of the slave, in the same way as a calf belongs, not to the owner of the bull, but to the owner of the cow. But if the master of the slave, in consideration of some present, has consented to the marriage, then some of the children belong to the free man and others to the master of the slave. If a woman marry a stranger, not knowing that he was a slave, the children must be divided between the mother and the master of the slave.

XIII.

If a new-born child is given to a woman to nurse, and the parents do not ask for it till it has arrived at puberty, then the value of its body is divided into four parts, of which three belong to the nurse and one to the parents. But if the child was not given into her care till it could call upon its father and mother by name, or get up the steps of the house, then three parts only are to be made of the value of the body, of which two must be given to the woman and one to the parents. If, finally, the child could dress itself, the value must be divided equally between them.

XIV.

When the child of a slave is thus given out to nurse, one third of the price must be given to the nurse, when it is reclaimed.

XV.

If a person hires a boat to take him to any place, and after his arrival it is lost, he is bound to make good the damage, besides paying the hire agreed upon. When any one hires a cart to carry his merchandise, if the driver goes by frequented roads, he is not responsible if the goods are stolen ; but if he chooses a new and unfrequented track, or driving very furiously causes some damage, and the goods are thus lost or spoilt, he is obliged to repair all losses.

XVI.

If a person has borrowed a vessel from another to wash his head,* and it happens, that after it has been restored, its owner falls sick, the borrower is obliged to furnish all the medicines ; and in case the man dies, to pay the value of a man and a half to his relations. The same is the law respecting clothes borrowed to accompany a funeral.

XVII.

A man may reprove and even slightly beat another whom he has hired to cultivate a field, if he is lazy or negligent in his work. If it happens that a hired labourer is drowned, or breaks a limb, or is eaten up by tigers, or meets with any other accident, the owner of the land is not bound to anything, if he has paid him all the wages agreed on ; otherwise he must pay the value of his body, or only half of it, if he was his debtor for only half his wages. If in working in a field any precious

---

* Sometimes the Burmese wash their heads, to free themselves from an incantation, to which they believe themselves subject.

thing is found, half goes to the labourer and half to the owner of the land.

XVIII.

If a man hires another man's slave, who runs away after he has received his wages, he is not bound to pay any fine to the master of the slave. But if, knowing him to be a slave, he did not ask the permission of his master, then if the slave runs away, or dies before he has received his wages, the master may claim the value of his slave.

XIX.

If a Mandarin obliges a man to climb up a tree, and he falls down, the Mandarin must pay double the value of his body if he is killed, and the simple price if he is only bruised.

XX.

When a strange ox gets into a fold, the owner of the fold must give notice of it to the chief of the village, who is to look out for the owner of the ox, and restore it to him. If an ox gets into a field and eats or tramples down the crop, the first time, warning must be given to the owner of the ox, and if after that, the ox still continues to do the same damages, the owner of the field may kill it, and, giving half to the chief of the village, may keep the other for himself.*

If two oxen or two buffalos begin to fight, and one of them is killed, their owners are not subject to any fine; but if a loose ox kills one that is tied, then the owner of the first is bound to pay the value of the other. When the masters of both incite them to fight, and one of them is killed, the master of the other is bound to pay triple the value of the one that is killed. For any other damage that these animals are the cause of, their respective masters are responsible.

XXI.

When a labourer who has been hired for six months demands his wages at the end of three, he loses all further right to it.

---

* This custom is out of use at the present day.

Vol. IX.

I.

When a man beats a woman or a child, or two men beat one, in these three cases, by reason of the inequality of strength in the parties, the guilty must be condemned to pay a double fine. If a woman through contempt throws women's clothes on a man's head, she must pay fifteen ounces of silver. If any one, man or woman, pulls another's clothes so as indecently to expose his body, if the offending party be poor, the fine is an ounce and a half of gold, and two ounces and a half, if rich.

II.

When a lawsuit has been settled finally before a judge, it must not be renewed ; and the party seeking to revive it may be punished with the loss of his tongue, and if he obstinately persists in forcing his adversary into litigation he ought also to lose his hand. But although this punishment be just, the judge does not generally proceed to such severity. When a lawsuit is terminated, the fortunate party requires from the other the accomplishment of the sentence, for if he delays this for three years, or till the death of the Emperor, he can no longer demand it.

III.

When a poor man, or one of base condition, insults or offends a rich person, or one of a noble family, he must pay fifty ounces of silver. But if a rich man insults a poor man, he is only to pay three ounces and a half.

IV.

If a person has given an ox or anything else to another in sign of friendship, or if he has given him one of his female slaves for a concubine, and afterwards wishes to resume his gift, he must still leave half what he has given, or half of its value to his friends. In like manner if a person has in this way given, for example, a house to his friend, who, however, dies before him, the gift in this case does not go to the heirs, but returns into the possession of the former owner. But this is not the case with respect to things which are situated at some distance, and which the person to whom the present was made has acquired with difficulty and danger, as the property then descends to his heirs.

V.

When a master commands a slave to marry one of his female slaves, both are thereby made free.

When a master has had a connection with one of his female slaves, he has no claim to the price of her body ; and if she was a virgin, and born of honest parents, he must let her go where she pleases.

VI.

When a lawyer promises his client to finish a lawsuit in a certain number of days or months, and does not fulfil his promise, he must pay twice the value of the fees he has received.

VII.

Whoever falsely asserts that another owes him a sum of money, must pay to the person he has accused double the debt he had charged upon him.

And if a real debtor denies his debt, he must pay double in punishment.

If a person dies in debt, and religious and pious men charitably defray the expenses of his funeral, they are not subject to any claims from the creditors ; but if they were friends or acquaintances who performed this office, they must pay a quarter of the debts, and half of them if they were relations.

VIII.

If a boat, laden with merchandise, goes down, and the owners mark the spot by a pole or some other sign ; any one, afterwards recovering any part of the cargo, must be treated as a thief, if he keeps it in his own possession; but if he faithfully restores it to the owner, the latter in gratitude must give him a third part.

IX.

If a man has married a woman, not knowing that she was another's wife, and the rightful husband afterwards appears, she must be restored to him, even though she has had six or seven children by the second husband. But if the first husband knew that his wife was marrying another man, and did not protest against it, then after the lapse of three years, he loses his claim to her.

X.

If a master learns that one of his slaves is maintained in another's house, in a time of scarcity, and fraudulently allows him to remain there till the scarcity is over, he then loses his right to the slave, who becomes the property of the man who had fed him.

XI.

Whoever destroys or arbitrarily changes the landmarks that distinguish one property from another, such as trees, brooks, or public roads, must be condemned to pay a fine of seventeen ounces of silver and a half.

XII.

Of wagers.

There are two kinds of wagers: one made by the spectators upon rowing-matches, or races of men, oxen, or horses; the other, made for the display of a man's own strength or agility, in which latter there is generally a risk of life; such are challenges to wrestle, run, or swim. Of the first kind of bets, the winner can only claim two-thirds, but the whole of the second.

If a man who has got no money, in the presence of some person of note, says to another, 'Let us bet what I have in my hand,' then in penalty of his deceit, he must pay the half of what he pretended to hold.

The obligation of debts contracted by betting does not pass to a person's heirs; so that if the loser runs away or dies before he has paid, the money lost cannot be exacted from his wife or children, unless they have been surety for its payment.

When any one is hurt in wrestling, or in any other similar game, he cannot claim damages from his opponent; only in case of the death of one of the parties, the other must pay the value of his body.

When the winner in a wager pursues the loser, who is running away or hiding himself, and upon overtaking him strikes or wounds him, he not only loses the bet, but must also be punished by the judge.

Vol. X.

I.

If a person buys another man's daughter before she has arrived at the age of puberty, and afterwards, when she has reached it, makes her his wife or concubine, without advertising her father of it, the children of this marriage must be divided between the master of the girl and her father. But this does not hold when the girl had attained the age of puberty at the time of the sale.

II.

If a master pursues his fugitive slave, and finds him in some village, he may not of his own authority seize him, or bind him, but he must give notice to the chief of the place, who, in virtue of his office, is obliged to seek out the slave, and consign him to his master.

III.

If a man takes a fugitive slave for his companion in remote and uninhabited places, but was ignorant that the man was a slave, he is not guilty of any crime: but if he was acquainted with his condition, he may be accused of theft.

A master may also accuse a person of theft, who, being the relation of his fugitive slave, meets him in unfrequented places and converses with him : but not if he does it in the public streets or porticos.

IV.

If the relation of a fugitive slave receives him into his house, and then conducts him back to a particular spot, he cannot be treated as a thief, because he was the relation of a slave.

V.

When a slave, who has had several children during his captivity, desires to purchase his freedom, he must pay twice the value of his own body. Formerly he had, besides the value of his own body, to pay that of all his children.

VI.

A master is not responsible for the crimes committed by his runaway slave ; and if for his crimes the slave is condemned to labour, the profits of it must be divided between the judge and the master.

VII.

When a person incites another to steal, and himself buys the stolen goods ; upon the appearance of the real owner, the thief must restore what he has stolen, and the receiver is to be punished as the thief.

Also when a man steals the female slave or the daughter of another, and gives her to another man to keep for him, if the latter did not know that she was another's slave or daughter, he is not guilty of anything ; but if he knew it, he must pay half the accustomed fine, and the real thief the other half.

VIII.

If a man quarrels with a woman or a child, or two persons with one in a remote place, and the affair is brought before a judge, if the persons injured depose to having been struck or wounded, and can show any marks of it upon their body, the judge must give credit to their assertion, even though no witnesses can be brought forward. But he must not believe a man who says he has been struck by a woman or child, even though he may show marks of violence upon his body, unless he can produce some testimony.

IX.

In cases of quarrels, that party must be thought guilty which began with insults and blows, or which returned a slight insult or blow with more serious ones.

It is not so unbecoming for a man to be first in abusing a woman or a child, but it is very unbecoming for a woman to begin to rail at a man, or for a youth thus to offend an old man ; a poor one, a rich one ; or a vulgar person, one more noble ; and if in these cases the offended party, unable to bear the insult, slightly strikes the offender, he must not therefore be punished.

X.

When two people of equal condition mutually insult or strike each other in a quarrel, neither of them can be considered guilty; but if one of them calls in his slave to his assistance, he may be fined by the judge.

XI.

This paragraph contains the regulations concerning appeals from one judge to another. When it is evident that a judge has given an unjust sentence, an appeal may be made to a superior Mandarin; and if he also decides unjustly, recourse may be had to the queens, or to the heir to the crown ; from them there is an appeal to the Emperor ; and from the Emperor to the Brahmins, Talapoins, and other just men, who must then go to the Emperor and persuade him to rescind his unjust decision ; and the queens and the heir to the throne must likewise assist in this, when he is unwilling to retract his sentence.

XII.

If a boat in ascending the river meets another, and they run foul of each other, so that the one which was going against the stream is sunk, and the cargo lost, the owner of the other is not responsible; but if the one which was coming with the stream goes down, the owner of the other must make good the loss, unless the accident was caused by the violence of the wind or because the rudder was broken. With respect to two people meeting on land, of whom one has the sun in his face, the other on his back, the former must give way; and if they run against each other and any hurt happens to the one with the sun at his back, the other is bound to pay the damage, unless he was seized with a sudden fear, which hindered him from seeing what was before him. When two carts meet on a road, of which one is heavily loaded, the other not, the latter must make way for the other to pass.

XIII.

The keeper of an elephant or an ox is obliged to hinder his beast from passing through places where people either sick, or mad, or drunk are lying; otherwise, if any one is killed by the animal, he must pay fifty ounces of silver, or twenty-five if only some serious injury is caused; if, however, the animal was furious and unmanageable, he is not subject to this fine.

XIV.

An accusation against a man who has stolen flowers during the night must be made before mid-day; and an accusation of fruit-stealing must be made before the fruit has been eaten, as afterwards it is unlawful to accuse a person. It is no crime to take fruits which are lying under the trees.

XV.

If two people quarrel and fight during the royal festivals, they must pay a fine of 250 ounces of silver for having shown contempt of the imperial majesty.

S

XVI.

Whoever commits a nuisance within the enclosures of the Pagodas, or Baos, or in any other place which ought to be kept clean, must be punished by the judge, provided it was not involuntary.   They also must be punished who sit down or sleep in the places appropriated to the Talapoins, the Brahmins, or the Mandarins.   Those too are liable to punishment who dare to put on the dress of a Mandarin, unless in case of a war, when this is lawful.

XVII.

It is not lawful for creditors to exact debts in the following places: In those where the royal festivals are being celebrated, in those where the customary oblations are made to the Nat, the guardians of the city or town, in the places where the Talapoins recite their prayers, finally, in other people's houses. If a person offends against this law, he may be punished.   And if he not only asks for his money, but seizes and binds the debtor, he then loses the whole debt.

XVIII.

When a person discovers a treasure in the earth, if he is a rich man, the treasure must be divided into twenty parts, eight belong to him and twelve to the Emperor; if he is a poor man, he must give two thirds to the Emperor, reserving only one for himself.

XIX.

If the contracts, made in the sale of slaves, or in concluding any other bargain, which are generally cut upon a palm-leaf, become old and worn out, they cannot be renewed upon another leaf by private authority ; and writings thus unlawfully renewed have no weight in a court of justice.

XX.

If a person who holds another's money in trust puts it out to interest, and the owner after a short time demands back his money, he must immediately restore it, together with the interest he had received upon it; but if he does not ask for his money for a long time, the holder of the trust may lawfully make use of the interest received.

XXI.

When a brother takes his share of the paternal inheritance before the regular division has been made, and engages in trade with it, all the profit belongs to him alone, and the other brothers have not the least claim upon him.

XXII.

When any one buys any merchandise with the promise of paying at a definite period, if he lets the time go by without payment, the creditor may exact the accustomed interest.

XXIII.

In any lawsuit where witnesses are required, those ought in the first place to be chosen who are just, pious, and religious, who give alms, and do other good works, who are men of honour, and conscientious, or else rich men and those in dignity. But in case the transaction has taken place at a distance, where witnesses of this character were not to be found, the testimony of such as were present may be received.

XXIV.

The following persons must not be listened to by judges, but must lose their cause: 1. Those who, after having taken the oath, of themselves bring forward witnesses; 2. those who having promised to produce witnesses, are afraid to interrogate them; 3. those who having promised to take the oath, in the act of taking it, put in words which do not signify what they are swearing to; 4. those who, having pointed out a witness, will not permit him to be interrogated in the court, but bring forward others.

XXV.

In this last paragraph the price of men and animals is determined. A male child of free parents, as soon as it is born, is reckoned at four rupees; a female child, at three; a young man of free condition is valued at thirty rupees, a girl at twenty-five: and thus the value of rich men, Mandarins, queens, etc., goes on increasing, each superior rank being valued at twice as much as the one below it.

As for slaves: a new-born male infant ranks at three rupees, a female at two; a boy is worth ten rupees, a girl seven; when arrived at puberty a man is worth thirty rupees, a woman twenty. The value of the body of a dead slave is ten rupees.

With regard to animals; an elephant is worth 100 rupees, a horse fifty, a buffalo three, an ox two, and a pig two. A goat, a peacock, a dog, and similar animals are worth the quarter of a rupee, and the price diminishes in proportion to the smallness of the animal.

A rupee of gold is equal to twenty-five of silver; and a rupee of silver to fifty of lead.

The price for daily labour is a quarter or the eighth part of a rupee for a woman, and twice as much for a man. But at the present day these prices have very much varied from the ancient standard.[1]

---

[1] See Appendix III. for some general remarks on the Burmese Code. The notes to this Chapter, and elsewhere, marked with asterisks, are reprinted from Dr. Tandy's translation.

NOTE A

As native Christians are often mentioned in the course of this work, it will not perhaps be uninteresting to give a short account of the origin and progress of Christianity in the Burmese Empire. Our information is in great measure derived from unedited sources.

In the year 1719 Pope Clement XI. sent a solemn embassy to China, consisting of the Patriarch of Alexandria, Monsignor Mezzabarba, and several zealous ecclesiastics. They had a gracious audience of the Emperor at Pekin on the last day of the following year; but, their affairs having subsequently taken a less favourable turn, the Patriarch returned to Europe, after having distributed his clergy in different countries. Two were appointed to the kingdom of Ava, Pegù and Martaban, the Reverend Joseph Vittoni, a secular priest, and F. Calchi, a member of the Barnabite congregation, and a young man of very superior parts and acquirements. On their arrival at Siriam, then the principal port of Pegù, they found there two Portuguese clergymen, who acted as chaplains to the few descendants of their countrymen who yet remained there, but were wholly ignorant of any language but their own. After much opposition from several quarters, which they vanquished by a personal conference with the sovereign, they were authorised to erect churches and preach the Christian religion. The King even despatched the Abbate Vittoni with a present of precious stones to His Holiness. F. Calchi proceeded to erect a church in Ava; but worn out with fatigues he died, March 6th, 1728, in the forty-third year of his age. About the time of his death a small supply of missioners arrived, and the result of their labours became sufficiently cheering to induce the zealous Pontiff Benedict XIV. to appoint a Bishop as Apostolic Vicar in that mission, and to intrust its management to the Barnabite Fathers. F. Gallizia was the first Bishop; but the most distinguished labourer in that mission was F. Nerini, who, being a man of great eloquence, publicly preached, with great effect, the doctrines of Christianity. Many churches were now erected, and the Catholic worship publicly exercised ; funerals and processions marched through the streets without giving the slightest offence. Upon the capture of the city of Siriam, the churches were entirely plundered, and with difficulty saved from destruction. In 1745, the Christians received a severe blow, by the massacre of the Bishop and two missioners as they were accompanying some Dutch officers, who had gone to court upon a safe-conduct from the Emperor himself. The Christians were dispersed, and F. Nerini only saved his life by flying to India. He returned to Siriam in April 1749. Being now in great favour, he erected the first brick building ever seen in that country. This was a church, eighty feet in length, and thirty-one in breadth, with a large house adjoining for the residence of the clergy. One Armenian merchant, who had no children, contributed upwards of 7000 dollars to these pious works.

The following are the principal Christian establishments, existing or erected about this time.

In Ava was the first church, destroyed afterwards when the new capital was erected. From a letter of F. Amato in 1822, it appears that a church and house has been built in this.

At Siriam a house and church built under the direction of F. Gallizia. Another church and house built by F. Nerini. A college containing forty students. An establishment for orphan girls. This city is now nearly destroyed.

In the city of Pegù, a church and house.

At Monlà, a church, presbytery and college, erected in 1770. The Talapoins claimed the ground on which this was built, and it was consequently thrown down. A much larger one was accordingly built by F. Cortenovis, who tells us he had fifty boys residing in it.

In the environs of the city six other churches. In Subaroa two churches.

At Chiam-sua-rocca are six churches, which in 1822 were served by F. Amato.

Finally, in Rangoon, a church and house, with a convent and orphan school.

Subsequently many able missionaries laboured in this country, among whom deserve notice the two Cortenovis, F. Sangermano, author of the foregoing history, who returned to Europe in 1808, and F. Amato, who was still alive and zealously exerting himself at the close of 1828, though seventy years of age. He was then the only European clergyman in the country ; as, in consequence of the dissolution of the religious congregations, under the French occupation of Italy, the Barnabite Fathers had not been able to supply the wants of the mission. In 1830 the state of this mission was taken into consideration by the Propaganda, and four clergymen of distinguished merit, who offered their services, were despatched thither. They all arrived safe, and a further supply will perhaps be furnished before long.

NOTE B

SEE CHAPTER XV.

OUR readers will probably have observed the resemblance that exists between the practices described in the last chapter, and some of the institutions of the Catholic religion. In the Buddhaism of Tibet, which is the same as the religion of the Burmese, Godama only being another name for Buddha, this resemblance is still more marked. 'The first missionaries,' says Abel Remusat,[1] 'were not a little surprised to find in the heart of Asia, monasteries, processions, pilgrimages, festivals, a pontifical court, a college of superior lamas electing a chief, who was ecclesiastical sovereign and spiritual father to all the Tibetans and Tartars. But, as good faith was a characteristic of the time, as well as the profession of these men, they contented themselves with considering this Lamaism as a sort of degenerate Christianity, and as vestiges of the former settlement of Syrian sects in those countries.'

But this resemblance was afterwards used as a controversial weapon, and the French Philosophers pretended to find in Lamaism the origin of Christianity. But the celebrated Orientalist just quoted has completely confuted these assertions from the works of native authors. In his memoir he has made us acquainted with a valuable fragment preserved in the *Japanese Encyclopedia*, which contains the true history of the Lamaic hierarchy. The first seat of Buddhaism was India, whence its patriarchs migrated to Tibet and there established their religion, but still in dependence upon the civil power of the State, till the house of Tchingkis Khan delivered them from it and invested them with dominion. It was the grandson of the conqueror who first bestowed this sovereignty on the head of the religion, who then took the title of Lama, which signifies a priest, as his peculiar designation. The account given by Abel Remusat of the origin of the Lamaic dynasty accords perfectly with another interesting document, brought to light, and translated into Russian by the Archimandrite F. Hyacinth Pitchourinsky,[2] and from Russian into French by M. Julius Klaproth.[3]

At the time when the Buddhist patriarchs first established themselves in Tibet, that country was in immediate contact with Christianity. Not only had the Nestorians ecclesiastical settle-

ments in Tartary, but Italian and French religious visited the
court of the Khans, charged with important missions from the
Pope and St. Lewis. These carried with them church ornaments
and altars to attempt a favourable impression on the minds of the
natives. For this end, they celebrated their worship in presence
of the Tartar princes, by whom they were permitted to erect
chapels, within the precincts of the royal palaces. An Italian
Archbishop, sent by Clement v., established his see in the capital,
and erected a church to which the faithful were summoned by the
sound of three bells, and where they beheld painted edifying
representations.[4]

Nothing was easier than to induce many of the various sects,
which crowded the Mongol court, to admire and adopt the rites of
this religion. Some members of the imperial house secretly
embraced Christianity, many mingled its practices with the profession of their own creeds, and Europe was alternately elated and
disappointed by reports of imperial conversions, and discoveries of
their falsehood.[5] It was such a rumour as this, in reference to
Manghu, which caused the missions of Rubriques and Ascellius.
Surrounded by the celebration of such ceremonies, hearing from
the ambassadors and missionaries of the West, accounts of the
worship and hierarchy of their countries, it is no wonder that the
religion of the Lamas, just beginning to assume splendour and
pomp, should have adopted institutions and practices already
familiar to them, and already admired by those whom they wished
to gain. The coincidence of time and place, and the previous
non-existence of that sacred monarchy, for it has been well shown
by Fischer that no writer anterior to the thirteenth century gives
a hint of this system, amply demonstrate that the religion of Tibet
is but an attempted imitation of ours. It is no less probable, or
rather certain, that the inferior branches of the same religion
either copied these institutions from Tibet, or received them
directly in the same manner.

---

[1] Abel Remusat, Aperçu d'un Mémoire intitulé ' Récherches chronologiques
sur l'origine de la Hierarchie Lamaïque,' in the *Journal Asiatique* for May 1824,
tom. iv. p. 257 *seq*.

[2] St. Petersburgh, 1828.

[3] In *Nouveau Journal Asiatique*, Aug. and Oct. 1829, tom. iv. p. 81 *seq*.

[4] Abel Remusat, p. 267, compare Assemani, inf. cit.

[5] Assemani, *Biblioth. Orient.* tom. iii. Pa. 11. ccclxxx. *seq.* *Di Marco Polo
e degli altri viaggiatori Veneziana più illustri.* Dissertazoni del P. Ab. (now
Cardinal) Zurla, Venez. 1818, vol. i. p. 287.

NOTE C

By John Jardine, Esq., H.M. Bombay Civil Service, M.R.A.S., President of the Educational Syndicate of British Burma.

The Right Reverend Monsignor Bigandet, Bishop of Ramatha and Vicar Apostolic, Vice-President of the Educational Syndicate of British Burma, and author of *The Legend of Gaudama*, has put in my hands an Italian book containing an account of the origin of the Italian mission in Burma, and with it much interesting information about the earliest inquiries into Burmese literature, and the earliest attempts to give the Burmans and Karens the benefits of European teaching and European medicine.

It is entitled *Della Vita di Monsignor Gio. Maria Percoto*, of the Congregation of St. Paul, Missionary in the Kingdoms of Ava and Pegù, Vicar Apostolic and Bishop of Massula, written in three books by Father D. M. Griffini of the same congregation. It was printed at Udine in Venezia, by the Fratelli Gallici in 1781, after approval of the Inquisitor-General of the Holy Office at Venice, and under the licence of the Reformers of Studies at Padua. It is dedicated to the Deputies of the City of Udine, who are told how Bishop Percoto, 'an intrepid soldier of Christ, who through love to his Prince had sailed the stormy seas, crossed dreadful deserts, lived alone in barbarous lands, in dangerous climates, in the midst of tigers and of crocodiles, and, what is worse, among a people full of superstitions and of vice,' was ' not only your fellow-citizen, but, what is more, was pupil and fruit of these schools, which are yours, and are kept safe under your guardian care.'

The first book describes the early life of Percoto. He was born in 1725 at Udine, of a noble family of that city. Being drawn to the religious life from his childhood, he entered the Congregation of St. Paul at Monza, and, after taking the vows, spent some years in the study of philosophy at Milan, and of theology in Bologna. On being called to the mission, he went to Rome, and received the blessing of the Pope, Clement XIII., before starting. He sailed from Leghorn to Smyrna and Aleppo : thence he travelled on camels through Damascus and Bagdad to Bussora, where he found an English ship, which took him round Cape Comorin to Bengal. After staying four months at Chandernagore with the Capuchins, he sailed from Calcutta to Rangoon, which he reached in October 1761, two years after leaving Italy.

The second book opens with some account of the country and the people. Rangoon is said to have become the great port because of the fall of Syriam. Crocodiles and elephants were common ; and people built their houses on piles, not because of the waters, but for security against tigers. Instead of medicine, the people had an infinity of foolish superstitions, for which reason the missionaries usually managed to bring some one who knew medicine and surgery, and in this way attracted the people to hear the gospel. The dislike to killing animals was general, and the Europeans were known as the killers of fowls.

After this description of the country the writer describes the origin of the mission. In 1720 there were two Portuguese priests, one at Syriam and one at Ava ; but in 1721 the Propaganda sent Fathers Calchi and Vittoni to supersede them. They were well treated by the King of Ava, and helped by the Armenians. Calchi built a church at Ava and died there in 1728. After two months Padre Gallizia arrived, and was made Bishop of Elisma and Vicar Apostolic. After him came Father Nerini, who had taught in the schools at Milan, and, among others, Brother Angelo Capello, ' a clever chemist, skilful in surgery and medicine.' The zeal of Nerini took him among ' some savage populations who lived separate from others in full liberty, and are called Karens ' (Cariani). All the functions of the Church were allowed with full publicity, and schools were established at Syriam. In 1745 there suddenly appeared at Syriam eight ships, with a little squadron of soldiers, commanded by the Cavalier di Sconemille, Governor of Bankibazar, a city belonging to the Germans (Alemanni) on the Ganges. The Governor of Syriam under the King of Pegù sent Nerini on board, and they told him they had been driven out of Bankibazar by the Moors, and had come to seize Syriam, and hand it over to the King of Ava. Nerini dissuaded them, and they came ashore and lived peaceably. After this they went with some of the mission to Pegù to get leave to establish a European colony ; on arrival they were told that the king had gone to hunt elephants, and that they could only be received in audience two at a time with heads uncovered and barefooted. The Cavalier suspected treachery, and refused to comply with such disgraceful conditions. The Bishop and the Fathers Mondelli and Conte advised them not to trust the short faith of the barbarians, but to get back to Syriam. They agreed to do this; but on starting they were taken by surprise and killed. 'They had hardly entered into the ship when out of the thick bushes that border on the river there came an ant's nest of soldiers, some on horses, but the most part on foot : and immediately the marsh was covered with armed men, crying for their death, and stopping their way with stones and arquebuses.' The ship could not go fast as the water was low and the tide on the ebb; the Cavalier and his men took to the shore, but made little speed in the thick jungle. 'After many conflicts they were beaten, and almost all were killed with the Cavalier, and only four crossed those savage places and reached Syriam to tell the sad news.' The bishop and the two priests were all killed in this slaughter.

Father Nerini thought it necessary to obey orders and put the mission in safety. He sent off Father Angelo to India, and soon followed *viâ* the Siamese port of Mergui to Pondicherry and Chandernagore. Nerini returned to Syriam in 1749; and—a rich Armenian and his wife finding the money—he built 'a splendid church, with only one nave adorned with arches and columns within and without,' and with a bell-tower so high as to make the Peguans marvel. A Latin inscription of 1750 commemorated the Armenians, whose names were Nicholas de Aguilar, and Margarita, his wife. 'The people met in the church at the sound of the bell; baptisms were performed with solemnity; they made processions, and went singing psalms through the squares and the streets, and everything was done as in Italy. For the boys many schools were made of geography, arithmetic, navigation, and such sciences and arts as might be useful to them, and over all Father Nerini presided, untiring, day and night.' The King of Tavoy had sent for one missionary, and promised to build a church at his own expense; another was to go to Pegù to re-open the church there, and a third to the new English colony at Negrais. The Pope had made Nerini a bishop; and he was hard at work making grammars of the Burman and Pegù languages, dictionaries, and prayer-books. Every day seemed a thousand years to his ardent desires.

Then suddenly great disasters occurred. None of his mission-aries reached their destinations. Two others were killed at the sack of Martaban, the Padres Quadrio and Gazzeri. In 1756 the Burmans took Syriam after a long siege, defeating the King of Pegù. The old church was burned down ; some of the pillars of the new church were broken. A spent bullet killed Father Angelo as he was tending the wounded.

It happened that a French ship came into the port, and the Burman King, Alompra, suspected that Nerini had got it to come there to succour the King of Pegù. He ordered his soldiers to fetch Nerini's head, but out of reverence for him they disobeyed the order, and carried to the king the head of a Portuguese priest whom they killed instead. Alompra, knowing that this was not the head of Nerini, ordered the soldiers back to the church to fetch it. They were met at the church door by the Bishop, who asserted that he would protect the women who had taken refuge there. Hereupon a soldier wounded him with a spear : other wounds were given, and when he fell, they cut off his head and bore it to the king. This happened in the beginning of 1756. The same incidents, the arrival of the *Galatee*, sent by Dupleix from Pondicherry at the instance of M. Bourno, chief of the French factory at Syriam, the seizure of the ship by Alompra, and the massacre of the French, are described in the *British Burma Gazet-teer* and in Sir A. Phayre's history.

In 1760 two new missionaries arrived,—Donati, who went to Ava and died in 1761, and Gallizia, nephew of the bishop of that name. He was joined by Percoto, who on his way out had learned French and Portuguese, but found Burmese a greater trouble. The author describes the talapoins or pongyis as the custodians of the learned language, and suggests that they are a remnant of the *Samanei*, or ancient Hindu philosophers described by the Greek writers (see *Ancient India as described by Megasthenes and Arrian*, by J. M'Crindle).[1] The word *sramana* occurs in the Wagaru Dhammathat, and it would be interesting to know whether in Percoto's time it was used as meaning a Buddhist monk. Percoto took immense trouble with pronunciation, going

---

[1] Bigandet does not appear to accept this opinion : but the facts in support of it are given by Colonel Sykes (*Notes on Ancient India* p. 134), and it is accepted by Hardy.—See *Eastern Monachism*, p. 10. Mountstuart Elphinstone discusses the question, but without any definite conclusion on the point, in his *History of India*. See his *Appendix on the Greek Accounts of India*.

about repeating words till he became a master of the language. His account of the Buddhist religion is inserted; he wrote a dialogue between a Christian and a pongyi. He translated the Gospel by Matthew, the Book of Genesis, and the story of Tobit, which latter delighted the king. After this he translated the Gospels, the mass and prayers, and made catechisms in Burmese. Another instance of his energy consisted in his making a complete tri-lingual dictionary in Latin, Portuguese, and Burmese, thus carrying into execution the idea of Calchi, Mondelli, and Nerini. Besides this he made translations of the sacred books of the Buddhists into Italian.

In the meantime the Fathers Avenati and Gallizia died, and Percoto was left alone. He followed the king to the royal city (Swemiudo), where he taught Latin and Portuguese in his schools. In 1767 Carpani and other priests came to the country. After his elevation to the episcopate, Percoto aided in starting a seminary for young Burmans aspiring to the priesthood at Monla under Father Cortanovis. There was some opposition from the pongyis, but the king decreed in favour of the mission, being influenced by a Frenchman in his service named Millard. There were some contentions with the Portuguese, who had a church of their own in Rangoon, where also Carpani had a beautiful church, and employed himself in teaching, and in practising medicine. This padre was appointed Judge of disputes among the foreigners there. When he left, a Christian Burman was found who had some skill in medicine.

Leaving Rangoon, where he was disturbed by some conspiracy against the king, Bishop Percoto continued his visitations, and at Monla returned to work at his great dictionary. The climate was against him and he worked too hard: he sickened, and soon after reaching Ava entered into his everlasting rest, on the 12th December 1776, in the forty-eighth year of his age. The Cavalier Millard performed the funeral with some pomp. A stone slab with a Latin inscription was placed over his grave, and was disinterred many years afterwards by Bishop Bigandet and Sir Arthur Phayre. Percoto was succeeded in the episcopal office by Padre Cortanovis.

The third part of Father Griffini's book is a treatise on the virtues of Monsignor Percoto, written for the edification of the pious. It contains a statement that when in Calcutta with Padre Avenati, he presented a letter of introduction to Lord Cleves (*sic*) from Lord Pitt, English Minister at Turin : the English ruler offered him a large amount of rupees, and was greatly surprised at his gift not being accepted. All the missionary asked was a letter to Captain Dundas, then living at Rangoon.

The *Vita di Monsignor Percoto* is written in a beautiful and reverent spirit, which it is impossible to reproduce in a mere abstract of facts. Some day the history of education in Burma will be written, and perhaps this note will guide English readers to the perils and sufferings, labours, martyrdoms, and successes sustained by the accomplished and ardent Italians who preceded Sangermano. The latter had a church at Rangoon dedicated to St. John, where the convent stands now. Bishop Bigandet has seen the foundations. Sangermano, like Herodotus, is usually correct in what he describes of his own knowledge, but like the Greek historian he sometimes makes misstatements when he goes beyond it, as for example when he remarks that the Burmese and Arakanese language differ greatly from each other. It is probable that a research among the manuscripts in the college of the Propaganda at Rome would give results of value to both the missionary and the educationalist, and throw light on the Burmese history of the eighteenth century.

APPENDIX I

SEE CHAPTERS VI AND XX

SINCE Sangermano's time, much has been added to our knowledge of the peoples and languages of Burma. The best accounts I have found are :—*Notes on the Languages and Dialects*, by Dr. Forchhammer, Rangoon, 1884 ; *Burma Census Report*, 1891, by H. L. Eales, I.C.S., vol. i. ch. viii. and x. They are full of most interesting facts, and it is from them chiefly that this note is compiled.

Out of a total population of 7,605,560, the Burmese tribes were returned as 5,771,594, of whom 5,405,727 were Burmese proper. Mr. Eales takes exception to Max Müller's calling the Burmese an agglutinative language, and placing it in the Lohitic branch of the Turanian stock. Burmese has affinity with Tibetan : and Mr. Eales proposes to call it and the other languages spoken in Burma, as well as Chinese, polytonic for the following considerations. Variety of meaning is got by varying the tone or pitch of each sound, especially of vowels, which may be ejaculated, whereas consonants require the use of the tongue or lips. To use a simile which exactly conveys the meaning, the savage, having but few sounds, was forced to make as many words as he could out of them by uttering the sounds in different tones, like Paganini, who could play on one string of his violin. To avoid ambiguity of sense, synonyms (of which Sangermano gives some examples) are used at a later stage : and this is the first step to the agglutinative language—the use of synonyms to help the failing power of the ear. This is the tendency of Burmese and Chinese, and is manifest in Talaing.

Arakanese, an older form of Burmese, is the language of about 350,000 people. The Tavoy dialect resembles it, being that of an Arakan colony planted there before the conquest of Pegu by the Burmans. Both dialects are being rapidly absorbed into Burmese. The Chaungtha, Yaw, Kudo (or Kadu) and Danu dialects are now spoken by only 271, 57, 114, and 1160 persons respectively ; and the Yabein, which Captain Forbes proved to be a separate language, has died out. Among the Yaws, wizards are still found.

T

The next division, according to language, of the Tibeto-Burman stock is the Chin-Lushai or Chin group, containing the following :— Southern Chin, Pallaing, Kun, Daignet, Thet, An, Mro, Kami, Haka or Baungshe, Siyin, Shandu, Kyau, Lushai. These are mostly hill tribes, and aggregated 113,000, of whom 23,000 were returned as Buddhists, aud the rest as Nat-worshippers. For some account of ' Chin Law and Custom,' see Forchhammer's *Jardine Prize Essay*, Rangoon, 1885, and my edition of Maung Tet Pyo's *Customary Law of the Chin Tribe*, a curious book, which, Sir H. S. Maine told me, was useful as helping him to understand the origin of the customs made law in the famous Code of Manu.

The next group contains the Kachin-Naga tribes, Kachin, Lishaw, and Sak or Thet. They are found on the borders of Assam, Yunnan, and Burma. A grammar has been compiled by Mr. Andrew Symington, Extra Assistant Commissioner, Burma Commission, and a long account of these people by Mr. George, I.C.S., is appended to the Census Report.

Leaving the Tibeto-Burman class, Mr. Eales says the next most important is the Karen class, of which the principal varieties are the Sgau, the Pwo, which includes Taungthu, and the Bghai or Bwe, which includes Karenni or Red Karen. The numbers in Burma speaking these languages are above half a million, mostly Buddhists, with above 40,000 Christians, belonging chiefly to the American Baptist Mission, which has done much to raise them from the despised state they held under the Burmans, and has checked later Burmanising tendencies. In 1834 this mission supplied the Sgaus and Pwos with a written language, adapting the Burmese alphabet. The present tendency is to coalesce into a Karen nation. The languages are thought by Forchhammer to be connected with those of Northern China ; and M. de la Couperie's researches point to the Karens being a pre-Chinese race, driven southward into Burma by the pressure of the Chinese.

The next polytonic class is the Taic-Shan, sub-divided by Mr. Eales as follows :—

NORTHERN, . .	Ahom (near Assam—extinct). Khamti. Chinese Shans, Maingtha. Burmese Shans.
INTERMEDIATE, . .	Khun. Lu.
SOUTHERN, . .	Laos or Yun. Siamese.

There are about 180,000 Shans in Burma, nearly all, except 400 Christians, being returned as Buddhists. Dr. Cushing gives proofs that these Tai races came from South-Western China, the migration beginning many centuries ago. Forchhammer states that most Shan words can be found under the same or nearly related letters in the dictionaries of the Amoy and Hok-Kyen dialects. The Burmese Shans use an alphabet derived from the Burmans, supposed to have been devised 300 years ago. They have some religious literature. The Tai contains five tones in three series, so there are fifteen possible different pronunciations of a single syllable.

The remaining polytonic class is the Môn Khmer or Môn Annam group, containing the Talaing or Peguan, the Palaung and the Khamu. The Talaings number above 466,000 : their language was discouraged by Alompra, and furiously proscribed after 1824. There was much Talaing literature : many palm-leaf manuscripts were hidden in the caves at Pagat, the birthplace of King Wâgaru, some of which were procured by Dr. Forchhammer, and are now in the Bernard Free Library at Rangoon. Complete sets are, it is reported, preserved in the King of Siam's libraries at Bangkok. The Talaing nation is being merged in the Burman ; and some think the language will soon die out. It resembles the Cambodian. For the connections of the Talaings with that race and with the ancient Hindu colonies on the Burman coast, the reader is referred to Forchhammer's *Notes* and *Prize Essay*. The opinion that the Talaings were connected with Telingana in India is shown to be baseless, the name being a Burman term of reproach, meaning people trodden under foot In the fifth century Buddhaghosa brought the Buddhist Scriptures from Ceylon to the Talaings. The Burmans have received these, as well as the Hindu Manu Code, from them, as also their alphabet, which was identical with the Indian Vengi characters of the fourth century after Christ.

The Palaungs are found near the Ruby Mines. The Khamus are stragglers from a tribe beyond the Mekong River.

The Selons or Selungs, sea-gypsies of the Mergui Archipelago, are believed to be Malays, and their language is not polytonic.

Besides all these there are many immigrants from China, the Straits Settlements, Bengal, Oude, the Madras Presidency and other parts.

APPENDIX II

In Crawfurd's *Journal*, p. 287, under date 3rd Dec. 1826, I find the following account of a fire at Ava, which caused loss to the widow of the King's tutor, who complained to the King that ' the ministers, and especially Kaulen Mengyi, who was her husband's successor, and of whom she was very jealous, were not at their posts ; for it appears that it is their special duty to attend upon such occasions. The King, who was still very much out of humour, summoned the ministers before him : sent for a sword, drew it, and ordered them, one by one, to come forward and swear upon it that they were present at the conflagration and assisting in extinguishing it. Kaulen Mengyi came forward and avowed that he was not present; but that he had gone as far as the Rungdhau, or town-hall, to give the necessary instructions upon the occasion. He was immediately ordered to be taken out of the Audience Hall; and to avoid being dragged thence by the hair of the head, according to usage, voluntarily made as rapid a retreat as could be expected from a man between sixty and seventy, and of a weakly constitution. An order was given that he should be punished after a manner which I shall presently describe. The other ministers, none of whom were present at the fire, escaped under various pretexts of business or sickness. The punishment now awarded to the first minister is called in the Burman language *Nepu mha lhan the*, or spreading out in the hot sun. The offender who undergoes it is stretched upon his back by the public executioners, and thus exposed for a given number of hours, in the hottest part of the day, with a weight on his breast, more or less heavy according to the nature of the offence, or rather according to the King's opinion of it. It was at first thought that the sentence, on the part of the King, was a mere threat. Not so; the most faithful and zealous of his ministers underwent the punishment this afternoon from one to three o'clock, and not, as is customary on such occasions with culprits of distinction, within the palace enclosure, but in the public road be-

tween the eastern gate of the palace and the town-hall, and in
the view of a multitude of spectators. The old malefactor, whom
I once or twice before mentioned as being at the head of the
band of' executioners, superintended the infliction. This person
and others of the same class are themselves not entitled to a
trial ; but may by the law of the country be put to death by any
of the ministers at pleasure and no questions asked. Here was
the first minister, then, delivered over into the hands of this
ruffian, in whose power it was to make the punishment more or
less severe. Such are the anomalies of this truly rude and
barbarous government. The stretching and sunning process, I
ought to have mentioned, is the punishment of mere peccadillos,
and is a very frequent infliction on persons of condition.
Kaulen Mengyi has since appeared in Lut-dhau, and in the King's
presence, and has been carrying on the business of the government just as usual. It cannot be supposed, however, but that the
ignominy of such a punishment is felt by the person on whom
it is inflicted : and consequently those who had seen the minister
since described him as being low-spirited and downcast.'

While our envoys give general views of the administration, the
letters and journals of the early American Baptist missionaries can
be consulted for what I may call daily peeps at life in Burma
under the reign of King Bodoahpra, described by Sangermano.
They were eye-witnesses of two execution scenes presented in the
note at p. 84. Mrs. Judson confirms Sangermano about the great
local power wielded by the Viceroys and Governors. She, like the
Italian, found a friend in the Viceroy's wife at Rangoon ; and from
this lady, not from the Viceroy himself, she obtained the requisite
permit to depart to Bengal. These high officials were often related to the royal family by birth or marriage ; and as the
revenues of districts used to be given for their maintenance to
queens and other great ladies, these acquired much knowledge of
what went on in the districts, and influenced litigation, as shown
at p. 272. The Judsons had personal experience of heavy and
arbitrary taxes. In 1825, when the King Hpagyidoa was at war
with the British, the Rev. Adoniram Judson was, with the other
Europeans and Americans at Ava, suspected as a spy; and after being
roughly arrested and pinioned by the executioner, the malefactor
with the spotted face, he was cast into prison, and put in irons and
in the stocks. For some time his life was in danger ; but it does
not appear that the king desired the death of the captives ; and

the cruel suggestion of the successor of Bandula in the command of the army retorted on himself. Phayre's account agrees with Mrs. Judson's. The Pukhan Prince had been in disgrace, and was for some time in prison, along with the Europeans. 'He was a man of relentless cruelty. On being appointed commander-in-chief, he determined to inaugurate the assumption of his high office by putting the European prisoners to death—a horrible superstition, altogether outside and opposed to the national religion. The prisoners were sent to Aungpenglè, where this dreadful act was to be perpetrated. But the Pukhan Wungyi had many enemies. Having been twice punished by the king, it was suggested that he designed to raise himself to the throne. The dark deed he meditated seems to show a deeper design than that of success in the field. His house was searched, and it was said that royal insignia were discovered. He was trodden to death by elephants.'—Phayre, p. 251. At this period the queen, who was of low birth, had gained such entire influence over the king, that she was known as the 'sorceress,' it being seriously believed that she worked by witchcraft. Her brother, once a petty fish-monger, was then the most powerful man in the kingdom. Mrs. Judson writes : ' The king's mother, sisters, and brother, each in their turn, exerted their influence in our favour, but so great was their fear of the queen, that neither of them ventured to make a direct application to his Majesty.'

In the advertisement to Mrs. Judson's *Account of the American Baptist Mission*, dated 1827, I find the following notice of taxation and slavery :—

'Slavery is carried on, similar, in many respects, to that which prevailed under the Mosaic dispensation. When the father of a family is overwhelmed with debt he has recourse to the sale of his wife and children ; and if the sum he receives for them be not sufficient, he offers himself in order to balance the account. Not unfrequently, under the despotic government of the empire, a tax is levied on an individual far beyond his ability to pay, and he is put to the torture until he has entered into an engagement to produce the sum required ; the sale of his wife and children takes place for this purpose. Hence there are multitudes of slaves in the Burman Empire. But those slaves whose situation is peculiarly calculated to excite compassion, are children whose parents die involved in debt. The creditor immediately lays claim to the helpless orphans, and either retains them for his debt, whatever

may be its amount, or sells them for an equivalent sum.' Mrs.
Judson proposed to apply the profits of her book to ransom some
of these orphan girls. She describes the people as lively, industrious, energetic, frank, and candid, and neither pusillanimous nor
revengeful. When, in another passage, she 'presumes to say'
that there was not a single Burman who would not commit theft
or falsehood, given a good opportunity, the statement appears too
sweeping, and to require the qualifications which the great Indian
statesman, Mountstuart Elphinstone, sets forth in the chapter in
his *History of India*, where he treats of Hindu character. Alien
missionaries, police magistrates, and tax collectors, he reminds
us, do not see the most virtuous portion of a nation ; and under a
vicious government the lowest villager is often obliged to resist
force by fraud. Such was the case in Siam, where, as Bishop
Pallegoix, writing about the year 1854, tells us, the people while
detesting theft, were robbed by the Mandarins of every grade.
Falsehood was rare among equals ; but lies were told to superiors
in order to escape punishments. The Siamese, he says, are re-
markably humane, affectionate to parents, kind to wives, and good
to slaves, whom they treat better than servants are treated in
France, and not like the negro slaves in other countries.

A perusal of Elphinstone's well-known *Report on the Deccan
Territories* would enable an interesting comparison to be drawn
between the Burmese administration and that of a contemporary
Indian monarch, the Brahman Baji Rao, last Peshwa or King of
Poona. The Maratha government seems to have been by far the
more excellent, vigorous, and just of the two.

Leaving the subject of administration for that of philosophy,
which has a wide influence among the peoples of the 'brooding
East,' we can supplement Bishop Bigandet's statement of Burman
Buddhist metaphysics in his chapter on the Seven Ways to
Neibban, by some of the actual arguments used by Judson's
acquaintance. Mrs. Judson calls the Buddhist system of ethics
pure but powerless, 'like an alabaster image, perfect and beautiful in all its parts, but without life.' The Burmans are styled a
nation of atheists ; and I think that Sangermano in Chapter xiv.
is rather misleading, when he uses the word 'god' in translating
the Burmese term 'superior' or 'highest being' as applied to
Gaudama and other Buddhas. The people with whom Judson
argued about religion appear to have been startled by the concept
of a supreme and eternal intelligence, as contrary to their own

dogma, which substitutes a law or principle in lieu of a personality. The logic of one convert reminded Judson of the Idealism of Berkeley and the Scepticism of Hume. Another inquirer rejected the argument that fixed fate implies a being who fixes it. But by fate they meant Karma, the influence of good and bad deeds, under which the punishment follows the crime as surely as the wheel of a cart follows the footsteps of the ox. Bigandet mentions, however, that the notion of a supreme Buddha, akin to the Adi-Buddha of the Northern school, has taken root in the philosophy of Burma; and since my note at p. 103 went to the press, Mr. Taw Sein-Ko has informed me of his own conjecture that what vague belief in a supreme intelligence is diffused in Burma may be a survival of a form of the religion brought into Upper Burma from Northern India with the Sanskrit language, many centuries ago. Some devout respect is also paid to Maitreya and other existing beings now dwelling in the heavens, who are destined to become the Buddhas and saviours of those worlds to come, which will take the place of the present universe.

The two most contrasted schools of Indian philosophy are the Sankhya and Vedanta. The first maintains the eternity of matter, and its principal branch denies the being of God. The other school derives all things from God, and one sect denies the reality of matter. Elphinstone, from whom I am quoting, says that the doctrines of the Sankhya school seem reflected in the atheism of the Buddhists. These speculations are remote from the ordinary thought of men, but are commoner in the East than those who have never lived there are aware. As instances among my own friends I may cite the late Gokalji Jhala, minister of Junagadh, and Gauriashankar Udayshankar, the distinguished Regent of Bhavnagar, both Nagar Brahmans, who found repose in the Vedanta, among weighty cares and private anxieties. Rhys Davids remarks on the difficulty which a mind impregnated with Christian ideas finds in realising the Buddhist tenet that self or soul has no existence. The true Buddhism alleges that man is never the same for two consecutive moments, and that there is within him no abiding principle whatever. The philosophy is said to mitigate the fervour of the believers; and it is easy to indorse the observation in the Census Report of 1891, that such a movement as the Crusades in Europe, or a jihad in Arabia could never be excited by Buddhist monks. No Buddhist could have written the *Gerusalemme Liberata*, or drawn the character of the noble Godfrey. The expression of Christian heroism and hope, found in that warrior's oration over his dead comrade Dudone in the third Canto, seems the literary antipodes of Buddhist sentiment. Likewise Godfrey's belief in the active providence of God, of whose will what men call Fate is a mere servant.

'Anzi giudice Dio, delle cui voglie
Ministra e serva è la Fortuna e'l Fato.'
—CANTO VII. 70.

APPENDIX III

SEE CHAPTER XXIV

In spite of the absence of reasons based on theology, philosophy, and grammar, the learned reader of Sangermano's Burmese code, will, as noticed on pp. 87 and 221, readily recognise its general resemblance to Hindu law. As it is an abstract and not a translation, it is impossible to make a textual comparison with the Hindu codes and commentaries. This laborious work has, however, been done by Dr. Forchhammer for the Wagaru Dhammathat in his *Jardine Prize Essay*, pp. 44-59, where the parallel texts in the Institutes of Manu are given, as also the similar dicta in Yajnyavalkya, Katyayana, Narada, etc., which cover a considerable number of rulings of the Wagaru not found in Manu. The same has also been done for a great part of the Wonnana Dhammathat, compiled by Wanna Kyaw Din about the year 1772 A.D., in my *Notes on Buddhist Law*. But, as Forchhammer thought it important to notice, ' the deviations in the textual wording in the Sanskrit and Pali originals are far greater than the differences in the two languages require ; if the latter were a translation of the former, or based upon a corresponding Sanskrit version, a considerably closer approach in the wording of the texts would have been the unavoidable result.' Again, ' A marked difference, however, distinguishes the Dhammathat of the Talaing king from the Hindu Sastras ; the total absence, namely, of all that appertains to the Vedic and Neo-Brahmanic cultus. The Wagaru mentions neither Brahma, nor the Vedas, nor the sacerdotal class, and its innumerable rights and privileges, nor the sacrificial fire, or any other point bespeaking the influence of Brahmans and the religious and civil institutions peculiar to Brahmanic India.' One result in Burma is that marriage is not a sacrament, but an institution based on legal contract. Heirship, again, is not dependent on the offering of the funeral cake, as in India. In the Wagaru the direct religious element is almost absent ; but, as Forchhammer explains at length, its peculiar nature is nevertheless the result of a religious tenet ; and that tenet is the Buddhist Karma, or the efficacy of good and bad works, a doctrine inseparably bound up with that of transmigration or renewed existence. According to Professor James Gray, a similar treatment has been applied in Burma to the ethical maxims of the Sanskrit Manu found in the literature called *Nīti*, or proverbial philosophy, to bring them into accord with Buddhist tenets.

The Menu Kyay collection of laws, compiled about 1756 A.D. by order of the Emperor Alompra, introduces religious reasons freely, including long quotations from the sacred literature of the Buddhists, of which some specimens are given in the *Notes on Buddhist Law*. The jurist went to the *Suttapitakam* for the discourse of Yasodhara, the wife of Gaudama, before he became a Buddha, on the seven kinds of wives, those who are respectively like an executioner, a thief, a ruler, a mother, a sister, a faithful friend, and a slave. In another passage, the principle of government, that 'all men whatever, even of the most degraded class, are worthy to be raised to rank and station if the habits are good,' is enforced by the story of Gaudama's success in wooing and winning a lady of high degree, although in that former existence the embryo Buddha was veiled in the family scavenger. It is not easy to avoid suspecting that the Buddhist jurist, like his Brahman predecessors in India, found a number of common secular customs, and supplied religious reasons for them. In my preface to the *Customary Law of the Chin Tribe*, I have drawn attention to the resemblance of the rules of Burmese law to those of the *Thesawalame*, which is a compilation, made by the Dutch Government of Ceylon in 1707, of the law of the Tamil Hindus of Jaffna, and which that great authority, Mr. J. D. Mayne, thinks may be taken as a fair statement of the Hindu law of Southern India before the English Courts with their Brahman assessors began to apply the rules of the Sanskrit books. I must add that the religion of the Jains of India is, like Buddhism, opposed to Brahmanism. Yet they are governed by the ordinary Hindu law. Hitherto, I have found no trace of a specially Jainist law-book.

The greater portion of the Burmese law is now abrogated. British Indian statutes of general incidence make up the law of crimes, procedure, evidence, contract, and relief in equity. Tort and damages are dealt with on English principles. Adultery is a penal offence, and slavery is abolished. Privileges and sumptuary laws are done away with. But our Courts are required by statute to administer to the Buddhists their own laws about marriage, inheritance, and adoption: and the Dhammathats regulate these important matters, with the general assent of the people, given because of the conformity of the rules to Buddhist ethics. Thus women are placed in a favourable legal position, property is divided almost equally among the children, and husband and wife both retain rights over the property gained by their joint labour or capital. The contract of marriage now generally follows the consent of the parties themselves, and not that of the parents, as in older times, and among the Hindus still. The English rulers have found almost nothing to repeal in these provisions of the law: and the tendency of the native judges is to reverence the Dhammathat, as was shown in their objections to a proposed statute of distributions as unnecessary. One judge called the Dhammathat the Great Will. Another wrote—'It is very just, very subtle, very good, and very clear. All disputes on such matters can be settled by it. It is a second sun to the earth. Where then is there a Buddhist who can renounce the Dhammathat?'

The apparent likeness to the Hindu law is thus varied by means of Buddhist opinions, and also by the existence of Burmese and other customs, which are incorporated in these codes. It is, for example, a common practice for a young married pair to dwell with the bride's father (see pp. 228, 257, 258, etc.); the youthful wife is thus ensured more consideration and protection than in India and China. At p. 255, sections 18 and 19, we find recognition of damage caused by an unfriendly spirit, and a sanction given to private war and revenge. These sentiments belong to a lower stage of civilisation, like that of the Kachin and Hpun tribes, as appears from the highly interesting reports on them from the pen of Mr. George, Deputy Commissioner of Bhamo, appended to the Census Report of 1891. He states that among the Kachins the law of reprisal is the only one to which ultimate appeal is made, and that slavery is prevalent. Mr. George quotes informants who say that among the Kalangs, Kanons, or Kamans, and the Lings or Liangs, the old men and women are got rid of by being killed, cooked, and eaten. For a middle stage of civilisation, the *Customary Law of the Chin Tribe* may be consulted. No attempt has yet been made to collect the tribal laws of the Karens and the Shans. Much information about the wilder tribes is to be found in Mr. A. R. Colquhoun's work, entitled *Amongst the Shans*, to which M. de Lacouperie has written an introduction.

It remains to add that, according to Dr. Rost, the law of

Siam is based on the Dhammathat. The alleged Indian origin of the Code is mentioned by our envoy, Mr. John Crawfurd, in his *Embassy to Siam in* 1821, as also by Bishop Pallegoix. Many practices are common to India, Burma, and Siam, as appears by comparing the similar works of the Abbé Dubois, Pallegoix, and Sangermano. The kings of Siam, like those of Burma, often promulgated new codes, by which system the Siamese Manu is said to have been reformed and amplified. Java and the neighbouring island of Bali were for centuries the seats of Hindu colonies and governments, which were originally Buddhist, but in the course of centuries became subject to the religion of the Brahmans, and at a later period to that of the Mohammedans.

APPENDIX IV

SEE CHAPTERS XIV, XVII, AND XIX

DR. RHYS DAVIDS, in his work on *Buddhism*, writes—'It is probable that the idea of transmigration first originated in that curious trick of the memory, by which we sometimes feel so sure that sensations we are experiencing have been experienced by us before, and yet we know not how or when. Several interesting instances of this are given by scientific psychologists. See the cases quoted by Dr. Carpenter, *Mental Physiology*, p. 430, *et seq.*, and Sir B. Brodie, *Psychological Inquiries*, Second Series, p. 55.' The mystery of *Karma*, on which the Buddhist dogma of transmigration is based, has, he thinks, the same foundation of truth which lies at the bottom of the widely prevalent belief in fate and predestination. The ancient Egyptians believed in transmigration : and the Greeks, according to Herodotus, derived the doctrine from them. The poet Ennius introduced it among the Romans. See Dr. Paley's article on ' Metempsychosis ' in the *Encyclopædia Britannica* and Grote's *Plato*. There are traces of it in the *Apocrypha* ; and it was held among the Gnostics. Origen adopted the belief as the only means of explaining some scriptural difficulties, such as the struggle of Jacob and Esau before birth, and the selection of Jeremiah (Jer. i. 5). Lessing taught it, and it forms part of Swedenborg's system. Montaigne in his essay on ' Raymond Sebond ' calls it ' the most universal and received phantasy, and which endureth to .this day,' and goes on to quote Pythagoras, Plato, and the rest of the ancient believers.

While there is abundant literature about the *doctrine* of transmigration in its various forms, I can find no notice of the *effect* on character and conduct of this great tenet of the Brahmans, the Jains, and the Buddhists. This is one reason for my inserting here the following estimate of its influence on the people of Burma, given me by an officer, who, from long service in that country, has had many opportunities of studying their character :

' The belief, most truly held by the Burman Buddhists, that the present earthly life is but one of many that have passed, and of many that are to come, in which the individual has had and will have a place and a share, has a distinct influence on the personal and national character. It enters into every thought of their past, present, and future condition ; and produces in them a frame of mind affecting their whole life which it is difficult for those outside the faith to understand. The fact that, to them, the existing life is only a small portion of their experience of the earthly world, so enters into their estimate of life and character, that they may be said to find in it the most powerful factor in their acts as well as their thoughts.

'That their past must influence the present is to them a living truth, and the wide results that flow from this cannot be easily described or realised. The first thought of a mother, with her new-born child, is turned to the unknown past whence it has brought into this world a legacy of merits or demerits. She is certain that the course of its life depends on the deeds of former days, and she anxiously watches for symptoms that may indicate whether these have been good or evil. If the child develops a bad disposition, she will conclude that its demerits are great : if a good disposition, she rejoices that its merits preponderate ; for she knows that all she may do for her offspring will profit little against the results of its previous existences.

'But the acceptance of this truth does not lead to apathy or despair : on the contrary, there are no people who more thoroughly indulge in the constant expectation of some sudden reward accruing to them from the accumulated merit with which they may be endowed. The prospect of this happy turn which will bring with it an improved worldly position, or, better still, a step towards the great deliverance, is far more potent than any feeling of depression on the prospect of suffering in this life the burden of demerit. As between the two alternatives, the Burman Buddhist looks rather to the better issue.

'The merit which follows a good deed will certainly bear fruit. Hence a hidden hope always rests in the mind of the amelioration of present trouble. The hope of a better life is never absent from the thought of a Burman Buddhist.

'The knowledge that the vicious acts, or the misfortunes of individuals in their present condition, are not solely due to the existing faults of character, but rather that these faults are the results of former misconduct, leads to a lenient view of a fellow-creature's apparent wickedness, and from this comes the marked tolerance displayed by the Buddhist.

'One result of the belief in successive births is the consequent feeling of the comparatively unimportant nature of the present existence. It is natural, to those who look on the narrow span allotted to man as his one and only existence on earth, to attach a supreme importance to the conduct of this life. But this is a condition of mind very little experienced by the Burman Buddhist. He therefore takes life more easily, and exhibits a light-heartedness which is the special characteristic of the race.

'In addition to the blessings of a tolerant mind and light heart, the Burman Buddhist possesses the further virtue of being open-handed. By the ethical teaching of his faith he is impelled to generosity and consideration for others, and he is also influenced by the assurance that the exercise of these virtues will bring its reward. From this springs the current admonition, "Before you are old, before you are sick, before you die, perform good deeds, and so lay up merit." The Parables of Buddha-ghosa (which are supposed to have been uttered by Gotama, the founder of the Buddhist religion) show how deeply interwoven into the ordinary events of life are the results of former good or evil deeds, and prove how powerfully the Buddhist mind must be influenced, even in small matters, by the belief in successive existences on this earth, and by the relation which these bear to one another.

'From this belief can be traced the salient points in the Burman Buddhist's character and impulses, as seen now among the people. There may still be found the light heart and the open hand, the generous view of others' faults—the tolerance towards all creeds, and the hopeful spirit which spreads a cheerfulness over their whole life.'

Another reason for presenting this unique inspection of one of the great factors of character is connected with the view taken by some writers that the religion is without life and power, or at most only a 'thin veneer' spread over the real basis of older superstitions; a view that seems wholly at variance with the above. (See p. xiv.) Sir James Mackintosh, the historian of Ethical Philosophy (in his Note on Jonathan Edwards) lays great stress on the religious opinions of Augustine and Calvin about predestination as a powerful influence in the moral education of the Scots, the Dutch, and the people of New England. The two influences of dogmatic religion and empiric superstition exist together in

Burma as elsewhere, but are easily distinguished. Bishop Pallegoix, in his *Description of Siam*, mentions the Brahman fortunetellers, and the occult practices of Indian, Chinese, and native origin; but observes also, that the *superstitions* one sees among the Siamese form no part of their *religion*, since Buddha has forbidden his followers to consult soothsayers, or put faith in omens, or, generally, to give themselves to any superstitious practice. Sangermano, while himself entirely free from any belief in such things, as shown by his remarks on witchcraft (pp. 149, 172) never suggests that the more credulous Burmans are not Buddhists. In *Hudibras*, as also in Burton's *Anatomy of Melancholy*, the reader will find an immense store of learning, displaying the prevalence of the same superstitions in Europe. Samuel Butler treats them with his usual burlesque humour in the second part of *Hudibras*, where the knight and the squire discuss whether a saint may resort to a sorcerer. In his Partition on 'Cures' Burton raises the questions, whether it is lawful to ask a wizard's advice, or to pray to saints—like St. Vitus or St. Valentine —in cases of sickness; and while pronouncing against both such means of remedy, refrains from shutting the believers in such practices out of the pale of Christianity. Nor does that learned canonist and upright judge, Abbot, Archbishop of Canterbury, go that length in his curious minutes in the divorce case of the Earl and Countess of Essex in 1613, found in the State Trials: he seems, indeed, to be in advance of his time, as he speaks of sorcery to thwart the chief end of marriage as a rag of Popery, and doubts whether, in England at any rate, the black art can create an impediment, now that we have the light of the Gospel, meaning the Protestant religion. The common law judges, however, went on treating witchcraft seriously, until Lord Holt left it as a matter of fact to the jury in a famous case where a woman had been illtreated as a witch. Serious cases of such maltreatment are not uncommon in the Indian tribunals; and I lately adjudged one of homicide, in which a sick woman was killed by men whose aid she had implored to cast a devil out of her. They pretended to become enthusiast or possessed by good spirits for the occasion of the cure. Mysticism and magic have still a hold over the nations of the East, with regard to whom Whewell remarks, that we have no evidence, as with regard to Europeans we have, that they are capable on subjects of physical speculation of originating sound and rational general principles.

U

Another proof of the close and general influence of Buddhism in Burma is found in the constant reading and teaching of the Niti literature, the system of prudence and morality found in proverbs and aphorisms. Professor James Gray, the translator of these works, tells us of the charm they have for the Buddhists, as guides to good conduct in this life, and thus helps to a better life beyond. The Buddhist, he says, firmly believes that his future happiness depends upon his behaviour in his present life, and relies more on practical deeds rather than on the faith which his religion demands. In Chap. xx. Sangermano gives some quotations from these aids to virtue. The Lokaniti is still taught in almost every monastic school in Burma.

Buddhaghosa's Parables, translated from Burmese by Captain T. Rogers, R.E., have been published with an Introduction by Professor Max Müller. Many of the stories relate to Gaudama's former existences. It is in this Buddhist literature, the Jatakas especially (see p. 180), that many of the nursery songs and the fairy tales, the comic stories and the fables, which are now the common property of Europe, are found in their oldest form. The Buddhist dogma disappears under Western influence. See Max Müller on the Migration of Fables, iv. *Chips from a German Workshop*, p. 175. The same essay relates how the transmigration of Gaudama Buddha himself into the Saint Josaphat of both the Greek and Latin Churches came about, an interesting story not generally known to the Buddhists of Burma now, nor to European scholars before 1859, when the *Lalita Vistara* was pointed out as the source of the *History of Barlaam and Josaphat*, the narrative of a hermit and an Indian king, written by Johannes Damascenus early in the eighth century. Thomas Warton had long before drawn attention to this work as containing the originals of many stories found in the *Gesta Romanorum*, in Boccaccio and Gower, in Caxton's *Golden Legende*, and elsewhere. Says Warton: 'As Barlaam's fable is probably the remote but original source of Shakespeare's "Caskets" in the *Merchant of Venice*, I will give the readers a translation of the passage in which it occurs, from the Greek original, never yet printed.' See Price's edition of 1840 of Warton's *History of English Poetry*.

WHEN I wrote the Introduction to this Edition, the long and valuable essays by Francis Buchanan, M.D., on the religion and literature of the Burmans, and by John Leyden, M.D., on the languages and literature of the Indo-Chinese nations, printed in the *Asiatic Researches,* vols. VI. and X., had not come under my notice. They are not mentioned by Cardinal Wiseman or his colleagues. Dr. Buchanan had accompanied our envoy, Major Symes, to Burma, where Sangermano gave Symes three treatises, composed by him in Latin, on Burmese Cosmography, the Religion of Gaudama, and the Ordination of Buddhist Monks. In Buchanan's essay, English translations are given, which contain substantially the information given in the present work. The dialogue found in Chapter XIV. is said to have been written by the king's confessor; and Leyden says the object of it was the conversion of the English, Dutch, Armenians, and others to Buddhism. Among many other interesting matters, Buchanan supplies a comparative vocabulary of languages, and an account of astronomy, with a fine engraving of the sixty-eight constellations.

Buchanan, at p. 304, makes the following statement about the law literature of Burma :—

'On law, the Burmans have many treatises, both containing the laws of Manu and copious commentaries upon these. Whether they still have any copies of the law as originally imported from Ceylon, I know not; but I was told that the Damathat-gye, or Code in common use, has suffered several alterations and additions made by the decrees of various princes.' Compare Sangermano, p. 223, Notes, pp. 87 and 221, and Appendix III. Leyden, whose essay was printed in the *Asiatic Researches,* vol. X., in 1811, the year that he died, had read Buchanan's article, and a number of works written by old Catholic missionaries in Burma. He mentions the Code of Law, and Sangermano's Compendium, but does not discuss its origin.

Probably when a practice became general, and had been recognised as a custom, it became incorporated in the next edition of the Code. One of the rules in Section 8, on p. 228, is better understood after reading Buchanan's account of the physicians. One curious custom, he says, may be mentioned : 'If a young woman be dangerously ill, the doctor and her parents frequently enter into an agreement, the doctor undertaking to cure her. If she lives, the doctor takes her as his property ; but if she dies, he pays her value to the parents ; for in the Burma dominions no parent parts with his daughter, whether to be a wife, or to be a concubine, without a valuable consideration. I do not know whether the doctor is entitled to sell the girl again, or if he must retain her in his family ; but the number of fine young women which I saw in the house of a doctor at Myeda makes me think the practice to be very common.'

John Leyden, better known to Scotsmen as the poet of Teviot-dale and the friend of Sir Walter Scott, sailed in 1802 for Madras, as an assistant-surgeon. His health giving way, he went to Penang, where he studied the Indo-Chinese languages. He was afterwards a professor, and then a judge at Calcutta. In 1811 he accompanied the Governor-General to Java, and died from a fever caught in the bad air of a warehouse of books at Batavia, which he had rushed to examine. Sir John Malcolm and Sir Walter Scott both honoured Leyden's memory with notices of his genius.

> ' Quenched is his lamp of varied lore,
> That loved the light of song to pour :
> A distant and a deadly shore
> Has Leyden's cold remains.'

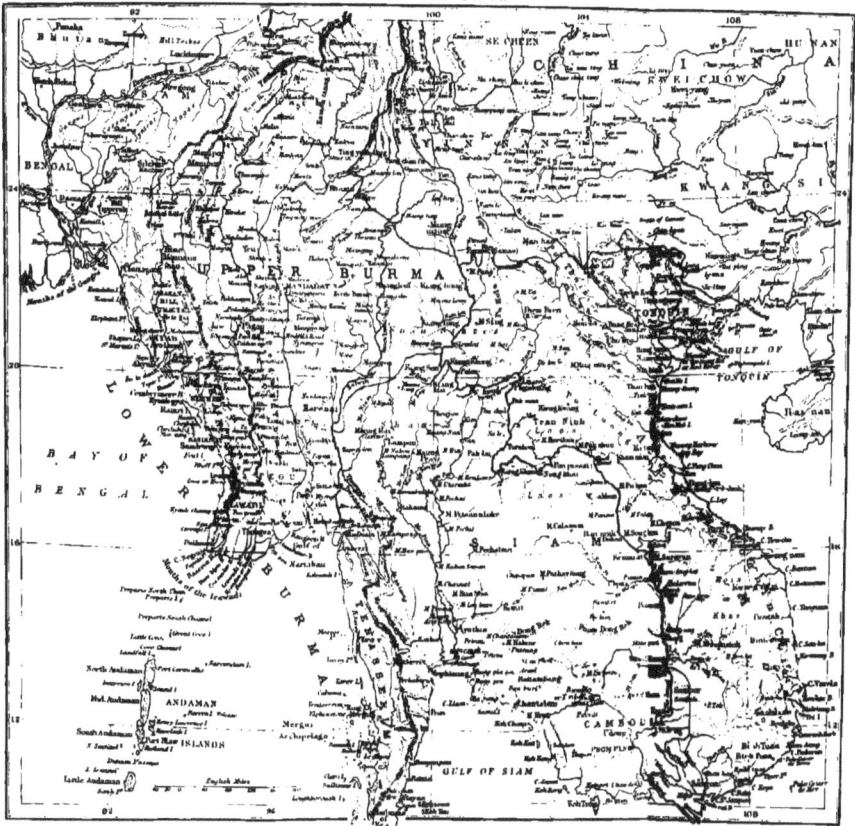

INDEX

Printed by T. and A. CONSTABLE, Printers to Her Majesty,
at the Edinburgh University Press.

www.ingramcontent.com/pod-product-compliance
Lightning Source LLC
Chambersburg PA
CBHW021112270326
41929CB00009B/847